Tokyo

World Cities series

Edited by
Professor R. J. Johnston and Professor P. Knox

Published titles in the series:

Mexico City *Peter Ward*
Lagos *Margaret Peil*
Tokyo Roman Cybriwsky

Forthcoming titles in the series:

Rome *John Agnew and Calogero Muscarà*
Budapest *György Enyedi and Viktoria Szirmai*
Lisbon *Jorge Gaspar and Allan Williams*
New York City *David Johnson and Eugenie L. Birch*
Vienna *Elisabeth Lichtenberger*
Hong Kong *C. P. Lo*
Paris *Daniel Noin and Paul White*
Melbourne *Kevin O'Connor*
Warsaw *Joanna Regulska and Adam Kowalewski*
Taipei *Roger M. Selya*
Calcutta *Ramendra De*
Seoul *Joochul Kim and Sang-Chual Choi*
Dublin *Andrew MacLaren*
Brussels *Alexander B. Murphy*
Randstad *Jan van Weesep*

Other titles in preparation

Tokyo

The Changing Profile of an Urban Giant

Roman Cybriwsky

G.K. HALL & CO.
70 LINCOLN STREET, BOSTON, MASS.

Published in the United States by
G.K. Hall & Co.,
70, Lincoln Street, Boston, Massachusetts.

Published simultaneously in Great Britain by
Belhaven Press
(a division of Pinter Publishers)
London and New York
ISBN 0–8161-7329–X

Library of Congress Cataloging-in-Publication Data

forthcoming

Printed in Great Britain

kodomo to kanai e,
Adrian, Alex, beautiful Mary, and Olga-*sama*
with love

Contents

Contents

List of figures

List of tables

Preface

This book began in 1984 when my employer, Temple University, offered me an opportunity to move to Tokyo to be one of the faculty at its new extension campus. I had no previous experience in Japan, but am afflicted with the geographer's malady of going at first chance to any place where one has never been before. It was a marvelous encounter with a fascinating society and the greatest city in the world, so that after an initial stay of one year, I returned there for a summer, and then later again for a little more than three years. Therefore, the total stay in Japan has been about four and a half years. I now consider Japan, and East Asia more generally, to be a permanent part of my professional repertoire, and have specific plans to return soon to the region for research for another writing project that is beginning as this one winds down.

But while Japan is a new topic for me, the study of cities is not. My previous urban research has been in Philadelphia, the historical industrial city on the East Coast of the United States, where I have worked for many years, and in such diverse cities in other parts of the country as San Francisco, Pittsburgh, Corpus Christi, and Milwaukee. I have also lived in Vancouver and Victoria in Canada, and have done research there as well. Consequently, even though Tokyo is very different, I felt at home with the idea of comparative urban studies, and was able to employ some of the same skills for research that served me well before. So, too, I was able to learn about Tokyo by extensively walking its streets and neighborhoods, and riding from district to district by motorbike. This is a kind of geographical exploration that requires a careful eye for the details of urban landscape, as well as such tools for the field as camera, notebook, good maps and an ability to engage strangers in conversation. I call this 'doing geography,' and readily admit it has been an avocation of mine for many years. Tokyo has been far and away the most interesting experience of this type that I have ever had.

One of the greatest difficulties that I experienced in preparing this book was with language. I began my inquiries into Tokyo not knowing any Japanese, but saw immediately that this was a crippling liability and began seriously studying the language. I am still far from fluent, but proud that I can get around the city and talk to people in Japanese, including business meetings and interviews that related to this book, and that I am beginning to read. However, the reader should know from the start that most of my bibliography is in English. Most of what I read in Japanese, including some very helpful sources about city planning in Tokyo, was with the assistance of a number of my students, to whom I am most grateful.

Therefore, I think it appropriate that I begin my acknowledgments by thanking the students who helped me. Not only did they assist with translations, but some of them also wrote extremely interesting term papers about Tokyo neighborhoods that gave me new insights to the city, or conducted informative field trips to different parts of Tokyo as one of the assignments in my 'Metropolitan Tokyo' course. Other students helped me find data or bibliographic sources. I was always impressed with the kindness they showed me and the extra efforts that many of them made on my behalf. I am proud to have them as my friends, and pleased to comply now with a promise I made to mention each of these fine individuals by name: Tomohiro Akutsu; Taro Ando; Michiko Araki; Miho Ayabe; Yukiko Ban; Miwako Go; Mikako Hamasuna; Junko Hayashi; Jun Honna; Akiko Iizuka; Mio Ito; Ayumi Kanzaki; Shin'ichi Kashiwara; Rika Kazami; Akiko Komoto; Yuri Kondo; Tomoko Koyama; Junko Kusakari; Naoko Matsumoto; Kazumi Matsuo; Sadahiro Matsushita; Mikie Mesuda; Mami Miyamoto; Yuichi Miyashita; Izumi Morioka; Yuka Mukai; Satoru Murakami; Ryoji Nakamitsu; Akihiko Naito; Satomi Ogawa; Brigitte Regier; Kaori Sakai; Ikumi Sato; Aoi Shimizu; Osamu Shimizu; Seisho Sugimoto; Yoko Suzuki; Tomoko Takizawa; Kazuko Terada; Yoshimi Tamai; Mikiko Togo; Naoko Uehara; Liling Wang; Satoko Watanabe; Tomoyuki Yamazaki; Yumiko Yano; Akinori Yokosawa; and Tatsu Yoshida. I especially want to single out Yuri Kondo for being an outstanding research assistant with unusual skills at data-finding; and Ayumi Kanzaki, Mami Miyamoto, Aoi Shimizu, and Mikiko Togo for the many last minute errands relating to data, illustrations, and permissions they carried out for me as I was preparing to leave Japan.

There are several other fine people at Temple University to whom I am indebted for help with this book. I especially want to mention two excellent Deans, first George Deaux and then his successor Bill Sharp, who were very supportive of my plans to write this book, and who helped me with their encouragement; Associate Dean Bill Young, who was also very encouraging and who arranged a convenient teaching schedule; two incredibly busy women in the office, Yoko Makishima-Young and Michiko Usui, who helped in a thousand ways, ranging from frequent on-the-spot explanations about things Japanese to daily words of encouragement and friendly smiles; the Director of the Library, David Green and other members of the library staff who took good care of my acquisitions and interlibrary loan requests; my teaching colleague, Mona Pederson Toyama, who often kept my mailbox filled with useful news clippings about Tokyo; and another colleague, Jeff Kingston, teacher of the ever-popular 'Japan Today' course, who read an early version of my manuscript and made valuable suggestions for improvement.

Other people who helped me include Professors Noriyuki Sugiura and Paul Waley, both of Keiō University, who read parts of the manuscript and offered suggestions for improvement; Professor Takashi Yamaguchi of Tokyo University, who gave me early advice about studying Tokyo and who first outlined the complex lineaments of the city's geography; Mr. Akio Hosoya and other librarians at the Japanese Studies Center at the Japan Foundation Library in Chiyoda Ward, Tokyo; several kind librarians at Sophia University; Ms Kazuko Koitabashi and Ms Keiko Fukaya, both of the Liaison and Protocol Section of Tokyo Metropolitan Government, who provided me with data and publications about Tokyo, and assistance with illustrations; Ms Kazuko Horie, who was previously with the Liaison and Protocol Section of Tokyo Metropolitan Government and who provided me with data and readings about Tokyo; Itsuo Kiritani, an extremely talented artist who generously allowed me to use two of his drawings of Tokyo's older neighborhoods as illustrations in this book; Elizabeth Kiritani, who with her husband gave me a fascinating interview about neighborhood preservation in Tokyo; and Father Bill Grimm, M.M., the activist priest who introduced me to the streets of Sanya and who reviewed those pages of my manuscript that dealt with that remarkable neighborhood. I am also grateful to John Western, a social geographer at Syracuse University, on whom I relied at critical junctures for expert advice about book writing because of his own experiences with books about Cape Town and London. So, too, I want to thank the editors of the World Cities series, Professors Paul Knox and R. J. Johnston, for their help and encouragement, and for numerous improvements to the manuscript. Illustrations were prepared by Andrew Ellis, Gareth Owen and Don Shewan from City Cartographic and DTP Unit, City of London Polytechnic.

Some individuals were truly special. Bill Young and his wife Yoko were my closest friends in Japan. I depended on them often to keep me on an even keel (as much as this is possible), and relied on our regular lunches together as a break from hard work and a treasured source of enjoyment. Kaori Kato, resident of Sagamihara and Sarasota and 'future famous professor', has also been a special friend. She encouraged me from the start to write this book, and has stayed with me all along with countless valuable insights to Japan and sound advice on a number of important topics. I am also extremely thankful to Aoi Shimizu. She too has been a very special friend, both in Tokyo and in Philadelphia. She sat with me for hours as I finished the manuscript and reviewed it, and helped me immensely with a great many last minute details. Her excellent research paper about the Shioiri district of Tokyo was especially useful, and is clear proof that she has a brilliant future as a social geographer or urban sociologist.

Preface

Last but very definitely not least are the best friends of all, my family. I dedicate this book to my wife Olga, and my three children, Adrian, Alex, and Mary, and am profoundly appreciative of all they have given to make this book possible. They are the ones who had to endure my many shifts of mood over more than three years of writing, and who had their lives disrupted, first with a move to Tokyo from Philadelphia, and then with a move back to Philadelphia after they had begun to think of Tokyo as home. I am especially grateful to Olga for perceptive criticisms of the parts of the manuscript I put on her desk. She is an excellent reader and a fine editor. She is also the person who introduced me to the wonders of word processing. Without her, I would still be writing this book by hand into little notebooks. I am glad that my family came to enjoy Tokyo as much as I did, and I hope this book will be a fitting keepsake of that wonderful experience.

RC, March 1991
Fort Washington, Pennsylvania

1
Introduction

Introduction: a neighborhood tour

To be in Tokyo is to experience one of the most dynamic and changeable cities of all time. The city is also uncommonly rich in traditions. This is a duality that, I think, represents the essence of Tokyo and makes it so incredibly interesting and such fun. At one instant, one thinks of Tokyo as a thoroughly modern, international place that belongs very clearly at the forefront among the greatest cities of the world. It is superbly style-conscious, is perfectly attuned to the latest trends in fashion and technology from around the globe and it is an unsurpassed mecca for culture. It is thoroughly delightful for its many spectacular examples of the most contemporary architecture, its wonderful department stores and shopping centers and its many other attractions. But in the next instant, there is a change of scene and something happens to present Tokyo as a small town rather than a giant city, and as a place forever tied to the past rather than at the cutting edge of the future. So, too, one is reminded again and again that the city has been shaped very much by forces that are distinctively Japanese and very alien to the habits of other realms, especially those of the West. Yet, in these instances too, Tokyo displays uncommon greatness. As a result, it is hard not to love the city and harder still to avoid becoming immersed in its myriad details.

There are more than a thousand ways to show Tokyo's complex nature. A modest example begins just outside the window of my house as I write. There is a big Denny's restaurant there, the same US franchise establishment with mostly the same foods that one finds all over America, especially at exits of interstate highways and next to suburban shopping malls. Its large red and yellow sign dominates the view from my living room and lights up my daughter's bedroom above. There is also a private tennis club on the same parcel. The eight courts are almost constantly in use whenever weather permits, as tennis is now an extremely popular, albeit costly, sport

1

Figure 1.1 The two towers of the new City Hall in Shinjuku nearing completion. They are located between Shinjuku Chūō Kōen (Central Park) at the lower left and other high-rises of this urban renewal district in the upper right. (Courtesy of the Office of Information, Tokyo Metropolitan Government)

in Japan. Many of the players arrive in BMWs and other expensive cars. Next door to the restaurant and club, and also visible from my home, is a high-rise office building. This is the headquarters of the Lotte company, a giant, multinational corporation famous for candy and chocolates, other foods, and ownership of a baseball team in Japan's major league. Often in the mornings I see the company's executives, uniformed office girls, and other employees lined up outside for group exercise and a pep talk from their boss.

A little further down the street, about five minutes walk from my house, Shinjuku begins, one of the busiest commercial centers in Tokyo and during business hours perhaps the most crowded place on earth. The part of Shinjuku that is closest to my house is a prominent cluster of ultra-modern skyscrapers – the most famous skyline view in Japan (Figure 1.1). It is the site of some of Tokyo's best international hotels and offices for the biggest corporations, and also where a new city hall complex is being built for Tokyo government. The design, by Japan's master architect Tange Kenzō,[1] promises to make this place a leading landmark. One of its twin towers will rise to 243 meters, just high enough to be the tallest building in the city. I walk past the construction site nearly every day and keep watch on

[1] Japanese names are given in this book with the family name first.

2

the progress. As I do this, I am always reminded of how dramatically Tokyo is changing, even within the short span of the four years that I have been in the city, and feel particularly lucky to be a witness.

I am also fortunate to experience the different aspects of Tokyo that are seen in the other direction from my house. I can't pretend it is old Tokyo there, because the neighborhood itself is not very old, and because most of its oldest features, such as its first generation of houses and shops, have long since disappeared. The area's hot real-estate market and the cataclysmic destruction that visited the city during the bombing raids of 1945 have seen to that. Nevertheless, there is much remaining that is a reminder of an earlier time, when Tokyo was a smaller city and there were no high-rises, and when internationalization was not such a common buzzword. The house next door, so close that we can almost reach from a window and touch it, is an older building belonging to our neighbors the Tamura family. Tamura-*san* is a *tatami* maker. This is the thick straw mat used as the floor covering in traditional Japanese rooms. His workshop is the front of the house, in a room that opens directly on to the street and is fully exposed to all passers-by. He does his craft by hand, in much the same way that his father worked in the same room before him. There is no shortage of orders, and he stays busy every day well into the evening.

The neighborhood shopping street is at the end of the block (Figure 1.2). It is a narrow lane, barely wide enough for one car to pass, and is lined on both sides with small shops whose fronts open widely to the street like the Tamura's, and invite customers in. There are more and more boutiques and other new arrivals on the street, including an extremely busy supermarket, but there are still quite a few of the older establishments left as well: fishmongers, rice sellers, a noodle maker, a cracker bakery, a cubbyhole that sells only buttons, a glazier's shop, and countless other, small places for the local market. Tucked away to the side is the neighborhood's Buddhist temple. It is a new building but designed in a traditional style, and has a welcome open space for community fairs and other gatherings in front, and a lovely Japanese garden at the back. The garden is such a contrast to the harsh lines and bustling activity of the surrounding city that at times it seems to me to be the most secluded and contemplative place in the world. Around the corner from the stores is the local public bath, where neighbors from some of the older houses and tiniest apartments, as well as many other people who simply prefer the facilities and neighborliness of the *sentō*, go regularly to wash.

There is a strong feeling of community on this street. It is a friendly place that is the scene each day for hundreds of conversations among neighbors out shopping, and a play street for the many children who zip around on their bicycles or run about underfoot amid all the other activity. During the daily shopping rush just before supper time the street is closed to vehicles and becomes a pedestrian mall. A merchants' association makes sure it is always decorated for the appropriate season, and that loud-

Figure 1.2 A typical neighborhood shopping street. The street is closed to cars during the busy time near the end of the day when there is a rush to prepare dinner. The decorations on the lamp standards are a project by the shopkeepers association

speakers on the utility poles always play popular tunes when pedestrians are out in force. This is the first week of spring, and the plastic snowflakes that had hung overhead for the past few weeks have just been replaced with plastic cherry blossoms. Yesterday, the tune I heard was the brassy hit single 'Tattoo' by singing idol Nakamori Akina.

In the fall, in conjunction with a popular Shinto religious festival, the shopping street becomes the scene of a noisy procession that is known simply as *aki-matsuri* or the autumn festival. The highlight is the carrying of a heavy *mikoshi*, or portable religious shrine in which the spirit of a special deity is said to reside during festival days (Figure 1.3). It is toted on long poles that are held above the shoulders by neighborhood men, and moves along slowly for well over an hour down this street and into some of the side lanes. Shouts of *Washoi! Washoi!* ring out a cadence that keeps the mob moving. Women, children and other men press in on this procession, and sing and dance alongside in colorful costumes. Neighbors have considerable pride in the *mikoshi* itself, which is the property of the local shrine, because it is highly ornate, beautifully crafted, and expensive, as well as distinctive in design detail. Sometimes outsiders from other neighborhoods come to see these festivites and to admire the *mikoshi*, as there are many 'matsuri aficionados' in the city who travel from neighbor-

4

Figure 1.3 Carrying the *mikoshi* on busy Yamate-dori during the autumn festival

hood to neighborhood according to a publicized schedule of festivals (Bestor, 1989a, p. 252), but they are very clearly just by-standers. In this neighborhood, as well as in every other local area, *aki-matsuri* belongs to insiders.

Foreigners are especially few and far between in this and almost any other neighborhood in Tokyo. The friendliness of the community is extended to them (or should I say 'to us') too, often to excessive degrees. For example, from time to time one is showered with gifts and offers of free meals and drinks from the Japanese as reward for just being in Japan, or for taking the time to engage in a few minutes of English conversation. In addition, there are many opportunities to form wonderful, lasting friendships. However, with most individuals there are also clear limits for foreigners and frequent reminders that in Japan any non-Japanese is forever an outsider. I remember a similar shopping street near my first address in the city, a more suburban-like setting in Setagaya Ward on the west side of Tokyo, where the dry cleaner returned a suit that I had taken in for pressing with a tag that identified me as *gaijin #2*, or 'foreigner #2.'

My first introduction to the dual nature of Tokyo came on my first morning in the city. My family and I had arrived in the city late the previous night and had been escorted to our new apartment by my employer, who had already taken care of housing arrangements. Having heard so much about the cramped 'rabbit hutches' that Tokyoites are said to live in, we were very pleasantly surprised to see on arrival that our assigned quarters were, in fact, reasonably roomy and comfortable, and that they had all of the necessary appliances for easy living, lots of big windows (but no drapes yet), and an attractive combination of Japanese and Western interior design. The neighborhood, we were assured, was an up-scale district in one of the city's 'better' wards, popular among aspiring professional people, and close to the international schools that my children were set to attend. In addition, we were informed that many of the neighbors had travelled abroad and spoke English, so it would be easy to make friends and get oriented. We were also told about the playground just outside the building where our children could play as my wife and I supervised them through the windows. Thus assured, we crashed into a deep sleep, our first ever on *tatami*, that lasted until mid-morning. What woke us was the commotion at our windows: a dozen or so of the neighborhood's school-age children had gathered outside our ground floor apartment, faces pressed against the windows, looking to see the strange new creatures who had moved in to Apartment 110!

And so it is that in Tokyo one experiences simultaneously the exciting dynamism of a major global metropolis and the intimate world of an unchanging small town that is somehow stuck in the past. The two are always side by side, or are intermixed in interesting ways, and give the city much of its distinctive personality. Moreover, occasional annoyances aside, it is almost always a very pleasing mix. This is one of the things that makes Tokyo exceedingly livable, even though it has such exacting problems as extreme crowding, high living costs, and dangerous air pollution. Perhaps the city could be described, as some other authors have done, as an over-grown village, but that sounds like a pejorative and is not what I intend. There is nothing out of whack about these combinations of contrasting images. To me, Tokyo's duality is a positive attribute that enhances the urban experience in every way, and provides a continual source of enjoyment and stimulation. It has also convinced me that the city is well worth writing about.

Landscape interpretation

This is a book about contemporary Tokyo, what it is like, how it got there and where it seems to be headed. These are ambitious considerations that began to attract me not long after I first arrived in the city in the summer of 1984, and that became increasingly irresistible the longer I stayed. From the very beginning, perhaps from the moment of that awkward first encounter with the children of Setagaya Ward, almost everything I saw in the city interested me. It was all so different from anything I had experienced before! I had always enjoyed exploring cities and getting to know their layouts and details about various nooks and crannies. However, in Tokyo the urge to get to know the city was stronger than ever, because no matter where I went a special kind of urban differentness would reveal itself and draw me closer in. Paul Waley, Tokyo expert, friend, and author of an enviable history of the city that I will cite several times, started his book with similar thoughts: 'Tokyo is different with a difference. The ways in which it is different from other big cities are such interesting ways. One wants to think about them and speculate upon them' (Waley, 1984, p. ix).

The approach I have chosen for these topics is to concentrate on the look of the city – on landscape or cityscape. This emphasis stems from the broader interests I have in the relationships between built environment and society, and reflects a belief that thoughtful examination of the former can lead to insights about the latter. Urban landscapes are especially interesting in this regard, because they reveal much about the people, including both present and past generations who shaped them. That is, the many layers of development and redevelopment one typically finds in a city tell of that it's history, and of the various influences from economics, politics, religion, culture and other realms that have combined to give it its particular character. Thus, the cityscape is a usable record of urban society, and can be read to introduce themes from any of a number of academic fields or topics of concern. For us, cityscape in Tokyo provides a convenient organizing theme that runs through all the chapters and makes the broad scope of this book manageable. This is an approach that academic geographers in particular often employ in analysing a city and relating an interpretation (Lewis, 1976; Relph, 1987).

Tokyo, however, poses some special problems in this regard. First, the city's repeated history of tragic disasters – huge fires that swept across entire sections of the city in the seventeenth, eighteenth and nineteenth centuries, earthquakes (especially in 1923), and wartime devastation (1945) – has destroyed most of the historic urban fabric that would otherwise be a material record of the city's past. Thus, there really is no 'Old Town' neighborhood as such to wander around in and get a feel for the conditions of earlier times. In most areas of the city, almost everything is new, having been built in the past generation or so; there is comparatively little of the kind of mix of buildings from different periods, especially from earlier centuries, that one finds in most other great cities. However, this in itself is part of the record of Tokyo and a clue to its personality. Moreover, as we shall see, there is considerable history left in the landscape, even though most buildings are quite new, and it is indeed possible to imagine the past while exploring the city today.

Secondly, we need to understand that there is much in the landscape of Tokyo that is designed primarily for show and does not necessarily represent the true nature or innermost characteristics of the city. This is a difficult topic I can only begin to address, but it catches an observer's attention almost immediately when visiting Tokyo. Consider, for example, the rather striking but curious situation that exists for many of the city's most important public landmarks. In other great urban centers, such as New York with its Statue of Liberty and Empire State Building and London with Big Ben and the Houses of Parliament, public landmarks help define the city and identify some its key characteristics or economic roles. In Tokyo, however, this function is confused because most of its big landmarks are actually imitations of other cities. Tokyo Tower, for example, which I have calculated to be the most common postcard symbol of the city, looks too much like the Eiffel Tower to truly represent Tokyo; Tokyo Station, the city's central rail commuter interchange and one of its most distinctive buildings, is a copy of the main station in Amsterdam; Akasaka Detached Palace, the former residence of Japan's Crown Prince and now the official state guest house, is patterned after Buckingham Palace on the outside and the Versailles on the inside (Conner and Yoshida, 1984, p. 214); and the massive, new (1986) domed sports stadium, popularly called Big Egg, is clearly an offspring of similar shapes in Houston, New Orleans and especially Pontiac, Michigan. Even the sleek, modern skyline of Shinjuku, the giant commercial center near where I live, is often thought of as the city's answer to the glamor of New York.[2] And then, of course, there is Tokyo Disneyland – a fantasyland designed to reproduce a fantasyland in, ahem, Southern California.

The point of this is to caution that the true essence of Tokyo is rather deeply held in the landscape; what is on the surface, while also a valid insight to the city, is just that – the surface image only. Thus, many first impressions of Tokyo, I think, can be misleading. For example, one might conclude from the city's famous landmarks, and from the hundreds of business enterprises (eg., restaurants and coffee shops) that use American and European themes in decor, that the city is truly international. However, as experience shows, it is much, much less this than it presents itself to be. I was dismayed when I learned on my first full day in Tokyo that no one at the Café Colorado, which I happened upon near my new home and hoped would be a place where I could effortlessly order a meal, spoke English (or Spanish). Despite the name and an architectural style straight from the shopping malls of America, this was Japan. So, too, all the other restaurants named Colorado (it's a chain), the countless Kentucky Fried Chicken outlets, the coffee shops called Miami, and the billiards bars named Chicago (in Kichijōji), Los Angeles (in Harajuku), or New York (in Shibuya) that I would encounter later, would make Tokyo look international (or American), but on the surface only.

Peter Popham, author of another of my favorite books about Tokyo, has also thought about these subjects, and has written about how they apply to the famous high-rise skyline of Shinjuku. Here is a place that is 'very eagerly modern' and that represents 'the embodiment of the city's Manhattan fantasies,' but on closer inspection (Popham, 1985, pp. 101–2):

[2] I recently received a Christmas card that shows the impressive skyline of Shinjuku on a quiet snowy night, Santa and the reindeer in the sky above, and the unmistakable reflection of *the Statue of Liberty* on the glass skin of one of the high-rises! Also, I have a keychain that says 'Tokyo Megalopolis' and that shows a montage of Tokyo landmarks and New York's Chrysler Building. Finally, I note that there is a waterfalls-fountain in *Shinjuku Central Park* that is called Niagara Falls.

... it's not like Manhattan at all; it's just like Japan, only fifty stories high. That most venerable Japanese magic trick, in frequent use since at least the eighth century, by which they solemnly and meticulously copy some product of another culture and wind up with something that is unmistakably Japanese is at work again.

Perhaps the best way to express this characteristic of Tokyo is to introduce the distinction between what is said to be *omote* and what is *ura*. The literal meanings of these words are 'front' and 'back', respectively, or that which is 'outside' versus what is 'inside'. The two apply to many varied situations, are always an inseparable pair, and are mutually dependent and supportive of each other: *omote*, for example, is the 'official, public aspect of a person, place or institution' while *ura* is unofficial and private; *omote-ji* is the outer cloth of a kimono and *ura-ji* is the layer closest to the skin; and *Omote-Nippon* is Japan's urban-industrial eastern side that trades with the world, while *Ura-Nippon* is the more traditional, secluded, western side of the country. With respect to cityscape, we see that *omote-dōri* is a wide, public thoroughfare with important offices in tall buildings and fashionable shops, while *ura-dōri* are the private residential backstreets hidden behind the big streets (Tasker, 1987, p. 78). Thus, in my own neighborhood, we saw the great contrasts that exist between the big streets with exotic businesses and huge public commercial center on the one hand, and the intimate backstreets that are the domain of neighbors only on the other. The former represents the easily evident surface of Tokyo that makes the city look thoroughly modern and even Western, while the latter shows that Tokyo remains profoundly traditional. The city is actually comprised of both facets, but the surface is nothing more than the skin: the real heart of Tokyo, *ura*, is nestled in the interior, shielded from attention by the glitter of *omote* and more difficult to get to know. Our job in this book will be to consider both.

However, *omote* and *ura* are just part of the picture, and Tokyo is even more complicated than that. What is more profound about the city, and even more complex about understanding its landscape, is the contrast of images that one typically sees at any one place. This is true even deep in the heart of Tokyo, far off the beaten path in neighborhoods of *ura-dōri* where outsiders almost never go, and where one feels convinced that here, at last, is the real Tokyo. I will never forget one such contrast that I saw during one of my first visits to *shitamachi*, the low-lying rivermouth area on the east side of the city that is one of its major plebian quarters. One of the first photographs I took there was of a small clothing shop on a sidestreet of Kuramae, a small neighborhood with a concentration of toy and doll wholesalers. Out front on hangers over the sliding door was a selection of *happi* coats[3] and one bright-red, slim-size Santa Claus outfit! Likewise, I remember my first visit to Sensōji, the old and important temple

---

[3] A short slipover jacket with an employer's crest on the back often worn by workmen. It has become popular among youths during festivals in which a portable shrine is carried.

to Kannon, the goddess of mercy, in the Asakusa area of *shitamachi*.[4] On its Nakamise-dōri, the 'street of the inside shops,' which is a long lane of retail stalls leading to the foot of the temple, I was amazed to see a selection of posters for sale of the 1950s American pop idol, James Dean. A recent visit to Nakamise-dōri, nearly five years after the first, showed James Dean to be there still, but also that one shop had added 'Gorby Dolls,' after Soviet Premier Gorbachev, to its inventory of things for sale.

The crazy aspects of Tokyo's modern vernacular represent but a small fraction of the total scene. However, it is an important and telling fraction nonetheless, and to my mind the most compelling evidence of Tokyo's exceedingly engaging personality. Here is a city – clearly one of the most important in the world – in which major landmarks, much less many hundreds of smaller establishments such as restaurants and other businesses, take on the physical form of structures that represent places elsewhere! Everywhere I went in the city there would be some surprise – some example of cultural confusion – to greet me. If it wasn't James Dean at a major temple, then it would be one of a hundred or more other startling juxtapositions or bizarre landmarks: Japan's 700th (considered to be a lucky number) McDonald's restaurant, located in Shinjuku, with life-sized

Figure 1.4 Marilyn Monroe and sumo wrestler on a revolving fountain near Takadanobaba Station, Yamanote Line. The telephone number is for a pawn shop

[4] This place is not off the beaten path at all, but is instead a popular attraction for worshippers and tourists alike.

sculptures of the four Beatles near the entry and Superman crashing through a window on the second floor; the headquarters building of Fuji Latex Company, manufacturer of prophylactics, that is shaped like its main product (unrolled); or the pawn shop in Takadanobaba, an area of universities and special 'cram schools' (*juku*) close to where I teach, with a huge, neon-lit, revolving fountain on its roof showing a much-bigger-than-life-sized, naked Marilyn Monroe squared off for combat against a hulking Japanese sumo wrestler (Figure 1.4).

What kind of city is Tokyo really, and why does it behave this way? It might be that not all these aspects of the city are meant to be understood, but I was hooked on these questions nevertheless and decided to get to know the place as best I could.

2
Orientation to Tokyo

Japan's primate city

Perhaps the best place to begin is to write about the extraordinary size of Tokyo and its great influence in Japan and the world at large. If we look first at the international picture and at population totals, the most common measure for urban importance, we see that here is truly one of the World Cities. According to the most recent census (1985), the administrative unit that is Tokyo, a 2,162 square kilometer territory known formally as *Tokyo-to* (see below), has a population of 11.8 million. This ranks third in the world in a comparison that lists the most recent census totals for the world's largest cities and their suburbs (Table 2.1). However, the urbanized area of Tokyo is much bigger than just *Tokyo-to*. If we define the metropolis as *Tokyo-to* plus the three surrounding heavily urbanized prefectures, an area of 13,508 square kilometers, then the total population increases to 30.3 million. A comparison of 'urban agglomerations' by the United Nations, which attempts to standardize such definitions for urbanized areas, ranks Tokyo as first in the world in 1985. Table 2.1 shows this as well.

Even more to the point about Tokyo's global importance than its population size is its huge role in the world economy. This, is widely reported, as year after year Japan registers its famous trade surpluses with the rest of the world and garners for itself more and more wealth. The city is now the world's principal lender and biggest creditor, as well as the number-one ranking city in terms of large corporate headquarters, total bank deposits, and numerous other economic measures (Marlin, *et al.*, 1986, pp. 549–50).[1] The Tokyo Stock Exchange, once only of interest within Japan,

[1] This is based on numbers of corporations with annual 1982 sales in excess of US$1 billion. Tokyo had 81 such companies, London was second with 67, and New York third with 44. However, New York ranked first in total sales by these companies, London second, and Tokyo third. Tokyo has doubtlessly improved its position since 1982.

is now monitored worldwide, and ranks alongside the stock exchanges of New York and London in size and global influence.

Table 2.1 Tokyo as a world city

A Populations of cities and their suburbs

rank	metropolitan area	year	population
1	New York City	1980	15,590,000
2	Mexico City	1980	13,354,000
3	Tokyo	1985	11,828,000
4	Sao Paulo	1985	10,099,000
5	Buenos Aires	1980	9,766,000
6	Seoul	1985	9,646,000
7	Los Angeles	1980	9,480,000
8	Calcutta	1981	9,194,000
9	Paris	1982	8,907,000
10	Moscow	1985	8,873,000

B Populations of urban agglomerations (defined by United Nations) (in millions) (rank as of 1985)

rank	urban agglomeration	1955	1970	1985	2000
1	Tokyo/Yokohama	8.59	14.87	19.04	21.32
2	Mexico City	3.77	8.74	16.65	24.44
3	New York	13.22	16.19	15.62	16.10
4	Sao Paulo	3.60	8.06	15.54	23.60
5	Shanghai	10.60	11.41	12.06	14.69
6	Buenos Aires	5.86	8.31	10.76	13.05
7	London	10.25	10.55	10.49	10.79
8	Calcutta	4.95	6.91	10.29	13.00
9	Rio de Janeiro	4.13	7.04	10.14	12.97
10	Seoul	1.55	5.31	10.07	12.97
11	Los Angeles	5.15	8.38	10.04	10.91
12	Osaka/Kobe	4.73	7.60	9.56	11.18
13	Greater Bombay	3.43	5.81	9.47	15.43
14	Beijing	7.06	8.29	9.33	11.47
15	Moscow	5.54	7.11	8.91	10.11

Sources: A Showers, V., *World Facts and Figures, Third Edn.* 1989. New York: John Wiley and Sons, pp. 404–5.

B United Nations Department of International Economic and Social Affairs, *Prospects of World Urbanization, 1988.* New York: United Nations, 1989, pp. 76–7.

One way to visualize the practical implications of just how important Tokyo has become on the world scene is to consider what would happen if, suddenly, the city were gone. This is not just a fanciful exercise to think about: such a fate is a distinct possibility with Tokyo, if not a likelihood or certitude, because of the extreme risk from earthquakes. On 1 September, 1923, the city was almost totally destroyed by the Great Kantō Earthquake and the fires that raged for forty hours thereafter. It could be levelled again, with even more damage, at any moment. This is one of the most fundamental facts about the city and, as we shall see, the shaper of much of its personality. It is also something for much of the rest of the world, outside Tokyo, to be concerned about. This is not just out of humanitarian concern for the hundreds of thousands of lives that are known to be at risk, but also because of the global economic repercussions that would doubtlessly follow Tokyo's annihilation. In 1923, the disaster cost over 100,000 lives and property damage that taxed the nation. However, because the city had but a tiny role in the world at large, little impact was felt outside Japan. Now, by contrast, because Tokyo has risen to such gargantuan economic heights, the impact of a giant shake will be felt immediately around the globe.

Given the importance of the topic, it not surprising that there are quite a few predicitions about it. One scenario, put together by Oda Kaoru, a young economist at the Tōkai Bank in Nagoya and retold in a most entertaining manner by Michael Lewis (Lewis, 1989) is especially engaging.[2] It foresees a series of economic shock waves from the Tokyo quake that begin with the very instant that the city is destroyed, including its stock exchange and all records of transactions, which in Japan are primitively kept. The value of the yen nose-dives as investors scramble to unload Japanese stocks, except for the stocks of the giant construction companies, which increase in value just as the dust settles around the collapsed buildings they had erected. Then, because of immediate plans to rebuild the city (estimated cost, $1.3 trillion!), Japan begins to liquidate its foreign assets: stocks, bonds, currencies and commodities, including real estate. These, it turns out, represent the 'national nest egg' to be used in the event of just such an emergency, even as the rest of the world has come to depend on them (Lewis, 1989, p. 76). The result is a disaster on Wall Street, in London and other financial centers, high interest rates and economic depression in the US and other 'dependencies', and a long period of declining growth in those countries. In the meantime, Tokyo, which has a history of fast reincarnations, re-opens for business and its new stock exchange begins to record immediate gains.

The impact of a giant quake would be even greater domestically. This is because Tokyo is far and away the nation's leading urban center, both in terms of numbers of people and its vastly disproportionate influence on almost all aspects of daily life in Japan. The 11.8 million total for *Tokyo-to* represents nearly 10 per cent of the population of the country, and overshadows not just the provinces but also all of the other giant urban centers such as Yokohama (2.7 million), Osaka (2.6 million) and Nagoya (2.1 million). The 30.3 million Tokyo metropolitan area (*Tokyo-to* plus Chiba and Saitama Prefectures, and Yokohama's prefecture, Kanagawa) is

---

[2] See also: 'When the Great Quake Comes to Tokyo,' *Tokyo Business*, Vol. 3, No. 7 (Summer) 1989, pp. 5–10.

even more dominant. It represents about 25 per cent of the national total. This is a remarkable concentration, given the fact that the city and the metropolitan area comprise only 0.6 and 3.6 per cent of Japan's total land surface, respectively. What is more, the degree of concentration has been increasing in recent years.

The statistics cited here are from 1985, but as recently as 1970 the urbanized area's share of Japan's total population was only 23 per cent, and in 1960 it was only 19 per cent. This reflects the fact that the Tokyo area continues to be a magnet for migrants, as it has been for nearly all its history, albeit at a decreased rate recently because of overcrowding and high costs. Geographers have long referred to such cities that are overly large in comparison to others in their country, that therefore take huge shares of a nation's resources and investments and exert exceptionally great domestic influence, as primate cities (Jefferson, 1939).[3]

The disproportionate influence of Tokyo within the nation applies to nearly all important economic and cultural functions. Among other distinctions, the city is the political capital of Japan, the headquarters of its largest economic enterprises, its main contact with the world abroad, the leading center of higher education, its largest manufacturer, the dominant media center, the locus of the largest number of cultural events ranging from concerts to art exhibits, sports matches and others. This is illustrated in Table 2.2. The historian Henry D. Smith II has gone so far as to describe Tokyo's relationship to the rest of Japan as 'urban tyranny'. He has pointed out, as an example, that because of the education and business contacts that are concentrated there in disproportionate amounts, the city is for all practical purposes 'the only road to success in modern Japanese culture' (Smith, 1973, p. 369). Consequently, anyone with ambitions has to spend time in Tokyo, if not actually to live there. Although most people in Japan think fondly of the city, there are many others in the rural areas and in some of the would-be rival cities who resent it for its primacy. For example, proud residents of Kansai, the Osaka-Kobe-Kyoto region, sometimes enjoy describing Tokyo as a young upstart without a deep history and lacking in style and grace.

Because so much that is vital to the economic and political life of Japan is concentrated in just one city, there are many appeals heard, both from inside Tokyo as well as outside, for decentralization. As we shall see, for Tokyo itself the problem is one of excessive crowding, chronic traffic congestion, high land costs and special difficulties in providing adequate supplies of water and energy and removing wastes for such a large population. For Japan as a whole, the problem of overconcentration in Tokyo is, in part, one of being 'more fair' to other regions. As in other countries, there is competition in Japan among local government units for the kind

[3] Use of the term primate city ignores the fact that in correct English the adjective 'primate' refers to a zoological category. It is never a synonym for 'first-ranking' or 'primary.'

Table 2.2   Tokyo as Japan's primate city (various years 1980s)

Item	Tokyo	Japan	percent
Population	11,906,000	121,672,000	9.8
Land area (sq. km.)	2,162	377,801	0.6
Company headquarters (over Ybillion capital)	495	857	57.8
Foreign companies	997	1,188	83.9
Foreign banks	81	127	63.8
Securities companies	1,188	3,751	31.6
Advertising companies	3,678	9,763	37.6
Information service companies	4,700	11,174	42.1
Newspaper companies	719	2,403	29.9
Publishing companies	3,376	5,202	64.9
Number of credit cards	11,593,000	67,004,000	17.3
Number of telephones	6,539,000	46,093,000	14.1
Monthly help wanted ads	123,227	1,050,909	11.7
Bank deposits (Ytrillion)	105.7	226.3	46.7
Number of college students	653,326	2,219,793	29.4
Number of foreigners	157,000	867,000	18.1

Sources: Tokyo Metropolitan Government, 1988, pp. 3 and 5; Yada, 1987, pp. 18–19.

of investment that provides jobs and builds economic growth, and considerable unhappiness in many parts of the country that one region (and to a lesser extent the Kansai area and the urbanized area around Nagoya) has taken the lion's share of this. Demands for 'spreading the wealth' are especially vociferous in the case of economically depressed regions such as Tōhoku (northeast Honshū, Japan's biggest island) and various remote islands and mountain districts that suffer a constant outflow of population, especially of young people, to urban magnets. Consequently, almost all prefecture governments and numerous municipalities (over 50 cities by count in 1988) operate offices in Tokyo to lobby in the Diet and among national ministries for deconcentration of the capital, as well as to entice private industry with offers of land and favorable tax advantages to relocate from Tokyo (Imaoka, 1988).

The other part of the problem for Japan as a whole of overconcentration in Tokyo is the considerable security risk involved. That is, having the vast majority of the nation's highest placed politicians and top business and industrial leaders, as well as many of its most influential journalists, writers, educators, researchers and other professionals, all gathered for most of the day within a few square kilometers of one another on a highly earthquake-prone site invites a national disaster of unthinkable proportions. This is not to mention the huge workforce that is also concentrated each day in this same area, and the presence there of most national records and the records of hundreds of private companies. Thus prudence itself calls for making Tokyo smaller and less of a primate city.

It is largely because of these and similar reasons that over the last 40 years there have been official policies in Japan, at least on paper, to contain Tokyo's growth and spread economic development nation-wide (Tamura, 1987). The first formal step in this direction was in 1950, with the passing of the first Comprehensive National Land Development Act. It came at a time when Japan was rebuilding from the war and migrants were flooding Tokyo for work opportunities, and was intended to assure a more equitable distribution of industry and other economic activity across the nation.

There have been four other National Land Development Plans since then (1962, 1969, 1977 and 1987), as well as a highly publicized 'last word' on the subject in 1971–72 by Prime Minister Tanaka Kakuei. This was his ambitious plan called *Nihon-Rettō Kaizō-Ron* and published in English as *Building a New Japan: Remodeling the Japanese Archipelago*. However, as we shall see, Tokyo kept growing through all of this, and, despite considerable earnest investment that went elsewhere, has strengthened its primacy over the rest of the country. Instead of deconcentration on a national scale, what took place was an unprecedented sprawl of the built-up area on to surrounding terrain, and incorporation of almost all the nearby cities, small towns and farmlands, as well as substantial portions of Tokyo Bay, into its urban-industrial orbit.

Plans and discussions about how to limit Tokyo's size and influence are still active. There is special urgency to this now because of the extremely steep increases in land prices that took place in the mid- to late–1980s. Indeed, as we shall see toward the end of this book, much of the attention on what is called 'the Tokyo problem' focuses these days on moving the capital of Japan, in whole or in part, out of the city to a new site or sites (Itō, 1988; Yawata, 1988). At the same time, we shall also see that Tokyo continues to expand, and that the actions of private developers, as well as government and official plans for the city, push growth in all directions: outward to previously undeveloped terrian and new sections of Tokyo Bay, upward to new heights of skyscrapers and downward to ever-deeper subterranean levels. We conclude that Tokyo is a giant city everyone knows is far too big already, but that simply won't stop growing.

Defining Tokyo

We can continue our orientation to Tokyo by clearing up some problems about definitions of the city and usage of the word 'Tokyo'. This is important because the city has a unique administrative status that makes it somewhat confusing to define, and that gives the legal entity called Tokyo some rather unusual borders. The first point to make is that, technically, there is no such thing as a city of Tokyo. This was abolished in 1943, and was replaced with a larger unit that combined the city with Tokyo Prefecture to make a new and unique unit of government called *Tokyo-to* or Tokyo Metropolis. We can think of this area as the old city plus many of its suburbs to the west, plus much other territory, most of which is further west than the suburbs and is not urbanized. This change was instituted by the national government during the height of World War II to facilitate defense of the national capital by streamlining local administrative structure, and has been retained ever since under a kind of 'regional government' model in which the central city and many of its suburbs function together as a unit.

One result of this is some confusion about the terminology of the word 'Tokyo'. There are at least three different definitions for places that are called Tokyo in casual usage, depending on whether one is referring to what is generally thought of as the central city only, to *Tokyo-to*, or to the whole metropolitan area. The smallest of these areas is the central city (Figure 2.1). This is what used to be the City of Tokyo before the change in 1943. It is often called 'the 23 wards' or, simply, 'the ward area,' after the neighborhood-scale administrative units left over from before the change, which now provide various services of local government. This definition of Tokyo is a densely built-up, compact area of 598 square kilometers at the head of Tokyo Bay that focuses on the Imperial Palace and the Tokyo downtown (e.g., the famous Ginza district). The total population is 8,351,893 (1989 official estimate). Table 2.3, which is keyed to the map called Figure 2.1, lists the 23 wards of Tokyo and gives the population and the geographical extent of each.

The second meaning of 'Tokyo' is *Tokyo-to*, the consolidated territory under the administration of the Tokyo government. In addition to the 23 wards, *Tokyo-to* consists of a large suburban and mountain area known as the Tama District and two groups of small islands far out in the Pacific Ocean. It is this geopolitical arrangement that has resulted in Tokyo's odd boundaries. The Tama District has a total area of 1,161 square kilometers and nearly 3.5 million inhabitants. It extends west like a finger pointed from the ward area for some 60 kilometers, well into a mountainous district known as the Kantō Mountains or Oku-Tama ('Deep Tama'). Most of the population is in the lower-lying eastern end of the area, adjacent to the ward area, and in a rapidly urbanizing central zone of hills and tablelands. The furthest point is Mt Kumotori, some 75 kilometers from the Imperial Palace (Tokyo's symbolic center), at the boundary between *Tokyo-to* and Yamanashi Prefecture. It rises 2,018 meters above sea level and is the highest point in the metropolis. Its area is fairly rugged terrain that is hardly built up at all, but it is still 'Tokyo' nevertheless. Administratively, the Tama District comprises 26 cities, five towns and one village. These are also listed in Table 2.3.

The islands of *Tokyo-to* lie far south of the city and are a world apart in terms of climate, physical appearance and lifestyles. They are joined administratively to Tokyo for convenience to provide their populations with local government services. The nearer group of islands, called the Izu

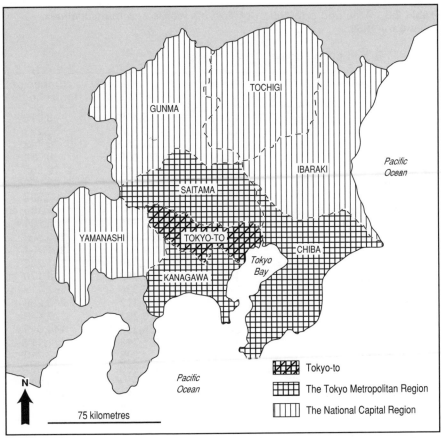

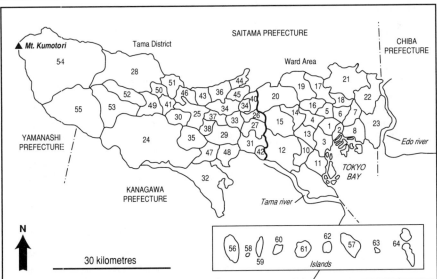

Figure 2.1 a. *Tokyo-to* and surrounding prefectures
               b. Administrative units of *Tokyo-to*

Orientation to Tokyo

Table 2.3 Area and population of Tokyo's wards and municipalities,
1 January 1988

● The area and population in the 23 wards

		Area (km²)	Population	Number of households
1	Chiyoda	11.52	45,458	18,072
2	Chūō	10.05	75,136	30,293
3	Minato	19.99	181,263	78,143
4	Shinjuku	18.04	323,635	148,392
5	Bunkyō	11.44	192,062	79,503
6	Taitō	10.00	172,157	68,259
7	Sumida	13.82	227,475	82,597
8	Kōtō	37.13	393,154	145,165
9	Shinagawa	20.91	351,575	148,291
10	Meguro	14.41	262,557	115,509
11	Ōta	51.02	659,687	261,784
12	Setagaya	58.81	810,344	351,203
13	Shibuya	15.11	231,753	108,170
14	Nakano	15.73	330,930	152,713
15	Suginami	33.54	539,113	243,238
16	Toshima	13.01	276,297	127,449
17	Kita	20.55	365,293	144,649
18	Arakawa	10.34	187,718	71,118
19	Itabashi	31.90	514,346	202,738
20	Nerima	47.00	607,950	227,991
21	Adachi	53.25	628,939	216,942
22	Katsushika	33.90	421,868	151,293
23	Edogawa	48.26	538,327	189,607

● The area and population in the municipalities

		Area (km²)	Population	Number of households
	(Cities)			
24	Hachiōji	187.79	442,045	145,330
25	Tachikawa	24.21	150,490	52,734
26	Musashino	11.03	139,152	60,049
27	Mitaka	16.83	166,854	68,258
28	Ōme	104.01	117,098	35,246
29	Fuchū	29.86	207,045	76,703
30	Akishima	17.20	101,611	34,597
31	Chōfu	21.79	196,137	76,632
32	Machida	71.54	337,177	107,937
33	Koganei	11.35	105,089	42,091
34	Kodaira	20.85	159,679	56,481
35	Hino	27.11	160,419	57,834
36	Higashi Murayama	16.58	128,756	41,855
37	Kokubunji	11.40	98,737	38,669
38	Kunitachi	8.08	65,139	24,715
39	Tanashi	6.89	73,604	26,053

Table 2.3 *Continued*

		Area (km²)	Population	Number of households
40	Hōya	8.77	93,651	34,413
41	Fussa	10.41	53,946	18,921
42	Komae	6.15	75,017	30,060
43	Higashi Yamato	13.52	73,226	22,983
44	Kiyose	10.19	66,753	21,400
45	Higashi Kurume	12.98	111,479	36,496
46	Musashi Murayama	15.23	62,322	19,713
47	Tama	20.68	135,144	44,294
48	Inagi	17.61	52,701	17,539
49	Akikawa	22.14	47,331	13,348
	(Towns)			
50	Hamura	9.79	49,376	16,544
51	Mizuho	16.82	29,026	8,221
52	Hinode	28.18	16,317	4,156
53	Itsukaichi	50.96	21,053	5,783
54	Okutama	104.91	8,940	2,592
	(Village)			
55	Hinohara	226.44	3,812	1,006

- The area and population in the islands

		Area (km²)	Population	Number of Households
	(Towns)			
56	Ōshima	91.00	10,144	4,000
57	Hachijō	71.44	9,932	3,889
	(Villages)			
58	Toshima	4.19	315	140
59	Niijima Honson	27.24	3,613	1,154
60	Kozushima	18.59	2,311	660
61	Miyake	55.14	4,086	1,724
62	Mikurajima	19.69	266	134
63	Aogashima	5.23	205	110
64	Ogasawara	106.18	2,341	1,010

Source: Tokyo Metropolitan Government, 1989b, p. 47.

Islands, is a chain of volcanic islands stretching north-south from about 100 to 350 kilometers from the main part of the city. The other islands are the Ogasawara (or Bonin) Islands. They are situated some 1,000 to 1,300 kilometers south of the 23 wards and are tropical in character. There are more than thirty islands in this group, including Iwo Jima, the famous World War II battle site. Both groups add up to about 403 square kilometers (a little less than one-fifth of the total area of *Tokyo-to*), but number only 33,587 inhabitants.[4]

The third usage of the word 'Tokyo' refers to the metropolitan area over and above that included within the *Tokyo-to* administrative unit. This is the least precise of the three usages, because several definitions of the metropolitan area (the city plus its surrounding built-up area) are possible. Moreover, because of the proximity of the huge central city of Yokohama (nearly 3.2 million in 1989; 25–30 kilometers from city center to city center), the Tokyo metropolitan area more properly belongs to both cities. Therefore, one often hears terms such as the 'Tokyo-Yokohama conurbation' in connection with this area. However, because of Tokyo's far greater size and influence, the metropolitan area is most commonly labelled as if it were Tokyo's alone.

Some definitions of the Tokyo metropolitan area are quite technical. One delineation, by the census office of Japan, employs 'densely-populated enumeration districts' (over 4,000 persons per square kilometer) as the basis for delimitation. The result is an irregularly shaped area of over 3,100 square kilometers that stretches out radially for distances of up to 50 kilometers from the city center (Tokyo Metropolitan Government, 1990, p. 6). Another delineation, developed by Japanese geographers Ishimizu Teruo and Ishihara Hiroshi, employed commuting patterns to define limits for the Tokyo metropolitan area. In the mid–1970s, when their research was done, the Tokyo area extended as far as 55 to 65 kilometers from the center (Hall, 1984, pp. 179–80). Other definitions, employed most commonly by national and local planning authorities, employ prefectural boundaries to set limits for the metropolitan area. One such area, generally called the Greater Tokyo Metropolitan Area, is described as *Tokyo-to* plus the three adjacent prefectures of Kanagawa (which includes Yokohama), Saitama and Chiba. This is a territory of 13,508 square kilometers and nearly 31 million inhabitants. Because they are not extensively urbanized, the distant islands of *Tokyo-to* are sometimes excluded from this definition. The largest definition of the metropolitan area is the National Capital Region. This entity includes *Tokyo-to* (less the islands in some sources), the three prefectures just named, and four other prefectures in a surrounding 'outer ring' around the capital city. This territory dates back to 1956, when it was defined formally by national planners in an effort to regulate the expansion of urbanization. The population is now approximately 39 million. Table 2.4 summarizes the three definitions of 'Tokyo'.

[4] The fact that these islands are technically within the same entity of local government that is Tokyo gives the city a distinction that is probably unique among urban areas in the world: its territory extends for the greatest distance from end to end (approximately 1,300 kilometers); and it covers the greatest range of geographical environments, from tiny tropical isles rimmed with palms, white sands and coral reefs on the one hand, to heavily-forested mid-latitude mountain slopes with four well-defined seasons on the other.

Table 2.4 Three definitions of Tokyo

Definition and common terms	Area (sq. km.)	Population (1980) (×1000)	Population (1988) (×1000)	Rate
'The ward area' '23 wards' 'The central city'	598	8,352	8,337	−0.2%
'Tokyo Metropolis' 'Tokyo Prefecture' *'Tokyo-to'*	2,162	11,618	11,680	+0.5%
'Metropolitan Tokyo' A Greater Tokyo Metropolitan Area	13,508	28,697	30,762	+7.2%
B National Capital Region	36,834	35,700	38,993	+9.2%

A Greater Tokyo Metropolitan area includes *Tokyo-to* (including the islands) and Chiba, Kanagawa and Saitama Prefectures.
B The National Capital region is all of (A) plus Yamanashi, Gunma, Tochigi, and Ibaraki Prefectures.

Administrative structure

Because of the confusion that comes with having three meanings for the word 'Tokyo', it is especially important to clarify the administrative structure that governs the city. The designation *to* that is given to Tokyo is the only designation of this type in Japan and is quite complicated. In some respects it is equivalent to that of *ken* or prefecture; in others it has similarities to municipal government in Japan; and in others still it is totally unique. Most often, *Tokyo-to* (or Tokyo Metropolis) is grouped with the 43 prefectures of Japan and three other special designations (one *to* and two *fu*), to make a total of 47 prefecture-type entities that are collectively called *to-dō-fu-ken*. While there are some differences in detail between them, each of these units, including Tokyo Metropolis, has a governor elected by popular vote for a four-year term, and a legislative assembly, members of which are also elected for terms of four years. The Tokyo assembly has 127 seats. The assembly and the office of the governor comprise what in English is called Tokyo Metropolitan Government (TMG). *Tokyo-to* is like a prefecture because it contains many units of local government within it. This includes the various cities, towns and villages, as well as vestiges of an older system of counties (*gun*) and the governments of the 23 wards.

The establishment of *Tokyo-to* as a self-governing entity similar to prefectural governments dates from 1947 when the Local Autonomy Act was put into effect after the adoption of the post-war Constitution. This ended the period since 1943 during which the *to* was little more than an agency of national government. About the same time, the wards that had comprised the pre-1943 city were reorganized. There had been 35 of them (since 1932), but they were consolidated first into 22 wards and then 23 when Nerima Ward was carved out of part of an oversized Itabashi Ward. These wards have a designation as *tokubetsu ku* or 'special wards'. In theory this means they have responsibilities and powers equivalent to those of cities in other prefectures, as well as a structure of government like that of cities. For example, each ward has a popularly elected ward head (the *ku-chō*) with powers similar to that of a city mayor and an elected ward assembly. In this way, we can think of *Tokyo-to* as a prefecture made up of 23 'cities' from the old urban definition, plus the 26 cities, five towns, one village and some leftover counties in the Tama district.

However, *Tokyo-to* is also a municipality. Because of a complex division of responsibilities between Tokyo Metropolitan Government and the local government bodies, TMG administers many 'big-city' services in addition to having functions equivalent to those of a prefectural government. This includes such services as fire-fighting, police, public education, garbage collection and disposal, waterworks and sewerage, port and harbor administration, streets, many public transportation services (eg., subways), and a large fraction of all public housing, parks, large urban renewal projects and other works. Consequently, each of the 23 wards has fewer responsibilities in practice than one would normally expect from a city. What is left for them includes responsibility for local parks, smaller public improvement projects, some public housing, many health centers and other social services, building certification, vital statistics and record-keeping, and other local or specialized functions. The purpose of this division is to strive to have both the advantages of a large centralized government that can efficiently coordinate major tasks over a wide area on the one hand, and the advantages of a more intimate-scale local government on the other.

Finally, we should note that in addition to being a prefectural government and a municipal government, TMG has numerous unique responsibilities that come with being the national capital. These include the guarding of the National Diet and other government offices, protection services for foreign diplomatic establishments and official guests, protection of the Imperial Household, and 'the maintenance of Tokyo's cityscape befitting its status as the nation's metropolis' (Tokyo Metropolitan Government, 1984, p. 37).

The view from Tokyo Tower

One of the best places for an orientation to Tokyo is to take in the view from Tokyo Tower. This is the famous broadcasting and reception facility-cum-tourist attraction that looms over the center of the city, providing from its two observatories (150 meters and 250 meters) some of Tokyo's most sweeping panoramas. I go there from time to time to introduce the city to friends who come to visit me in Japan, to teach some urban geography to my students, and for a dose of inspiration when the writing of this book slows down. We shall go there now for (1) an orientation to the geographical layout of Tokyo; and (2) for insights to the kind of city that Tokyo has become after 400 years of development – and to see the way it continues to change today.

Geography

The first thing to learn about the layout of Tokyo is that the center of the city is the Imperial Palace (Figure 2.2). Its grounds appear from Tokyo Tower as a huge void in the middle of a gigantic urban expanse; they are the place from from which all compass directions and distances from the city are described. The site is less than three kilometers from the tower, and stands out as a massive island of green (even in winter) contrasting with the the densely built-up surroundings. The whole of the city seems to huddle around this space, as indeed was the intention of the shogun Ieyasu who created this unique arrangement four centuries ago. The boundary between the city and the palace compound is quite rigid, as one sees lengths of stone walls and moats still in place from the time when Tokyo was a

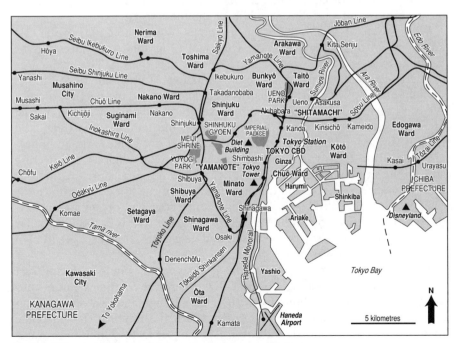

Figure 2.2 Locations of important places in Tokyo

castle town called Edo. With a little imagination, one can even see that today's road network, including the traffic-choked elevated expressways that snake through the crowded neighborhoods of the inner-city, comes together at the foot of the palace, at the business district that first formed just outside one of the main gates.

The area that adjoins the Imperial Palace to the south and east is the Tokyo Central Business District (CBD). This is an immensely crowded and internally complex area with numerous distinctive sub-sections defined by the specific economic activities they conduct. Our high vantage point allows us to pick out some of these. The area that is closest to us (i.e., between Tokyo Tower and the Imperial Palace) is the national government center of Japan. It covers two neighborhood-scale sections of Tokyo called Nagat-achō and Kasumigaseki, and has as its principal landmark the grey granite National Diet Building. The commercial focus of the CBD is to the east, on the other side of a sizable Western-style park called Hibiya Park. The principal office district, a place called Marunouchi, is just across a moat from the Imperial Palace, and is distinguished by a grid-street plan and block-like office buildings of almost equal height. Tokyo Station, the hub of the rail network, is just beyond. Other office and and retailing sections such as Ōtemachi, Nihombashi, and the famous Ginza are arranged in a kind of semicircle around Tokyo Station in the direction opposite from the Imperial Palace. As we shall see in later chapters, these were once parts of *shitamachi*, the low-lying river delta area at the head of Tokyo Bay that was the domain of commoner classes, and that evolved during the nine-teenth century into the business hub of the modern city.

What is left of *shitamachi* is on the other side of the CBD, to the east and north of the Imperial Palace. The main geographical features are the Sumida River and the dozen or more bridges that span it. This is the area of the so-called river wards (Sumida, Arakawa, Taitō, and Kōtō) and is thought of as Tokyo's historic district of old houses and old neighborhoods. We can't see the details from Tokyo Tower, but it is a highly mixed district of housing, warehouses and small factories, old commercial streets and famous shrines and temples. Some of the greenery of Ueno Park, an impor-tant recreation facility and major concentration of religious architecture and public museums in Taitō Ward, is visible near the horizon three or four kilometers north of the Imperial Palace. On the horizon itself are the eastern wards of Tokyo (eg., Katsushika and Edogawa), or, on a clear day, the suburban towns of Chiba Prefecture. In general, this is the blue-collar side of Tokyo, and many of the towns and neighborhoods there are known for industry and lower residential rents.

The Tokyo waterfront is visible from observation windows facing east and south. The area closest to the CBD, where the Sumida empties into the bay, is extensively built up with tall buildings and is ever more an extension of the business core. Further south the bayfront is called the Jōnan District and is mostly industrial. We can see factory buildings, ware-houses, gas tanks and port facilities all along the rail corridor that stretches

Figure 2.3 A view to the west from Tokyo Tower. The picture was taken on an unusually clear day, and Mt Fuji is visible on the horizon

near the center of Tokyo to Haneda Airport and beyond. This is all reclaimed land; on a clear day we can make out the geometric lines of ship channels that separate tightly packed industrial islands. Tokyo Bay itself is also a cluster of straight-line islands made of landfill. They are big, geometric, and for the most part are also given to industrial land uses. However, we shall see in a later chapter that there are ambitious plans underway to convert the Tokyo waterfront, including some of the largest new islands, into a new business and residential focus for the city.

The view to the west from Tokyo Tower (and a little to the north) looks out over many of the city's better neighborhoods and its sector of greatest spatial expansion (Figure 2.3). The area closest to the tower is especially nice, albeit crowded by most cities' standards, and includes such prestigious residential districts as Azabu and Hiroo, and the famous nightclub district called Roppongi. A little further away are the high-rises that mark Tokyo's fashionable new commercial sub-centers: Shinjuku, Shibuya, and Ikebukuro. Beyond them are miles and miles of city and suburb, as far as the eye can see. On a clear day, such as when I took the picture for Figure 2.3, one can see some of the residential areas of the Tama District of *Tokyo-to* and of Kanagawa Prefecture, as well as the distinctive profile of Mt Fuji nearly 90 kilometers away.

Table 2.5 Land use in Tokyo, 1988 (in hectares)

	Residential districts	Commercial districts	Industrial districts	Other developed land	Fields	Forests	Other	Total
Central Wards*	649	860	127	4	–	–	12	1,632
%	39.8	52.7	7.8	0.2	–	–	0.7	100.0
Other Wards	24,150	2,486	2,938	26	1,778	73	754	32,225
%	74.9	7.7	9.1	–	5.5	0.2	2.3	100.0
23-Ward Total	24,799	3,346	3,065	30	1,778	73	766	33,857
%	73.2	9.9	9.1	–	5.3	0.2	2.3	100.0
All *shi*	14,070	688	1,756	791	8,337	9,620	5,281	42,543
%	37.8	1.6	4.1	1.9	19.6	22.6	12.4	100.0
All *gun*	709	38	276	310	1,329	13,747	1,743	18,152
%	3.9	0.2	1.5	1.7	7.3	75.7	9.6	100.0
All islands	315	–	–	374	2,952	6,521	3,921	14,081
%	9.3	–	–	2.7	21.0	46.3	27.8	100.0
Tokyo-to Total	41,892	4,072	5,098	1,504	14,395	29,961	11,711	108,633
%	38.6	3.7	4.7	1.4	13.3	27.6	10.8	100.0

* Chiyoda, Chūō and Minato Wards

Source: Tokyo Statistical Yearbook, 1987, pp. 2–5.

Impressions

Perhaps the most striking impression of the view from Tokyo Tower is of the immense size of the city. This is no surprise because hugeness is a fundamental characteristic of Tokyo and probably the single most important fact about it. Yet the view is so impressive that I am still amazed with every approach to the observation windows, no matter how many times I go there. In every direction as far across the city's plain as the eye can see, as well as on new land reclaimed from Tokyo Bay, there is nothing but city! The built-up area extends for well over 50 kilometers in some directions, much further than one can pick out in urban detail, and seems almost limitless. Only on those days when Mt Fuji and the other mountains are visible does one actually see beyond the metropolis. Measurement is difficult because of problems with definitions, but it is safe to say that the total built-up area exceeds 3,000 square kilometers (Tokyo Metropolitan Government, 1990a, p. 6).

What is more, almost all this enormous territory is extremely densely built up. A great many of the buildings seen are high- or mid-rise structures, at least five or six stories tall, and there is almost no empty space between them. Where there are single homes, they are packed so closely together that one sees only an unbroken surface of contiguous roofs. To be sure, there are also some parks and other open spaces, including some quite large ones such as that for the Imperial Palace; but they stand out as dramatic exceptions to an otherwise oppressive mass of urban material. The buildings push right up against the edges of the open spaces, and form high, thick walls that define their boundaries precisely and enclose them almost completely. This accentuates the great volume of Tokyo, and adds to the impression, which is probably correct, that one can see from Tokyo Tower more city, as defined by a combination of spatial extent and building density, than from any other spot on earth.[5] Table 2.6 provides some data that illustrate the impressive physical dimensions of Tokyo's built environment.

A third thing one notices almost immediately is that this gigantic mass of urban material is growing even bigger. There is construction to be seen virtually everywhere! It seems that the whole city is pushing upward to new heights and outward in all directions, and that what was already enormous is becoming bigger still. Even Tokyo Bay is becoming urbanized, as large, new islands are being fashioned in the distance beyond other new islands. Everywhere else one looks, there are new buildings that are measurably taller than those of their surroundings, and many construction sites where steel frames are pushing skyward announcing buildings that are yet to be. One can easily spot more than 100 separate such projects from the Tokyo Tower observation windows alone. They are identified by

[5] On a clear day the view from The World Trade Center in New York shows much, much more greenery beyond the core of the city than one sees in Tokyo.

Table 2.6 Building density in Tokyo, 1986

	Number of Buildings	Buildings per hectare	Land Area per Building (m²)	Land Coverage Ratio (%)	Capacity Ratio (%)[a]	Height Ratio (%)[b]	Average Number of Stories
Chiyoda Ward	17,056	15.4	382.1	31.7	218.4	68.4	6.8
Chūō Ward	18,556	21.9	233.2	40.5	203.9	55.0	5.0
Minato Ward	35,670	17.6	342.4	25.8	117.2	45.5	4.5
23 Wards Total	1,686,750	28.7	205.5	30.2	81.0	16.0	2.7
Urban Areas in Tama District	793,740	9.6	285.0	10.1	19.0	6.2	1.9

[a] Total floor space in buildings as a percentage of land area.
[b] Percent ratio of buildings with 4 or more stories to all buildings. In terms of the number of building units and area space covered.

Source: Tokyo Statistical Yearbook, 1987, p. 10.

the presence of large, bright orange cranes and other construction machinery, and by the huge cloths, usually colored green or blue, that are widely used in Japan to shelter unfinished structures from the elements and shield passers-by from falling objects.

One is also somewhat taken aback by the incredible profusion of geometric shapes and building sizes that constitute the rising mass of the new Tokyo. Some of the new developments are quite large and stand out as megastructures towering over their respective neighborhoods and imposing on them a new authority. The Manhattan-like skyline of Shinjuku, seen in the middle distance to the northwest, is one example. Another is Ark Hills, the fresh cluster of high-rise hotels, office towers and giant condominium buildings just to the north of Tokyo Tower. It dominates the surrounding area and confidently proclaims itself in promotional advertising to redefine architecture for the 21st century and represent 'Where Tokyo is Headed'. Like so many of the other prominent new buildings in the city, the tallest towers in this development look a little like shoe-boxes standing on end.

On the other hand, many of the other new buildings are so slim they remind me of credit cards standing on end, or perhaps even pencils on end. Many are just barely wide enough to have elevators or stairways, and in quite a few structures the elevators are tiny and the stairways are affixed to the outside. Tokyo is so crowded and the cost of land so ridiculously high,[6] that one builds tall, even on the smallest of plots or the narrowest of land slivers, and does not worry so much about how the finished structure will be shaped or how furniture might be moved to the top floors. Nevertheless, one has to marvel at the skills of the city's builders as they maneuver cranes and other heavy equipment on to the most improbable sites, and create ways to squeeze in yet another high-rise where one would think that such a building could never fit. Often, the odd shapes that begin with a ground plan become even more convoluted at the upper stories, because of complex building regulations that control distribution of sunlight for street-level and neighboring structures. The view across much of the city, therefore, is one of sloped, stepped, and otherwise contorted upper levels on high- and mid-rise buildings. We can refer to this as Tokyo's 'angular vernacular' (Jinnai, 1988, p. 116). This is particularly so for the new multi-story condominium structures that abound in central Tokyo, called *manshon* (mansions) (Figure 2.4).

I should make it clear that building height is a relative concept, and that Tokyo, despite its impressive number of new, taller buildings, is not a high-rise city on the same scale as, say, Manhattan, Hong Kong or the fashionable stretches of Rio de Janeiro. Most new buildings are in the 6–15 stories range and only a small number are significantly taller. There are several limiting factors, not the least of which are extremely poor ground conditions and the ever present danger of earthquakes. To a lesser extent,

[6] A recent issue of *The Economist* (October 3 1987, p. 25) reports that a piece of land in the center of Tokyo about the size of this page would cost over $12,000 to buy.

Figure 2.4 New *manshon* amid tightly-packed houses in Kamiochiai in Shinjuku Ward. The *manshon* are examples of Tokyo's new angular vernacular

the lack of sizable development sites has also held back construction of super-tall structures. Consequently the tallest buildings are not in the core of the city at all, but in outlying commercial centers (Shinjuku and Ikebukuro) where bigger parcels were available for construction. Even then they fall short of the biggest structures in other leading cities (Table 2.7). In downtown Tokyo, the tallest building is only 152 meters (40 stories) high – only five meters higher than the first modern high-rise ever built in Tokyo, the Kasumigaseki Building completed in 1968 (147 meters; 36 floors).[7] However, developers are always on the lookout for engineering advances that promise to make tall buildings earthquake-safe, and many of them would hope to have super-tall high-rises in place in central Tokyo as soon as possible.

[7] The Kasumigaseki Building was a great novelty in low-rise Tokyo. There were long lines of curious visitors to ride the elevator to the observation area at the top for several months after the official opening. Moreover, because of its size, the building became such a prominent local landmark that it came to be used in the city, only half-jokingly, as a measure of volume: i.e., so many Kasumigaseki-Buildings of beer were drunk in Japan last year, etc.

Table 2.7 Tokyo's tallest buildings

Rank	Building name	Height (meters)	Height (floors)	Location
1*	Sunshine City	240	60	Ikebukuro
2	Shinjuku Center	216	54	Shinjuku
3	Shinjuku Mitsui	210	55	Shinjuku
4	Shinjuku Nomura	203	50	Shinjuku
5	Shinjuku Sumitomo	200	52	Shinjuku
6	Yasuda Kasai Kaijō	193	43	Shinjuku
7	NEC Headquarters	180	43	Shiba (CBD edge)
8	Keio Plaza Hotel	170	47	Shinjuku
9	KDD Building	165	32	Shinjuku
10	World Trade Center	152	40	Hamamatsuchō (CBD edge)
11	Kasumigaseki Bldg.	147	36	Kasumigaseki (CBD edge)
12	Shinjuku NS Building	134	30	Shinjuku

* Tokyo's new City Hall, which will tower to 243 meters, is now under construction and when finished will be the tallest building. It is in Shinjuku.

There are several other impressions that come to mind after these initial thoughts. One that follows directly from seeing the seemingly ubiquitous construction activity is that Tokyo is being given a whole new surface. As we survey the scene, we realize there are very few older buildings (say, older than 20 years or so) to be seen anywhere within a broad circumference around the tower, and conclude that yet another defining characteristic of the city, in addition to enormous size and density, is newness of the physical plant. The low-slung city of the past is almost completely gone: various parts of it were eradicated first by the earthquake and fire of 1923, then the 1945 disaster, and now by the super-active real-estate market. Even buildings that themselves are still fairly new and clearly serviceable, such as some of those built in the 1950s and 1960s, are being replaced by newer and bigger structures. The few historic buildings (i.e., from the early part of this century or older) that are visible are exceptions that have to be picked out from the scene after some study of the surroundings. Many of them, it seems, will soon be gone as well. This is particularly true for the general area where Tokyo Tower is situated. It happens to be an extremely expensive and popular section of the city, directly in the path of expansion of Tokyo's CBD, and growing especially quickly in numbers of tall office buildings, large international hotels, stores and other commerce, and *man-shon*. There is a certain irony, I think, that as Tokyo prepares to celebrate its 400th anniversary it is a rather new city.

Still another impression is that the overall form of Tokyo seems incredibly chaotic. This too is a fundamental characteristic that is part of Tokyo's general reputation. Not only is it a jumble of building shapes and sizes, it is also a maze of streets with no apparent plan and no relationship whatsoever to modern traffic needs. Most streets are small, narrow, and wind every which way in such fits and starts that no one even tries to give them names. The wider thoroughfares are different: they have names and follow courses that seem normal by the standards of modern cities. However, they are surprisingly few in number given the vastness of the built-up area and the demands of traffic; they stand out as somewhat ill-fitting additions slicing awkwardly through older neighborhoods. So it is not surprising that every one of these roads is exceedingly crowded. There are also several expressways visible from Tokyo Tower. They too are always jammed with slow-moving traffic, and follow narrow courses that are squeezed between tall buildings, meandering in great bends around prominent buildings as they pass through the center of the city. Perhaps it is the juxtaposition of so much that is new atop an old ground plan that reminds us of the city's past, and that convinces us (especially when we sit trapped in a traffic-stalled taxi with a meter running) that Tokyo is, in fact, a 400-year-old city dressed up for new.

Finally, we notice there seems to be little pattern to what has been built next to what. In a kind of a land use free-for-all that is also a fundamental characteristic of much of Tokyo, we see tiny single houses wedged between tall hotels or modern offices, or in the shadows of busy, elevated highways; shops and other businesses scattered all over what would seem to be housing areas; factories and warehouses sitting among private residences or apartments, or next to the newest gleaming office towers. There is little evidence of co-ordinated land use planning or the kinds of zoning restrictions that separate incompatible uses in most other cities – and even less evidence of attention to aesthetics in urban design. While some buildings stand out for their appealing architecture, the scene from Tokyo Tower is for the most part hard-featured and unattractive. The high-rises are mostly blockish and uninspired, and most of the rest of the buildings, the mid-rises, are cluttered with watertanks, television antennae and advertising billboards, and neons on their roofs. Utility poles and wires are everywhere. Almost everything, it seems, is meant to be purely functional, but little is built with the kind of architectural elegance normally accorded to structures that are meant to last. The whole scene is a careless jumble, because Tokyo itself is not meant to last, perched as it is between disasters and built for the moment (Popham, 1985, p. 34).

The area in the immediate vicinity of Tokyo Tower is a good example of Tokyo's frequently bewildering mix of land uses. We can look especially at Shiba Kōen, the large and now grossly disfigured park in which the Tower is situated. Although details are best studied on foot at street level, we can look directly down from windows in the lower observation level and see some of the odd juxtapositions that seem to be an essential feature of the city, and that make Tokyo such an interesting, albeit not necessarily attractive, place. The centerpiece is Zōjōji, one of the most important of Tokyo's many historic temples. It is famous for its old role as protector of Edo, as Tokyo was called in history, against evil spirits who might bring harm to the city from the southwest. It is distinguished visually by a great carved wooden gate that opens to the inner compound and a massive sloped tile roof on the main structure. Because of damage from the 1923 earthquake and fire and the bombing during World War II, Zōzōji is an historic site that was actually constructed in 1974. Next door, behind another historic temple gate, is a gigantic golf driving range. It has three decks of more than 50 drivers each, a bright green carpet covered with thousands of little white balls, a huge green net enclosing all of the action, and the word *Maxfli* in oversized red letters facing both the Tower and the golfers. This, in turn, is next to a large bowling alley with a huge tenpin on its roof. Next to that we see a wooded area in which some of the city's homeless men have built a small cardboard and plank shantytown. This and other sections of Shiba Kōen are bounded by wide, and incredibly busy highways, including an elevated expressway that winds around the southern edge of the park. There is still another big bowling alley almost straight down from the observation window with 'Tower Bowl' written in Japanese on the roof, and a television studio next door. A small pocket of tiny, single homes that somehow survived all the changes is just beyond. Off to the side is a luxury hotel (the Tokyo Prince) with a big, inviting swimming pool and a wonderful, quiet Japanese garden remaining from a feudal-era estate.

There is nothing particularly unusual about seeing a district of a city that is mixed, even with incongruities as striking as these. Cities, after all, are always giant repositories of complex history and multiple cultural influences. What makes this case special, however, is the contrast between the site as it is now and the role it played in history. In addition to Zōzōji, there were once *hundreds* of temple buildings there, as well as refectories and boarding houses for thousands of priests and novices (Waley, 1984, p. 359). Moreover, the grounds held the mausoleums of most of Japan's shoguns. In Waley's words, this was 'the citadel of Tokugawa Buddhism.' (Waley, 1984, p. 361). In just about any other culture, such a place would be considered a highly valued historic site, if not sacred ground, and would be preserved and protected forever. It would certainly not be an appropriate place for a tall steel tower, nor for bowling alleys and golf. But in the Shiba Kōen area, too, just as we saw at the start of this book with the example of my neighborhood and will see again in a number of other places to be visited, Tokyo is different: very different. It has its own sense of history and its own priorities for land use; it has developed its own distinctive urban form.

Physical geography

The physical geography of Tokyo has had substantial impact on the development of the city and its distinctive character. This is seen first of all in the location of Tokyo with respect to the rest of Japan. The fact that the city is near the center of the country, approximately midway along the Pacific coast of Honshū, the country's largest island, has helped it evolve into a giant national metropolis and to consolidate its influence as the national capital. So, too, Tokyo's growth has been enhanced by its setting in the Kantō Plain, the country's largest flatland. This area is a strategic hinge between the historic centers of Japanese culture to the west and southwest, and more recently integrated territories to the east and northeast. This aspect of geographic location accounts for the word 'Tokyo' itself, as well as for meanings implied in 'Kantō'. The former is translated as 'eastern capital', and contrasts with 'Kyoto', the city nearly 400 kilometers to the west, closer to the traditional Japanese heartland, that was the ancient capital. The word 'Kantō', on the other hand, means 'east of the barrier'. It is an older word than 'Tokyo', dating back to the Kamakura period of Japanese history (1185–1333), and reflects the fact that this large plain was once a frontier area located on the far side of a barrier station (sekisho) separating the established provinces from new lands.

Topography

The Kantō Plain covers parts of 7 of Japan's 47 prefectures, and measures approximately 13,000 square kilometers (Trewartha, 1965, p. 438). It extends from the coasts of Ibaraki and Chiba prefectures in the east for well over 100 kilometers to mountains in the west; and from Tokyo Bay in the south for 100 or so kilometers again to mountains in the north. The 23-ward portion of Tokyo occupies the southern part of this area, at the head of Tokyo Bay. The city's suburbs sprawl in all landward directions, but especially to the west, in the direction of the Tama area and adjacent parts of Kanagawa prefecture, where urban development abuts the Kantō Mountains and other highlands. The northern part of the Kantō Plain, above its longest river, the Tone, is heavily agricultural. However, urban growth is making rapid advances there as well.

The historic core of Tokyo is in that part of the Kantō Plain where three rivers, the Edogawa, the Arakawa and the Sumidagawa,[8] make their last meanders before emptying into Tokyo Bay. The land there is an extremely flat alluvial lowland, barely above sea level. It is highly susceptible to flooding and other hazards and has been the site of numerous disasters during the city's history. The original shoreline was marshy, but ambitious reclamation projects that began as far back as the late sixteenth century, when Tokyo was still a small settlement called Edo, changed all this and added considerable land to the city total. Other parts of the Kantō Plain in Tokyo are not so low-lying. Much of the territory is in the form of upland plains formed by changes in sea level over geological history and

---

[8] The suffix 'gawa' or 'kawa' means river. Thus, an alternative is Edo River, Ara River and Sumida River.

by shifts in the courses of rivers. The largest and most important is the Musashino Tableland, an expansive diluvial plain extending for some 60 kilometers west from the center of Tokyo to the mountainous rim of the Kantō region. Elevations range from approximately 30 to 250 meters above sea level. Its eastern reaches, set apart from the lower elevations by sharp escarpments, extend into the heart of the city. The result is a clear distinction between low-lying, flat sections of the city close to the bay and the river mouths, the *shitamachi*, and higher land inland, *yamanote*. We shall see that this is an extremely important distinction in the life of the city.

The Musashino Tableland covers the western side of Tokyo's 23 wards, as well as many of the towns and suburban developments in the central part of *Tokyo-to*, west of the ward area. Other more or less flat uplands are the Ōmiya Plain to the north, the Shimosa Upland in the outer suburbs in Chiba prefecture to the east, and the Sagamihara Upland in Kanagawa prefecture to the southwest. Each of these areas is covered with a thick stratum of volcanic ash (the 'Kantō loam') that is firm, dry, and otherwise physically well-suited for the urban development taking place there. In the past, however, settlement there was retarded because the land was poorly watered for irrigated rice. Other prominent features of the Tokyo portion of the Kantō Plain are heavily dissected hills in the south-central area and in the west before mountainous terrain begins. The former zone is especially important. This is the Tama Hills area across the Tama River floodplain from the Musashino Tableland. Today it is being extensively developed for housing and other urban uses because of its relative proximity to central Tokyo and Yokohama.

The mountains defining the inland limits of the Kantō Plain form an irregular semi-circle around the built-up area. The individual chains that make up the enclosure are the Tanzawa Mountains in the southwest, the Kantō Mountains in the west, the Mikuni Mountains northwest of the city, the Ashio Mountains to the north and the Yamizo Mountains furthest of all in the northeast. Some of these groups include prominent volcanic peaks. Mt Asama, at 2,542 meters in the Mikuni chain, is the highest. There are also several national parks and other attractive recreation areas (Figure 2.5). Mt Fuji, the graceful volcanic peak that is a symbol of Japan and the subject of so many paintings, photographs and postcards is beyond this mountain ring to the southwest. It is almost exactly 100 kilometers from the center of Tokyo, but visible from the city because its height (3,776 meters) rises above the intervening highlands. However, visibility is impaired by pollution. The best views are on crisp winter mornings and at dusk under clear conditions. In the latter case, the setting sun behind Mt Fuji presents Tokyo with a dramatic mountain silhouette.

Figure 2.5 The headwaters of the Tama River in Chichibu-Tama National Park, in the outer reaches of *Tokyo-to*

Climate

Tokyo's climate is influenced by the mountains and by the sea. It is a type of climate geography texts describe as humid sub-tropical; in many respects it resembles that of coastal locations in the southeastern United States. There is a clear distinction between the seasons. Summers are hot, humid and generally uncomfortable. Each year there is a month-long rainy season called *baiu* or *tsuyu* ('plum rain') from the middle of June into July. It is a most unpleasant time: the air is still and sticky, and the city suffers an annual invasion of ticks, mosquitoes and other tiny insects, as well as countless varieties of hardy and sometimes gigantic roaches. It is also a time when mold multiplies just about everywhere. On 20 July, a day called *doyō no hi*, the Japanese celebrate the end of this season by eating broiled eel to ward off mold-born diseases. Winters are cool, although only a few days have temperatures below freezing. Clear, sunny weather prevails, with little rain or snow. However, there is often a cold, dry wind that comes down from high elevations and puts a deep chill into the air. In the fall, there are occasional typhoons that come from over open water and bring heavy rains and widespread flooding. For many people, the favorite season is spring when the weather is generally good and the city seems especially pleasant. The few days in spring when cherry blossoms are in bloom (*sakura no kisetsu*) are particularly festive (Figure 2.6).

Figure 2.6 Partying under the blossoms during cherry blossom time in Inokashira Park. This is an annual ritual that is often a group activity. There is always a lot of beer and *sake* drinking and boisterous singing

Earthquake hazards

Perhaps no aspect of the natural environment of Tokyo is as momentous as the seismic characteristics of the site. As almost anyone who has spent more than a few days in the city learns by unnerving experience, Tokyo is at an extremely active earthquake zone and often undergoes subterranean tremors. This is true for Japan as a whole, because the country is where three tectonic plates (the edge of the Eurasian continental plate and the Philippine and Pacific plates) come into contact and create frequent spasmodic earth movements; but Tokyo is an especially dangerous site because of its proximity to the most violent lines of contact. In the summer of 1989, in an unusually active seismic experience, the Izu Peninsula, a weekend getaway area just south of Tokyo, with mountain hot springs and a rugged seacoast, was rocked with tens or hundreds of discrete shocks *each day*!

A second factor that makes Tokyo especially vulnerable to major earthquake damage in addition to the presence of the fault zone itself is that much of the city, including most of the downtown, most waterfront industrial districts and many crowded residential areas, are built on loosely consolidated landfill. When shaken by a quake, this material could mix with underground water and become a liquidy goo, causing the buildings that are built on it to collapse. This is a lesson Japan learned from a deadly earthquake in Niigata Prefecture in 1964, when steel-reinforced buildings, supposedly earthquake-proof, collapsed (Ueda, 1990, p. 26). The city's low elevation (sea level and below in some sections) poses still another threat: the possibility of tidal waves (*tsunami*) that would be triggered by a sea-floor quake in Tokyo Bay or elsewhere offshore. To protect against this, there is an extensive pattern of breakwaters in the bay, sea walls and river walls at the waterfront, and massive gates that can close off river mouths to prevent a flood tide from surging in.

There are approximately 30 to 50 perceptible shakes in Tokyo each year, two or three of which are strong enough to wake people from their sleep, rattle dishes and to do minor damage (Table 2.8). There is also a strong possibility that an even more substantial jolt could strike, causing wide-spread destruction and loss of life. This has occurred from time to time in the history of the city. The last such incident was in 1923, when the so-called Great Kantō Earthquake killed over 100,000 people in Tokyo and its environs, leaving much of the low-lying wards of Tokyo and Yokohama in ruins. It registered 7.9 on the Richter scale and was centered in Sagami Bay close to the Izu Peninsula.

Table 2.8 Number of earthquakes by magnitude, Tokyo, by year 1980s

	I	II	III	IV	V	Total
1980	15	9	5	2		31
1981	15	10	1			26
1982	16	13	4	1		34
1983	24	11	6	2		43
1984	18	13	11	2		44
1985	20	9	5	1		35
1986	17	7	2	1		27
1987	29	10	8	3		50
1988	36	9	6	1		52

I: Perceptible to people who are standing or sitting quietly.
II: Perceptible to most people; doors and windows rattle.
III: Houses shake; doors and windows rattle noisily; hanging lights, etc. sway; water moves in its containers.
IV: Violent shaking of houses; things tumble from shelves; people run from their houses.
V: Walls crack; gravestones and stone monuments tumble; considerable damage to buildings, etc.

Source: Rika Nenpyō (1989 edition), published by Maruzen Shuppan Co., Tokyo, 1989.

Experts agree that a major quake will strike Tokyo again. What is not known is when this will happen and how extensive the damage and loss of life will be. There seems to be a pattern of the biggest earthquakes, such as the one of 1923, occurring about every 70 years (1923, 1853, 1782, 1703, 1633), so it is possible that the next giant shake will come soon.

Such a possibility is very much a part of the background of living in Tokyo, and a major shaper of the urban personality. On the one hand, one sees that considerable energy is expended to prevent disaster and to be prepared in case the worst happens. On the other hand, one also discerns an air of fatalism in the city, not just because of earthquakes. Because of the devasting experience of wartime bombing raids in 1945 and a long history of destructive fires, there is an attitude in Tokyo that time between disasters is limited, and that the city should therefore hurry forward at full steam with its business, now, while it still can. Perhaps no other major city in the world defines itself as being so transitory as Tokyo; no other city views its own history so much as a series of urgent rebuildings between disasters. We will discuss these aspects of Tokyo more fully in the chapters that follow.

Social geography of the rails

In some ways the most important topic for orientation to Tokyo is the city's train and subway network. This is how the vast majority of Tokyoites travel from place to place, and the circulation system that is the city's lifeblood. A map of the ten subway lines that criss-cross under the inner part of the 23 wards is indispensable for getting around Tokyo, as is a plan of the many train lines that radiate in all directions outside the city and connect with the subway network. At first sight, the system appears complicated, but it is actually easy to use and extremely convenient. It is also meticulously clean, safe and on schedule. These aspects reflect an image of Tokyo as a perfectly tuned, smooth-running machine, a marvel of transportation planning, technology and social organization. However, the train and subway network is also hopelessly congested on most lines, particularly at peak times. Thus, the network also reflects an image of Tokyo as an overgrown giant.

It is not my intention to provide a detailed description of Tokyo's rail network. Visitors to the city have ample advice about this in guidebooks and maps, and from the continually improving bilingual signs (Japanese and English) at all the stations. However, there is one train line that I do want to mention. It is more important than the others not just because of the great number of passengers it carries, but also because it is something of a Tokyo landmark and performs a critical role in the geographical organization of the city. This is the Yamanote Line, a line that is distinguished by its green cars and the broad loop it forms around much of the center of the city (Figure 2.7). It is operated by Japan Railways (JR), the recently privatized rail system binding the nation. On a map the Yamanote Line looks a little like a fastened necklace with 29 beads corresponding to the 29 stations along the route. It takes 63 minutes to go round it completely, and during most times of the day, trains which themselves are a quarter-mile long, stop at the stations about every three minutes. Some

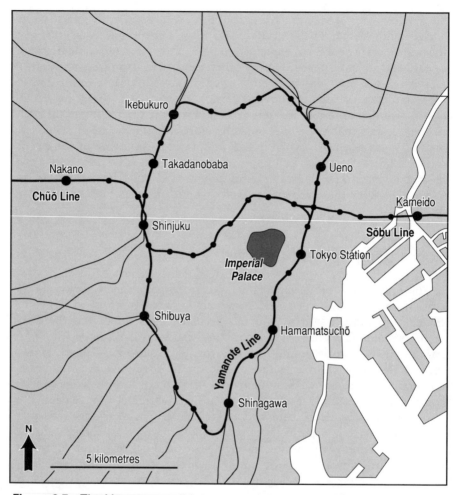

Figure 2.7 The Yamanote rail loop around the center of Tokyo and feeder commuter lines from the suburbs

of the stations, the bigger beads on the chain, are the most important stations in the metropolitan area. They are where the city's subways (most of them operated by Tokyo Government) and train lines from the suburbs (most of them private enterprises) come together, and where hundreds of thousands of passengers transfer between them or the loop line each day. Examples include Shinjuku, Shibuya and Ikebukuro on the west side of the loop, Shinagawa on the southwest and Ueno on the northwest. Tokyo Station, generally thought of as the city's central station, is also on the loop. It is on the east side where the Yamanote Line cuts through the city's Central Business District.

One of the most important bits of geographical terminology in Tokyo concerns the distinction between areas within the Yamanote loop from those outside it. The inside is a commonly accepted definition of the inner city; it includes all the Imperial Palace compound, much of the Central Business District, the national government center, and many historic sites and famous neighborhoods. The outside, particularly on the west side where the loop is stretched away from the center, marks the start of residential Tokyo and the direction to the suburbs. It is there that numerous rail lines come together from the elongated Tama area of *Tokyo-to* and from the expansive sector of suburban growth in neighboring prefectures. On the other hand, the parts to the eastern side of the Yamanote Line (and a little to the north) mark the boundary between the commercial core of the city on the inside and the historic neighborhoods of *shitamachi* on the outside. It is not the exact boundary, but is close enough and is sometimes described as if it were.

The shape of the Yamanote loop is widely recognized in Tokyo, especially when combined on an illustration with the corridor of the Chūō and Sōbu Lines (also JR). This slices east-west through the center of the loop and, as Figure 2.7 shows, has a distinctive crook, easily identified. These are features that residents look for when orienting themselves to almost any map of the city, be it of the street plan, the transit network or some other pattern. Advertisers often draw sketch maps of the loop on their copy so they can clearly explain the location of a business. In fact, Tokyoites know the loop so well that many of them, perhaps a majority, can recite the 29 stations in order without consulting a list and can name the other lines, both public and private as well as above and below ground, that intersect at all the transfer stations. So knowing the Yamanote Line is a matter of fundamental literacy about Tokyo. In the following pages there will be numerous references to places as being 'inside' or 'outside' the loop, and to various stations and station-front commercial centers along its course.

In addition to this geographical orientation to the rail system, I want to introduce some sociological observations. For one thing, we see from the train and subway network another example, as with earthquakes, of the precarious nature of Tokyo. The city is constantly on the edge of one type of disaster or another; with transportation the problem is that the system that works beautifully, like a flawless machine, for 99-plus per cent of the time, can fall apart completely almost at any moment. For example, on the rare occasion that there is a mechanical failure or an accident, a fast-moving ripple effect takes place across a wide area. Trains back up all up and down the affected line and sometimes on other lines too. As this happens, boarding platforms become dangerously crowded because pro-spective riders are continuing to arrive, as always, every minute, and access has to be closed. In the worst case, virtually the entire circulation system of a wide area would come to a complete halt. Fortunately, the employees of train and subway companies are well trained for such emergencies, and it never takes long before the problem is corrected and a reverse ripple brings everything back to normal. It takes incredible planning to keep the transportation system in tune, including strict maintenance schedules for the trains that probably rival those for jumbo passenger jets, and minute safety regulations that govern every motion, it seems, of the conductors on the trains and the railway personnel on the platforms.[9]

There are also certain expectations that are put on passengers to keep the Tokyo machine moving. For example, we see the reasonable requirements that passengers board smoothly during the few seconds that trains doors are opened at a station, and that they adhere to a certain level of quiet and other decorum. Violations are infrequent and are generally dealt with immediately and harshly. Not long ago I was fascinated by a story in the newspapers about two high-school boys who were exceptionally boisterous and rude on a train, and pushed aside an older man to grab a seat. By the standards of most cities, where much worse violations are common, this incident would hardly attract attention. But in this case the police were called in. After a few days of searching, they found the boys and made a lesson of them by publicizing their apologies to their victim and to the other passengers. (It was possible to trace the culprits because, like most Japanese youngsters, they wore uniforms particular to their school.) The purpose of calling the police and pressing the case was to make sure that problems of this type would remain minimal.

People who violate the system's rules in a more serious way, such as actually to delay trains, are dealt with even more harshly. Thus, in another incident an American schoolboy caused a panic among riders by releasing a garden snake on a crowded Chūō commuter train. This stopped the train and required its removal from the line until workmen could locate and dispose of the reptile. Newspapers next day were filled with outrage at the incident, and with wise editorial observations about how foreigners don't understand Japanese rules and have to be taught to fit in. One writer opined that while such 'a deliberate prank . . . may be rather common in American society . . . the humor was lost on most adults here' (*Japan Times*, 12 June, 1988). To make sure that there would be no future imitations of the incident, the boy's family was made to pay a heavy and well-publicized fine. In the same vein, when a person commits suicide by jumping in front of a train, which is apparently something that happens more often than officials care to admit, the family of the deceased is made to pay expensive penalties because of the disruption to train schedules.[10]

---

[9] All these employees, by the way, as well as all ticket sellers and attendants at the wickets where tickets are checked, are males. The rail system is so set in its ways that it stands out even in ultra-sexist Japan for its refusal to admit women employees. This criticism applies equally to the government of Tokyo, which operates most of the subway lines, to Japan Railways (JR), a newly privatized institution that runs most of the national rail network, and to the many private enterprises that make a business of providing commuter train services.

[10] I witnessed such a suicide once. It stopped the trains on this particular line for about 15 minutes and slowed them for about two hours while an army of railway employees and city police cleaned up the area. In an amazing example of the versatility of tools that are part of a nation's material culture, I was astounded to see that the smallest pieces of human tissue were collected with chopsticks.

What such examples show is one of the most fundamental lessons about Japanese society. We see that Japan, or Tokyo in particular, tolerates few deviations from a norm and expects faithful adherence to established routines. There is little tolerance for individuals who, for whatever reason, do not act like the others and would impede the general flow. People with serious injuries or physical handicaps, such as those that require a wheelchair, do not fit in to the transit system and are excluded from it by design. Without exception, every station has multiple stairways that have to be negotiated to reach the trains; has an elevator to the platform. So, too, slow-moving people, such as some elderly folk or people with bulky luggage, are discouraged from using the system. The only notable exception to such inaccessibilty concerns people who are visually impaired. In their case, the system is at least partly accessible because trains and stations are announced via loudspeaker, and stairways and boarding platforms have raised warning markings that can be felt with a cane. Overall, however, we observe that despite the great wealth of Japan and the considerable kindness most Japanese reveal in person-to-person situations, there is comparatively little effort made in the country to make public facilities accessible to movement-impaired individuals.

At the same time, some behavior that is not tolerated at all in other societies is, curiously, accepted as normal in Japan, or at worst considered to be nothing more than 'small problems' to be overlooked. It is well known, for example, that there is considerable sexual abuse of women that takes place on crowded trains by indecent touching. However, unlike the prompt action by police that follows other forms of misbehavior, this problem has been pretty much ignored by law-enforcement officials, and, most unfortunately, by other passengers as well. One of my female students, who like so many other young women has been a frequent victim of this, once explained that if she were to complain on a train about a wayward hand, she would become the center of attention among the passengers rather than the offender; that her requests for help from the people around her would be coldly ignored. In one experience, some fellow passengers insisted that she should stop bothering the man who was feeling her because he is 'obviously tired from a long day of work'. There are, as one can imagine, frequent complaints about this problem from women's groups and others, occasional sympathetic editorials in the media, and even some promises by police to act. Nevertheless, there seems to be little or no improvement in the situation, and the norm that it is better to not rock the boat (or moving train) continues to dominate.

Tokyo's address system

There is one last item left in this orientation to Tokyo: the city's address system. This is not a guidebook, so the purpose is not necessarily to help a person get around the city or to locate some significant attraction. Instead, it is to describe more fully the way the city is organized internally. This is necessary because the Tokyo address system is fundamentally different to the ones employed in most other countries, as well as different in detail from the norm for other Japanese cities. This creates problems for many newcomers to Tokyo, and adds to the reputation that the city's street plan is chaotic and impossible to negotiate.

What is perhaps most disconcerting to people who are unfamiliar with Tokyo is that except for a comparatively small number of wide, modern thoroughfares and a few other busy lanes, the city's streets have no names. We saw from Tokyo Tower that the streets below wind in such fits and starts that naming them and keeping track of which fork was a continuation of which street would be unworkable. Visitors to the city are also sometimes surprised to learn that it is their responsibility, instead of the driver's, to tell a taxi driver exactly where their desired destination is to be found. Well-known places such as major hotels or busy train stations pose no problems, but for small establishments such as a particular shop or a recommended pub (or heaven forbid, a private residence) the job of location is actually the passenger's. All that the driver is expected to do is to get to the right neighborhood fairly directly. Barrie B. Greenbie, author of an interesting recent book about Japanese space, has likened the experience of finding one's way around Tokyo outside the main commercial centers to being lost in the woods, even if one is with an experienced taxi driver (Greenbie, 1988, p. 55).

However, none of this is to suggest that addresses in Tokyo are all chaos and that people are always getting lost. In fact, quite the contrary is true. The address system works extremely well for people who understand its basic rules, and the expectation that taxi passengers should know how to find the precise location of their destination once the driver has got close to it is not so onerous if one is prepared for this. There are two underlying principles. One is that addresses in Tokyo are based on a hierarchy of named areas rather than streets; the second is that points (or individual buildings) within the smallest (or lowest-ranking) of these areas are generally numbered according to the sequence in which they were built or some other criterion, instead of according to location. We can illustrate this by going over how an address is written, say, on an envelope to be mailed.

The top of the address hierarchy is Tokyo or *Tokyo-to* itself, and this is written first. Then comes the name of the ward or the city, town, or village within the Tokyo metropolis. The level below that is the district of the ward or town. This is called *machi* and also has a name. For example, the address from which I wrote the introduction to this book (I have since moved to another area) begins *Tokyo, Shibuya ward, Honmachi*, with Honmachi (or Honchō as the combination of Chinese characters is also pronounced) being one of 29 *machi* within Shibuya ward. Below the level of *machi* is a hierarchy of numbered areas that continues the address. The largest of these is called *chōme*. Honmachi has six *chōme*, each about one-fifth of one square kilometer in size with several thousand residents. Mine was number 2 *chōme*. Each *chōme*, in turn, is subdivided into numerous smaller numbered areas called *banchi*. We could think of these units as being roughly equivalent to street blocks, except that most of Tokyo has nothing so geometric that the word 'block' could apply. Finally, there is the actual building. This is a point identified by the last number of the address, the *gō*. I had number 14. My full address, therefore, was written *Tokyo, Shibuya, Honmachi 2–2–14*.[11] However, this was also my neighbor's address, so it was required, as it is everywhere in Tokyo, to post the *banchi* and *go* numbers and the family name at the front of the house. When I procrastinated in posting my name at my new address (you are expected to have a special name plate made that costs much more than the material and labor are worth), one of my neighbors with the same address came by with a polite but insistent reminder that mail, various other deliveries and visitors would be confused as to which house was whose.

This explains how a letter finds its way to the right destination. But how does a person who is travelling from one part of the city to another find the right place? Even though it sounds facetious to say so, the answer is by consulting a map, or even a series of maps at ever larger scales. More than in any place I have ever seen, people in Tokyo depend on maps to get around or to give directions. Every book store has a special section devoted exclusively to maps, including many competing editions of thick map books that show considerable detail in color for every ward in the 23-ward area as well as for neighboring cities and towns. This is the kind of book people keep in their cars, and every taxi driver has on the seat beside him (always *him*, never *her*). Passengers on trains often have photocopies of needed pages from these atlases. There are also folded maps sold at every news-stand. Inset maps are printed on matchbooks, on people's business cards, on advertisements in newspapers and magazines, on advertisement posters that hang in subways and trains, and on the small tissue packets that one is always being handed on crowded sidewalks to promote some special sale or new business. There are even maps printed on to handkerchiefs.

So a person who needs to get to some unfamiliar place in Tokyo often consults one or more maps as a guide. The closer one approaches the destination, the more detailed is the map employed. Once in the right neighborhood, there will be large-scale maps posted on all-weather signboards showing locations for all the neighboring *banchi* and *gō*. These maps are located at subway and train station exits and at many prominent street intersections, and are usually maintained by the ward or municipality. There are also extremely detailed maps that are posted in individual neighborhoods to show all the buildings and property lines and to identify local businesses and residents. These maps are often the responsibilities of neighborhood associations such as local shopkeepers. They are especially

[11] There is also a postal code for each address. This is used only to assign mail to the correct post office.

helpful because *gō* numbers are often not arranged in logical spatial order, but scattered over a small area in unpredictable ways. And finally, if one still cannot find the right place, one can always ask for help at the local *kōban* or police box. There are 772 of these in the 23 wards alone. A major function, in addition to crime prevention and other police duties, is to maintain detailed maps of the surroundings and give directions.

What makes this system work so well is that Tokyoites (or maybe the Japanese generally) have exceptionally good map-reading skills. I see this in my students, who are far better at map reading than any group of geography students I have taught in North America, and from the many examples of outstanding informal sketch maps I have seen people in Tokyo make on little scraps of paper when giving directions. These impromptu drawings are always prepared so quickly and effortlessly, and they are almost always completely accurate! Usually, streets are drawn with double lines, and intersections are made neatly so that no line goes across them. There are always just enough landmarks to guide the way perfectly from the train station exit or some other well-known starting place, but not so many that the map becomes cluttered. A taxi driver who has brought his fare to the correct neighborhood would typically expect to be shown such a map (or at least have it described in words) so that he could drive the last distance to the desired residence or place of business (Figure 2.8)[12] Such cartography is a remarkable ability that comes from constant use of maps (and may also be because of practice at calligraphy and other arts), and that the anthropologist Roland Barthes has discussed as being one of the distinguishing cultural characteristics of Tokyo's inhabitants (Barthes, 1982, pp. 33–7).

[12] See also the map in Figure 4.12

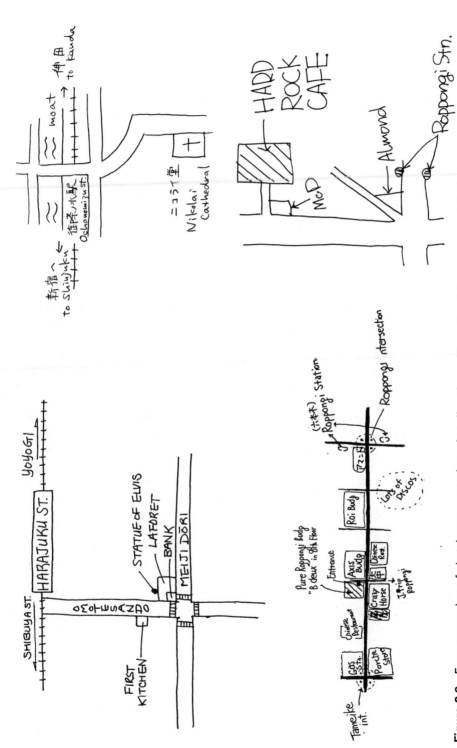

Figure 2.8 Four examples of sketch maps used to give directions. (From top left, courtesy of A. Kanzaki, M. Togo, A. Shimazu and K. Kato)

3
Historical development

Introduction

Tokyo is neither an especially old nor a new city, but instead has a history that is somewhere in between. It is older, for example, than all the cities of North America, but much newer than hundreds of other places, including such great capitals as Cairo, Beijing, Istanbul, Rome, London, and in Japan, Kyoto. However, the details of its history are as rich and interesting of those of any place in the world. They go on for page after page with captivating stories of political intrigue, powerful personalities and other exceptional characters, landmark events, great construction projects, and other details, all of them set in a context of a national culture that is unique and endlessly fascinating. Moreover, the Tokyo story stands out because it is the story of more millions of people than most other cities. It is also a story of more frequent urban destructions and rebuildings than any other place in the world. Finally, it is a story of unusually rapid and profound social change and modernization. As any proud Tokyoite will gladly point out, in just over four centuries, the city has been transformed from an insignificant castle town with only local impact to the huge, powerful capital of a populous nation – and then to one of the most important capitals in the world.

This chapter is a summary of those parts of Tokyo history that deal most directly with the physical development of the city. The goal is to understand the changing look of Tokyo over the four centuries of its existence, and to keep track of the sequential rings and layers of construction that constitute today's city. I have had considerable help with this from some excellent literature about the history of Tokyo that exists in English. Four writers have been especially important, and are cited often: Paul Waley, whom I have introduced before for his outstanding book *Tokyo Now and Then: An Explorer's Guide*, a book organized by districts in Tokyo (1984); Noel Nouët, whose 1961 book *The Shogun's City* has recently been translated from French to English and is a superb account of the city from its founding through the fall of the shogunate in 1868 (1990); Edward Seidensticker, author of two richly entertaining and fact-packed volumes about Tokyo's modern development: *Low City, High City* (1983) and the recent (1990) *Tokyo Rising*; and Henry D. Smith II, who has written numerous scholarly articles and book chapters about a variety of topics dealing with Tokyo history (eg. 1973; 1978; 1979; 1986).

Edo: founding and early growth

Archaeological evidence indicates that human settlement in the Kantō Plain dates far back into prehistory. However, the origin of Tokyo is quite recent. It is generally accepted that the start of the city dates to 1457, when a feudal lord named Ōta Dōkan chose the site for his castle. There had been a small fishing village there before called both Hirakawa, after the local river, and Edo. The latter means 'estuary' or 'mouth of the river', and was also the family name adopted by members of the Taira clan who settled there in the twelfth century. The name Edo stayed with the settlement after Dōkan's arrival and continued to be used for the place until 1868, when 'Tokyo' was adopted.

According to legend, Ōta Dōkan was led to Edo by the goddess Benten. Through the medium of a fish that jumped out of the water she signaled him to put up his castle on a specific low hill jutting close to the shore of Tokyo Bay. The hill was probably a wise choice, because even though it was low it commanded the head of the bay, the mouths of the local rivers and access to the broad Kantō Plain. There were also certain political advantages to the location, as it strengthened the defenses between rival feudal domains in different parts of Honshū, the large Japanese island of which the Kantō area is a part.

Relatively few details are known about the Edo of Dōkan's time. Nothing tangible remains, and what little record there is about the castle comes mostly from descriptions by visiting poets (Waley, 1984, p. xx). Even the river Hirakawa is something of a mystery. Its course was altered by Dōkan to improve navigation, and then changed again (along with that of Tokyo's other rivers) so many times in so many ways over the centuries that the original channel is now lost. However, as Waley tells us in his history of the city, the pattern of river engineering is so confusing in Tokyo that these are 'waters we would be wise not to try to chart' (p. 24).

The Edo of Ōta Dōkan and his immediate successors never developed into anything more than a castle town (*jōka machi*) of moderate importance. The city's rise to prominence did not begin until 1590, a little more than 100 years after Dōkan's death, when the next great figure of Tokyo's history appeared on the scene. This was the warrior chieftain Tokugawa Ieyasu, who would soon become absolute ruler of the whole of Japan and make Edo its undisputed capital and greatest city. The dynasty he founded,

Figure 3.1 Statue at Ōta Dōkan, founder of Edo, at the Tokyo Metropolitan Government headquarters

the Tokugawa shogunate, would rule the nation for almost three centuries. All of this would take place after 21 October 1600, following Ieyasu's victory at the Battle of Sekigahara, an epic struggle on the plains near Kyoto for control of the country.

What had brought Ieyasu to Edo in 1590 was his service in another battle to Toyotomi Hideyoshi, before Ieyasu's ascendancy the most powerful warlord in Japan. In particular, the city and the eight surrounding provinces of Kantō were Ieyasu's reward for having masterminded the successful military campaign against Hideyoshi's principal rivals, the Hōjō clan who had controlled all this land from its stronghold in Odawara. As the Hōjō castle was about to fall, the *taikō*, as Hideyoshi was called, personally announced the offer of his spoils of war to Ieyasu, who in turn suggested the bargain be finalized by the two of them urinating together in the direction of Odawara (Nouët, 1990, p. 25). Thus, as far as is known, Tokyo is the only one of the world's most important cities to have embarked on its course of modern urban development after a deal sealed with a piss.

As soon as he came to Edo, Ieyasu undertook to remodel the city. In doing so, he laid the foundations for urban form that would endure to the present day. Some of the best surviving examples are the altered courses of several rivers, the pattern of radial highways leading from the center to outlying prefectures, the reclaimed marshlands near Tokyo Bay that are some of today's major office and retailing districts, and the flat topography of the vitally important Kanda district. In the last of these, a low mountain (Mt Kanda, actually a finger-like protrusion of the upland behind Tokyo) was cut down to obtain fill for reclamation in the bay, as well as to make room for expansion of the city inland. The most important legacy left by Ieyasu is the vast open area in the center of Tokyo that was the site of his castle. It is now the Imperial Palace of Japan and its grounds. Most of the original buildings erected by Ieyasu and successor shoguns were destroyed by the fires that periodically burnt the city during the Edo era, but significant sections of wall and moat remain. The whole area measures substantially over 100 hectares, and stands out as one of the most highly revered places in Japan. It is also a striking void in the core of an enormously crowded city.

Construction of the castle was one of Ieyasu's first objectives. He did away with the rudimentary structure left by Dōkan, and began work on a very elaborate fortification on the same site. A large labor force was recruited from several areas of western Japan to do the construction work, and many thousands of stone blocks were quarried in the Izu region and sent by ship to Edo. When the work was finished some 50 years later (during the tenure of the third Tokugawa shogun), Edo Castle measured 16 kilometers around the outside defensive perimeter and 6.4 kilometers around the inner perimeter. It was the largest castle in the world. It was also noted for an ingenious defensive plan. Its distinctive quality was a maze of moats arranged in a spiral that unwound outward in a clockwise direction from the heart of the castle. There was also a supporting pattern of strategically placed bridges, gates, high stone walls and 36 lookout towers. In this way the center of the whole compound, where the shogun kept his primary residence, was most intimately protected.

The construction of such a gigantic complex was a massive undertaking that, by design, taxed the nation. Ieyasu used the project as a means to test the loyalty of supporters and to weaken the finances of political adversaries by demanding that they make huge outlays in material resources and corvée labor for the building effort. For example, he ordered each of the major *daimyō* (feudal lords) in western Japan to prepare a burdensome quota of thousands of large stone sections for the construction, and to provide all the required workers and means of transportation. The amount of the quota was pegged to the rice harvest in each domain. At one point in the construction, there were 3,000 vessels gathered in the various ports of the Izu Peninsula alone to deliver shipments of stone blocks to Edo

(Yazaki, 1968, p. 176). There was also considerable loss of life during the construction: ships loaded with stone sank at sea and took entire crews to the bottom, stones fell as they were hoisted to the top of walls and crushed workers below. After the earthquake of 1923 loosened some sections of stone, skeletons of workmen were discovered behind the walls. It may be that the victims had been deliberately sealed alive behind the foundations so their strength would pass on to the building. As Nouët reported, this was a common practice at the time. Interestingly, pillar men (*hito bashira*), as such workers were called, were sometimes volunteers (Nouet, 1990, p. 49).

Another calculated repression was a policy called *sankin kōtai*. Begun by Ieyasu but then formalized during the rule of the third shogun, Iemitsu (1622–1651), this was a practice that required all *daimyō* to spend alternate years in Edo, away from their own fiefs, in a specially designated section of the city. For *daimyō* from the nearby Kantō provinces, the change of residence occurred every six months. Even when they returned to their lands, they were required to leave behind as hostages their wives, children and samurai retainers. Moreover, *daimyō* and other high officials were expected to maintain an expensive lifestyle in Edo, complete with multiple mansions (*yashiki*) near the castle and in the suburban hills, casts of servants and many other luxuries. This stimulated demand for many types of goods and services in the city, and attracted thousands of craftsmen, merchants and other 'townspeople' to Edo to make a living. One particularly famous element in this population was business-minded people from Ise province (near Nagoya) and Omi province (on Lake Biwa near Kyoto). Described as 'Omi thieves and Ise beggars' by the citizenry of Edo (Waley, 1984, p. 79), they opened shops, banking houses and other commercial enterprises, especially in the Nihombashi area between the castle and the bay, that would provide the foundation for the city's rapid ascendancy to top rank commercial center.

Thus, not only did *sankin kōtai* help to consolidate the power of the shogunate, it also provided the basis for the spectacular population growth that characterized Edo from the 17th century. The settlement exploded in size from only a few thousand inhabitants in 1600 to nearly half a million by the 1650s. By that time it had surpassed both Kyoto and the merchants' city Osaka as the largest in Japan. The population rose still more to over one million inhabitants by the end of the century and then to 1.3 million by 1720. By then Edo was far and away the largest city in the world. Other leading cities at the time were London with about 600,000 inhabitants and Beijing with just under one million. For the next nearly 150 years the population of Edo was remarkably stable, and did not begin to change measurably again until the *sankin kōtai* requirements were relaxed in 1862 and the number of residents dropped sharply. In the meantime, London surpassed Edo in population totals early in the 19th century to become the new largest city (Smith, 1979, p. 51).

The spatial-ecological structure of Edo was a mirror of feudal society.

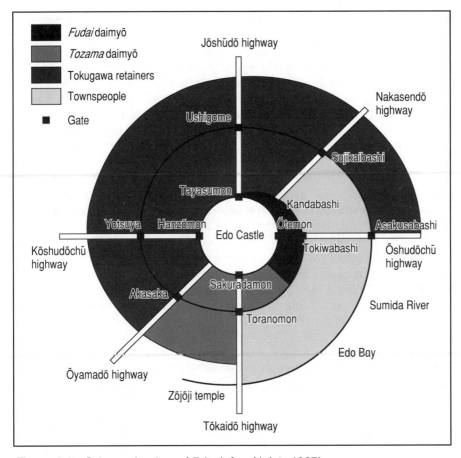

Figure 3.2 Schematic plan of Edo (after Naitō, 1987)

This could be seen by the scale of the castle complex alone, as well as at the scale of all Edo. In the former case, the hierarchy of status within the top echelon of feudal Japan was reflected faithfully by the location of residence with respect to that of the shogun. This was one of the intended functions of the swirl pattern of moats defining the core of the settlement. The shogun and his family occupied the inner-most compound (*honmaru*), while favored *daimyō* and other highest-ranking officials were just outside the main gate to this enclosure. Lesser lords were located further out along the spiral. Servants and others without status (eg. common soldiers) were outside this complex, where the swirl opened up to the rest of the city. The basic outline of this arrangement is illustrated in Figure 3.2, a spatial model of early Edo developed by architectural historian Naitō Akira (1987, p. 35). The distinction between *fudai daimyō* and *tozama daimyō* that is shown is one of closeness to the shogun; the former, who resided closest to the inner keep, had joined the shogun's forces before the Battle of Sekigahara, while the latter, the 'outside' *daimyō*, had joined up after the victory and were kept at a short distance.

There was still another spatial arrangement to Edo, one that existed as a superimposed pattern on the spiral pattern. In addition to the castle, which was more or less in the center, the city consisted of two broadly defined and vastly different districts, *shitamachi* and *yamanote*. The former means 'low city', and applies to the area of flatlands reclaimed from the bay and river deltas where the common people or townsfolk (*chōnin*) lived. *Yamanote*, on the other hand, is the 'high city', (literally, 'in the direction of the mountains') and was the higher ground inhabited by the samurai class. It was also the home of many shrines and temples. Other castle cities (eg. Osaka and Kyoto) had similar arrangements. In Edo, *shitamachi* and *yamanote* had roughly equal population numbers. In the 1720s, this was about 600,000 inhabitants each. The difference was in population density. *Shitamachi* comprised only 16 per cent of Edo's surface and had a residential density of some 69,000 people per square kilometer, while *yamanote* was 69 per cent of the city and had a density of 14,000 persons per square kilometer (Waley, 1984, p. xxvii). The rest of the city was the castle complex and water. Table 3.1 gives a breakdown of land use in Edo according to social class.

Table 3.1   Land use distribution in Edo (after 1818)

	Hectares	Per cent
Edo Palace	131	1.7
Upper *daimyō* residences	796	10.2
Middle *daimyō* residences	340	4.4
Lower *daimyō* residences	1,630	20.9
Samurai residences	1,878	24.1
Townspeople's residences	1,626	20.9
Government use	199	2.6
Additional *daimyō* use	5	0.1
Buddhist temples	1,112	14.3
Shinto shrines	70	0.9
Confucian temples	5	0.1
TOTAL	7,792	100.0

Source: Tokyo-to, 1989, p. 4.

The social hierarchy of Edo is seen in some interesting conventions regarding maps of the old city (Figure 3.3). To begin with, Edo Castle was, always shown at the center to emphasize its paramount importance. Then there were patterns to the way place-names were fixed on the maps. The ideographs, which are usually written vertically in Japanese writing, were made to point in different directions depending on the status of what was being shown. Thus, the names of Shinto shrines and Buddhist temples all

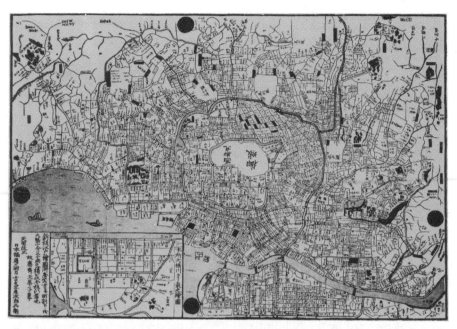

Figure 3.3 Edo in the early nineteenth century. Edo Castle is in the center, written with the name pointing west (toward the top of the map) in the direction of Kyoto. The orientations of other place names and the names of landholders are also symbolically arranged. (From a map in the author's personal collection)

point toward the castle because of their higher prestige, while those names that identified ordinary shops and residences were drawn to point away. According to the interpretation by Isoda (1987, p. 60), this was to show that the shogunate was 'sustained by divine protection' by shrines and temples, and that commoners' establishments were required to show their respect by 'bow[ing] their heads' toward the castle rather than pointing their 'feet' (i.e. the last characters of their names) in that direction. Moreover, these maps are always oriented with west at the top and with the characters for 'Edo Castle' written upside down. In this way, the name pointed west toward Kyoto, the imperial capital, 'trampling [it] underfoot . . . as a graphic expression of the tension between the mythic authority and actual power'.

Shitamachi

The low city was a world unto itself. Isolated as it was by the strict social and occupational segregation of feudal Japan, it charted an independent course of cultural development. Much has been written about this, a lot of which Waley correctly characterizes as too weighty academically or overly long on sentimentality (1984, p. xxvii). Suffice it to say that distinctive cultural characteristics were created among the *chōnin* of Edo, Kyoto and Osaka, and that these varied from city to city as well as between *shitamachi* and the high-crust districts within cities. The differences included manners of speech, styles of dress, forms of entertainment, traditions of cuisine, and if one is to pay attention to the substantial literature that debates details about the subject, even the physical attributes of young women (Takeuchi, 1987, p. 51). Moreover, ways of preparing *sushi* varied geographically. The *nigiri-zushi* style, in which the vinegared rice is formed by fingers (as opposed to a press) and the topping of (*tane*), usually raw fish, which is placed on top, was first developed in Edo in the early nineteenth century and came to be strongly identified with its *shitamachi* area.[1] So, too, such popular arts as *kabuki* (theater), *bunraku* (puppet theater) and *rakugo* (storytelling) were also distinctive *shitamachi* creations that varied in detail from one city to another.

The heart of *shitamachi* was an area of reclaimed land known as Nihombashi, or 'Japan bridge'. This was the city's most prosperous merchants' quarter. It stood at the entrance to Ōtemon, the front gate of the castle, and was bisected by the Nihombashi River, an extremely busy canal linking the city proper with the bay. The bridge that is referred to crossed the canal and became the area's first focus of commerce. It is most closely tied to a fish market that was begun there early in the city's history by Ieyasu to supply the castle's food needs, considered as the start of commercial enterprise in Edo. The excess catch was sold to the public at the foot of the bridge, initially by a group of 36 fishermen (all from one family named Mori) who had been given a license by the shogunate. As the population of Edo expanded, the fish market grew to encompass an ever-wider area and more and more stalls, and then to more and more food and non-food products. The bridge, however, was always thought of as the center. In this way, Nihombashi Bridge, actually a rather modest wooden span, came to be identified as the *symbolic* starting point for the radial roads leading out of Edo (i.e. these roads did not actually begin there), and the point from which all distances from the city to other provinces were measured. So powerful was the centrality attached to this point that even today, a 20th century descendant of that first bridge has the same symbolic meanings, while the Nihombashi district in general is still a main commercial area in the heart of the modern CBD.

Other sections of *shitamachi* were craftsmens' quarters. The earliest were at Kyōbashi, also on reclaimed land, to the north of Nihombashi, and Kanda, still further to the north. Each occupational group had its own quarter (*chō*) with its own gate and small guard house, and its own pattern of lanes and alleys, often an idiosyncratic maze. Many of these quarters

[1] This style of *sushi* has since spread widely to be the most popular type of *sushi* in Japanese restaurants around the world.

were set apart by the canals that criss-crossed the city and served as its principal lanes of traffic. It is reported that there were some 1,700 such *chō* in early Edo, each with some 300 to 350 residents (Rozman, 1973, p. 169; Yazaki, 1968, pp. 185–6). However, this pattern did not last long, in part because of the devastating fires that frequently swept through *shitamachi* and obliterated everything in their path. The Meireki fire of 1657, which caused the death of some 100,000 persons (one-fourth of the total population) and destroyed even the innermost keep of Edo Castle, was one of the largest and is best known. Nevertheless, many of today's place names in central Tokyo derive from the early occupational *chō*. Ginza (silver guild), Kon'yachō (dyers' quarter) and Kajichō (smiths' quarter) are but three examples.

As Edo grew and prospered, the original townfolks' areas spread out in various directions from the nucleus at Nihombashi. One form of growth was along the highways leading out of the city. Because of the *sankin kōtai* system, the number of travelers was always quite large, and post-stations at the approaches to Edo grew quickly into specialized towns of inns and various other businesses. This accounts for the start of such famous Tokyo districts as Shinjuku on the Kōshūkaidō highway to the west, Shinagawa on the Tōkaidō to the south, and Senju on the Nikko-kaidō to the north. Each of these places also thrived as edge-of-the-city entertainment districts for Edo residents. Other notable expansion of *chōnin* districts took place along the bayfront, where reclamation was continually providing new space for city growth, and in Honjo and Fukagawa across the Sumida River. Trans-Sumida urbanization was accelarated with the construction of three bridges, Eitaibashi, Shinohashi and Ryōgoku, completed after the Meireki Fire to reduce central city residential density and to give Edo residents a future escape route from fires. Fukagawa was to become especially important after 1780 for its lively pleasure quarter. There was also expansion of *chōnin* wards north of the core along the Sumida. The main center there, a temple district named Asakusa that originated hundreds of years before Edo, developed especially quickly and by the end of the eighteenth century came to rival Nihombashi as the focus of shitamachi cultural life and innovation.

Yamanote

In contrast to the crowded plebian flatlands of *shitamachi* members of the military classes kept their mansions on the higher ground of *yamanote*. In the case of *daimyō*, these were second or third mansions, to complement primary Edo residences close to the castle. Other mansions belonged to the thousands of *samurai* retainers of the shogun. Many of the properties were quite large, reflecting the wealth and prestige of the owners, and the whole area was generally thinly settled. The land was hilly and green with vegetation most of the year, and many of the slopes facing the west offered

Figure 3.4 A woodblock print (*ukiyoe*) by Utagawa Toyoharu (1735–1814) showing the life of Edo in the vicinity of the Ryōgoku Bridge across the Sumida River. (Courtesy of the Freer Gallery of Art, Smithsonian Institution, Washington D.C., accession number 03–217–1.)

spectacular views of distant mountains and the peak of *Fuji-san*. In the early Tokugawa period (before 1657), the mansions of the wealthiest families were extraordinarily luxurious. But even here there was devastation by the great periodic scourge of Edo, fire, and practices were adopted after the Meireki conflagration to build less sumptuous dwellings to reduce losses after they had burned down.

The *yamanote* district was also the location of many of Edo's shrines and temples. This was especially so after 1657, when many of these institutions were relocated there, to the outer reaches of the built-up area as a safety measure because of their deserved reputation as fire hazards. The Meireki Fire, for example, was also known as the *Furisode* (long sleeves) Fire, because it was said to have been caused by the accidental igniting of a flowing *kimono* during a religious ceremony.[2] The removal of shrines and temples was a great stimulus for development in *yamanote*, both because their numbers totalled in the hundreds and because of the many thousands of people who were attached to them. Moreover, all the largest temples spawned important commercial districts at their approaches. It was in this way that such famous sections of Tokyo as Shiba, Azabu, Yotsuya, Hongō, Ueno and Asakusa, mentioned above, came to be part of Edo's urban sprawl.

Yoshiwara

One other section of Edo should be mentioned at this point because of its tremendously important role in the social life of the old city. This is the famous pleasure quarter called Yoshiwara. It was established in the early years of the Tokugawa shogunate (1617) as a specially zoned district for prostitution and other entertainment, in part to keep an eye on the men of the city who might have in mind some plot against the shogun (Nouët, 1990, p. 90). The place prospered immediately, and during the eighteenth century became a city apart. It survived for well over 300 years. For most of this time, the number of prostitutes was between 2,000 and 3,000 and there were approximately 200 brothels. Then, as the merchant class of Edo prospered with the city's growth and found more time and money for diversions, Yoshiwara expanded and the number of prostitutes grew to around 4,000 in 1790, 5,000 in 1800 and 7,000 by 1868, the end of the Edo period (Kojiro, 1986, p. 47). The place was finally closed in 1957–8, after falling victim to modern-day legislation outlawing brothels. By then, however, it had declined greatly from its Edo heyday.

The original location of Yoshiwara was a marshy area close to Nihomba-

[2] It is not known exactly how the Long-Sleeves Fire started. While some versions have it that the kimono was being worn when it ignited, another story says that the kimono was deliberately set on fire in a religious ceremony because it had brought unusually bad luck to all previous owners. In either event, a great wind is said to have come along and spread the flames (Nouët, 1990, p. 105).

shi.[3] This accounts for its name which means 'reed plain'. However, since this site was one of the casualties of the great conflagration of 1657, a New Yoshiwara ('Shin Yoshiwara') was established shortly thereafter at the city's outskirts. The second site was a paddy field north of Asakusa, in a relatively out-of-the-way place favored by Edo officials because it effectively removed a nuisance from the heart of the city. Brothel owners were happy with the site because they were now allowed to stay open all night. This gave the place the nickname *fuyajō*, 'place without night'. A small moat was dug around the site to prevent customers from leaving without paying, and to keep the prostitutes from escaping. The latter was not an inconceivable possibility: most prostitutes were young girls from the countryside who were working involuntarily. In most cases, their services had been sold without consent to brothel owners by impoverished parents (Hane, 1982, pp. 207–17; Longstreet and Longstreet, 1988).

Despite the prominence of prostitution in Yoshiwara, it would be wrong to think of the place as simply a large collection of brothels. During Edo, Yoshiwara also offered many other diversions, and is more correctly remembered for having a broad range of entertainment in a setting of great splendor. Thus, in addition to its leading profession, Yoshiwara was also the refined world of the geisha and the tea house, and of various new genres of Japanese music, art and literature. Its cultural role expanded after 1841, whan kabuki theater was banished to a nearby section of Asakusa (Surawakachō). As a result, the two areas fed off each other as complementary entertainment centers. Great crowds trekked regularly from the city to Asakusa for a performance and then a bit further to Yoshiwara for different types of fun. What is most significant about this is that clients were drawn equally from the *samurai* classes of *yamanote* and the merchants of *shitamachi*. The only requirement for participation was to have enough money to pay the night's tab. Thus the social mixing that took place at Yoshiwara and Asakusa (as well as at some other pleasure districts) helped to blur the rigid social distinctions of the feudal order. This became one of the key preconditions for the making of modern society.

The making of modern Tokyo

The modernization of Japan is dated formally to 1868. This is the year the shogunate fell, feudalism officially ended, and a new era under restored imperial rule began. The main catalyst for change was the unexpected arrival in 1853 in Tokyo Bay near Yokohama of a small fleet of four ships from America under the command of Commodore William Perry. This show of force, which represented a sizable fraction of the small US navy, made Japan end its self-imposed, 250-year-long isolation from other nations and open its ports to foreign trade and ideas. It also showed to the

[3] The present Naniwachō district.

Japanese that their country lagged badly behind in military and technological development. The shogunate was beginning to weaken by this time anyway, because of internal problems ranging from a series of famines in 1833–6 to ever greater economic hardship among *daimyō*. The latter problem had been brought on largely by the extravagant financial requirements of the *sankin kōtai* system, such as keeping multiple mansions in Edo and at home, and costly processions with large retinues between the capital and the home province. Perry's ships added dramatic evidence from abroad that Japan's feudal order was flawed, and hastened the call for reform.

The new era that began in 1868 is called Meiji. The word means 'enlightened rule', a name given posthumously to the Emperor Matsuhito who, at the age of 14, then assumed the throne. He had a long reign until his death in 1912. The revolutionary changes in store for Japan under his rule were heralded in the Charter Oath he pledged to his ancestors on 6 April 1868, shortly after becoming emperor. Among other points, the Emperor promised to abolish feudalism and end social distinctions between 'high and low persons', to have a more open government based on public participation, and to advance Japan in all ways by seeking practical knowledge from every part of the world. He was directed to these objectives by powerful reformer-activists, most notably Saigō Takamori, Ōkubo Toshimichi, Itō Hirobumi and others, who set policy in his name and ran the affairs of government all through his era. The specific measures instituted included land and tax reform across the country (1873–81), establishment of prefectures with appointed governors in place of *daimyō* domains (1871), the start of universal schooling (1872), replacement of the hereditary *samurai* army with commoner conscripts (1873) and the promulgation of constitutional government (1879).

The impact of the Meiji era on Tokyo was especially profound. First and foremost, the city was made the imperial capital. This took place in 1868, when the young emperor was carried by palanquin from the traditional palace in Kyoto to the vacated shogunal castle in Edo. Secondly, the name Edo was dropped in favor of Tokyo, which means 'eastern capital'. Thirdly, the new government set out to modernize the city physically according to Western lines, and to reshape lifestyles and customs according to ideas borrowed from Western cultures. We shall see that one of the things that emerged from this was a modern downtown or Central Business District (CBD) in the city. Thus, in these ways and many others, the Meiji era was a period of unprecedented change in Japan. Nowadays it is often romanticized in films and on television, and is generally presented fondly as an extremely exciting time.

The changes in Tokyo were intended to draw attention to the city to make it an especially strong capital. This was to reunify Japan in the wake of fragmentation that had taken place during the dissolution of the Tokugawa era. Moreover, a certain amount of rebuilding was necessary in the city anyway, because of the declines it had suffered during the tumult of the shogun's undoing. One symptom was a sharp drop in population that took place as soon as the *sankin kōtai* sytem ended in 1862. There had been some 1.3 million residents in the city just before the change, but in the next years as many as 300,000 people left, as *daimyō* returned gladly to their home provinces with their entourages. In doing so, they left behind extensive tracts of vacant land. The city had also suffered considerable damage during the last years of the old order from an unfortunate series of disasters, both natural and cultural. The troubles began with pair of powerful earthquakes in 1854 and 1855, and were followed by incessant downpours and flooding and by a deadly cholera epidemic. Many residents blamed this on bad luck from Perry's ships (Waley, 1984, pp. xxix-xxx).

The changing face of Tokyo during the Meiji era is perhaps most clearly recorded in the famous woodblock prints called *ukiyoe*. These 'pictures of the floating world', which are so popular nowadays both among serious collectors and as reproduction-souvenirs of Japan, often depicted landscapes and showed how people lived and worked (Meech-Pekarik, 1986). Prints of Edo, such as those by the great masters Hokusai and Hiroshige, illustrate a city that is unambiguously pre-modern. The people illustrated in townscapes walk rather than ride, wear traditional clothing and work at their crafts in time-honored ways. Moreover, the city is seen to be a place of water, especially in *shitamachi*. Everywhere there are rivers and canals. In many prints these are shown to carry the city's commerce. In addition, the people are often shown to be either in boats or clustered at riverbanks or on bridges. We saw this in Figure 3.4. The city's buildings are almost always small, low-slung, made of wood and generally unimpressive (Lane, 1978).

All this changed during Meiji. We see this in prints such as those of the 1870s–1880s by Hiroshige III (a student of Hiroshige), Yoshitora and Kiyochika. They reveal a city based on streets and wheeled traffic, with such evidence of modern life as pedestrians in western dress, multi-story banks and hotels, brick-faced shopping streets, gas illumination and steam trains loading up in crowded stations. In some prints there are factories run by powerful machines. While these prints also showed that important bits and pieces of Edo still remained, for the most part they exhibited a new-style downtown in the place of old *shitamachi*, and a cosmopolitan air where the constricted world of the shoguns once dominated. Edward Seidensticker, without question the leading chronicler of Tokyo in English, has pointed out an interesting convention in many Meiji woodcuts of the changeover from a city of rivers and canals to one of streets on *terra firma*: 'When bridges are shown, as they frequently are, the roadway is generally an exhuberant mixture of the new and the traditional, the imported and the domestic; on the waters below there is seldom a trace of the new and imported' (1983, p. 53).

A favorite example of a Meiji woodcut of Tokyo is a triptych of the main street in Ginza in December, 1874 by Hiroshige (Figure 3.5). Called 'A Scenic View of Tokyo Enlightenment' (*Tokyo kaika meisho*), it emphasizes in all its aspects the great changes that had recently come to the city.

The focus is the crowds on the street and on the Kyobashi Bridge over one of the remaining waterways. Little is seen of the river, and there is certainly no important activity there. But on the bridge above, one sees a big omnibus filled with passengers and pulled by horses, rickshaws pulled by clothed men (pullers were mostly naked before the 'enlightenment'), and numerous stylish pedestrians, some in Western and some in Japanese garb. Moreover, there are gas lamps on the bridge to illuminate the scene. The street itself, which is lined with cherry trees in bloom, is paved and has sidewalks. On both sides there are new-fangled buildings made of brick and appointed with columns. There are also verandas, sash windows and other imported touches. As opposed to the mixed land-use patterns of the past, this is clearly a new type of urban district. It is commercial-only in use, and the people there have evidently come, as commuters, from neighborhoods elsewhere. The only feature that is not new and unfamiliar is Mt Fuji, placed in the background by the printmaker to give the scene orientation and stability (Meech-Pekarik, 1986, pp. 92–4).

The making of a CBD

The street depicted in 'A Scenic View of Tokyo Enlightenment' was but one part of a major restructuring of the old city during the Meiji period. Many other changes were seen nearby, in a broad area of *shitamachi* extending from the foot of the castle down to the waterfront at Tokyo Bay, that had at its center this Ginza street, the merchants' quarters at Nihombashi, the craftsmens' neighborhood at Kyōbashi and other plebian areas of Edo's core. This is the area that, in general, became the modern downtown or CBD of the city during Meiji, and that is still the city's principal business district. The transition was effected in pieces during different years and at various specific sites, and is attributed to a combination of planning or direction from central government, numerous independent actions by private entrepreneurs who saw new opportunities in the center of the city to make a fortune, and significant advice and architectural assistance from the growing numbers of Europeans and Americans who had arrived in Tokyo to teach just about everything.

Many of the first changes were seen in the area around the castle. This was where the reorganization of government took place and where the new government center of Japan evolved. The first step was the emperor's takeover of the shogun's castle as the new Imperial Palace. Because it was said the emperor did not require such elaborate defenses, some parts of the castle fortifications were dismantled and the stones were used to build bridges (Seidensticker, 1983, p.25). Secondly, the *daimyō* tracts immediately to the south of the castle that had been vacated with the abolition of *sankin kōtai* were claimed by the military for barracks and parade grounds, and then by various government agencies as office sites. The first were the Foreign Ministry (*Gaimushō*) and Finance Ministry (*Ōkurashō*) in 1869.

Figure 3.5 'Scenic View of Tokyo Enlightenment'. This is a woodcut print (*ukiyoe*) by Utagawa Hiroshige III from 1874, showing the bridge at Kyōbashi and the new brick and stone shops along the main street in Ginza. (Kanagawa Prefecture Museum)

Others, such as the Education Ministry (*Mombushō*), followed soon there-after when the cabinet system of government was adopted. Eventually, almost all of Nagatachō and Kasumigaseki were given over to government functions. This role was cemented in 1890 when the first Diet Building was erected there on a low hill. The only tract that was used differently was a *daimyō* estate turned parade ground in Kasumegaseki, opened in 1903 as Japan's first Western-style park. This is Hibiya Park with its formal gardens, large fountain, indoor and outdoor concert facilities, and some sports facilities and playgrounds, that still serves as a buffer between the govern-ment section and areas of the downtown given to commercial offices and shops.

A second focus of change was a district on Tokyo Bay east of the Palace known as Tsukiji. This is an area of reclaimed land that, like areas adjacent to the castle, had also been the private residences of feudal lords. It was rebuilt after the city's opening as a protected settlement for foreigners. The start of construction dates back to the last years of the shogunate and was a response by the old order to demands by foreign powers for extra territoriality, but its inhabitation by foreigners actually coincided with the first year of Meiji. One of the principal landmarks was the Tsukiji Hoteru-kan. This was a large hotel completed in 1868 just across a canal from the main part of the foreigners' quarter. It stood out because of its design. It was a striking brick building that combined curious Western accretions on a traditional Japanese timber-frame base. In doing so, it reflected the nation's first awkward encounters with the world beyond Japan. Even the word *hoterukan* was a stange new blend: the first syllables correspond to the Japanese pronounciation of 'hotel', while *kan* is based on the Japanese for 'inn.'

Another important landmark in the Tsukiji area was a place called New Shimabara. This was a pleasure quarter named after a district of the same type in Kyoto. It was staffed with close to 2,000 prostitutes (including 21 males) and was intended in large part to entertain foreign diplomats who would negotiate political issues with Japan. However, it was not a particu-larly successful place, as the foreigners were said to come in considerable numbers to look but not to play (Seidensticker, 1983, pp. 38–9). Neverthe-less, Tsukiji remained the principal residential district for foreigners until 1900, when the Unequal Treaties that so rankled the Japanese were revised and restrictions on foreigners' movements relaxed.

Very little remains of the old foreigners' settlement. The Hoterukan had an especially short history, because it was destroyed by fire in 1872, while New Shimabara was closed a short time later because it was a financial disaster. In fact, the only surviving institutions from when Tsukiji was a foreigners' enclave are places started by missionaries: a hospital (St Luke's) which is still at its original site, and a university (Rikkyō or St Paul's) which has since moved to a new location (Seidensticker, 1983, pp. 36–42). Nowadays, Tsukiji is most famous for the huge wholesale fish market that occupies a large corner of the area (but not the precise spot of the historic settlement), and for a mixture of edge-of-the-CBD land uses such as other wholesaling, various company offices, miscellaneous institutions and residences.

A tremendous fire swept through much of *shitamachi* in late February 1872. It broke out within the old castle compound at the headquarters of the Army Department, was fanned eastward to the bay by high winds and consumed nearly 100 hectares of the heart of the city. The Hoterukan was among the several thousands of buildings destroyed. Because one of the worst-hit areas was a modest commercial quarter called Ginza (after a silver mint established there as far back as 1612), this fire is generally referred to as the Ginza Fire, or the Great Ginza Fire. Like the Meireki Fire, this was one of a long string of conflagrations that had plagued the city throughout its history, and would not be particularly well-remembered today except for what followed. As Waley has pointed out, many of the new leaders of Japan during early Meiji had recently come to Tokyo from distant provinces, and were shocked to see the waste and destruction the city's frequent fires engendered (Waley, 1988b, p. 5). They were determined to make the city safer and used the opportunity of this disaster to begin. They were eager to modernize Ginza in particular, because this area had recently gained in strategic importance. It was between Tokyo's fast-developing central business district at Nihombashi on the one side, and its brand new central railway station at Shimbashi, completed just before the fire, on the other. This made Ginza a gateway to Tokyo and a grand project there a logical choice.

What resulted from these efforts is known as the Ginza Brick Quarter. A part of this area was described earlier as the scene of 'Tokyo Enlightenment' illustrated in the woodcut by Hiroshige III. The Brick Quarter was designed by the English architect Thomas Waters. He was retained by the governor of Tokyo to fireproof the district and make it a showpiece to impress foreigners (Smith, 1978, p. 54). Construction took nearly a decade and was extravagantly expensive. However, when it was finished, there were over a thousand brick buildings there and in adjoining sections of Kyōbashi Ward. This compared to fewer than twenty in the rest of the city (Seidensticker, 1983, p. 59). As the Hiroshige III print shows, many structures were two-story brick buildings with colonnades and balconies. The gas lights shown were the country's first. Furthermore, the streets were lined with maples and willows in addition to the cherry trees, and pine trees were planted at the corners.

It should have been very beautiful. Hiroshige III showed it to be so, but this is, in part, because he chose to omit the many problems that characterized this development in its early years. The other side of the story is described in a captivating paragraph by Waley about the Ginza Brick Quarter's growing pains. He relates that all the trees except the willows withered and died, homes were badly built and became damp and dangerous, lizards and centipedes multiplied and infested everything, and human residents became ill with dropsy. As a result, many houses were soon abandoned, only to be invaded later by 'acrobats, jugglers and other itiner-ant entertainers – including dancings dogs and wrestling bears' (Waley, 1984, p. 89). Even worse, according to eye-witness recollections recorded by Shibusawa, 'second and third-rate houses were turned into private schools by English teacher(s)' (Shibusawa, 1958, pp. 110–11). All this prompted the authorities to introduce special subsidies to attract residents back. Eventually, in the 1880s, Ginza got back on track, as businesses took advantage of inducements to open there, geisha houses returned from temporary exile after the fire, and its central location began to work more strongly in the district's favor.

But even as the Brick Quarter was experiencing its string of troubles, other parts of Ginza, as well as its northern neighbors Kyōbashi and Nihombashi, were recovering quickly from the fire (or had been spared the devastation) and were paving the way for a massive expansion of Tokyo as a commercial center. The leaders in this were the great financial houses built by lending money to *daimyō* and selling consumer goods. The richest of the entrepreneurs came from the Mitsui family. Their wealth derived largely from a dry goods store called Echigoya, opened in Edo in 1673, and from profits taken in the performance of banking services for the shogun between Kyoto, Osaka and Edo. During Meiji, this family became a stalwart financial backer of the government. In the course of introducing Western banking to Japan, the Mitsuis erected a massive, exotic-looking bank building in Nihombashi in 1872–3. This was quickly appropriated by the government as the First National Bank. It became the nucleus of a financial district that developed soon thereafter in western Nihombashi and then spead to Marunouchi, an adjacent area closer to the Palace. This district's distinction as a financial nucleus was cemented in 1882 with the opening there of the huge Bank of Japan, the nation's central bank and highest-order lending institution.

Echigoya, meanwhile, continued to prosper; evolved by the early twenti-eth century into Mitsukoshi, the first of Japan's great department stores. In many ways it was an imitation of the American store Wanamaker's, and drew crowds by presenting culture and entertainment as well as merchan-dise (Seidensticker, 1983, p. 111). Other department stores appeared nearby quickly thereafter. The second was Shirokiya, located just across a short bridge from Mitsukoshi in the direction of Ginza. It too evolved on the foundations of an old Edo shop, this one dating back to 1663. After-wards, other department stores opened, also in the direction of Ginza. These included Maruzen, Takashimaya and Ginza Mitsukoshi. The result is that a big part of the Nihombashi-Kyōbashi-Ginza area, including the territory of the Ginza Brick Quarter, became a large-scale retailing district.

There were many other examples in Meiji Tokyo of Western influence on the landscape. Another of the most memorable was the Rokumeikan, an elaborate hotel and gathering place completed in 1883 in the Hibiya section close to the government center. It was the work of another English architect, Josiah Conder, who was brought to Japan in 1877 at the request of the Ministry of Technology. He contributed immensely to the shaping of modern Tokyo by designing numerous striking buildings for the city, and by training a whole generation of Japanese architects. Like the Hoteru-kan, the Rokumeikan was an unusual structure, covered with stucco and combining Moorish, Mediterranean and other European styles. It was commissioned by the Japanese government to be a place where cosmopolitan citizens could mix with foreigners. During its heyday in the middle and late 1880s, the building hosted countless elegant balls, formal dinners, musical performances, charity bazaars and other Western-style 'high society' events. It was in this context that Shirokiya, the department store, came to specialize in Western-fashion women's apparel, and imported 'a certain Miss Curtis from Great Britain' to supervise its displays (Yazaki, 1968, p. 341).

This short-lived period is called the Rokumeikan Era. It is remembered fondly for its great splendor, and is often illustrated in films and television dramas that romanticize Japan's first successful experiences with Western ways. For the Meiji government, the purpose of having all this was to demonstrate to foreigners that the Japanese were civilized and enlightened, and to convince the foreign powers with whom Japan had been forced to sign unequal commercial treaties in the 1850s and 1860s (the United States, Britain, The Netherlands, France and Russia) that they should renegotiate. When the government failed at this, the Rokumeikan lost its popularity and began a decline that culminated in the razing of the building in 1941 (Barr, 1968, pp. 12–13 and 179–80; Seidensticker, 1983, pp. 68–70 and 97–100).

Another important example of how Japan's response to the west was seen in the built form of Tokyo was the development of a new district of the city that came to be called Mitsubishi Londontown. As the name suggests, it was a Japanese imitation of the British capital. Josiah Conder had a large hand in this, too, as did some of his students and other designers. Its main features were four-story, red-brick buildings vaguely reminiscent of Victorian Kensington (Figure 3.6). However, Waley's observations of photographs from the period conclude that the development lacked 'the architectural conviction and spontaneity that grows out of native soil', and that it revealed a 'pronounced sense of disconsonance'. Instead of trolleys and carriages, the streets were served by rickshaws; the passers-by must have been completely disoriented (Waley, 1984, p. 33).

In contrast to the Rokumeikan and Ginza Bricktown, which were government projects, Londontown was the creation of a private, family-owned business called the Mitsubishi Company. It was controlled by the powerful Iwasaki family, who conceived this plan purely and simply as a way to reap huge profits at real-estate development. The land was immediately south of the Imperial Palace, close to the main gate, and for many years was the preserve of top *daimyō*. It was vacated with the fall of the shogunate and, except for use as a parade ground for the army and some barracks, stood empty for nearly a quarter of a century after the start of Meiji. For

Figure 3.6 The Mitsubishi Bank building in Marunouchi's 'Londontown'. (From the 1899 book *Japan in Transition* by S. Ransome, published by Harper & Brothers)

reasons that make little sense now, when we have the advantage of hindsight, the government was unable to make good use of the land, and sold it in 1890 to the Iwasakis for little more than a pittance (1.25 million yen). Citizens referred to the purchase as the Mitsubishi Wasteland and wondered what good could be put there. The Iwasakis joked they might plant bamboo and introduce tigers (Waley, 1984, p. 32). Instead, they undertook to develop an office-commercial center that not only housed their headquarters (in a building by Conder), but also the offices of many other companies to whom the Iwasakis rented space in other structures. The project covered several streets and was the largest private development in Japan up to that time.

Even so, many vacant lots remained in the 'wasteland' until after 1914, the year when Tokyo Railway Station was opened adjacent to this development. The Iwasakis had arranged for its principal entrance to face their way rather than toward Nihombashi, and thus assured for themselves and all the Mitsubishi business concerns a central place in the life of Tokyo ever after. Today nothing is left of the original architecture of Londontown. However, the area is still Tokyo's principal office center, and the Mitsubishi Company, now a gigantic corporate concern famous world-wide, is still a major landowner. The separate headquarters buildings for each of the several companies that make up its 'family of companies' are scattered across the district and are especially prominent. The current name for the district is Marunouchi, a name that means 'within the circle of moats', but that in practice suggests a secure position within the inner circle of power in both the city and the Japanese nation at large.

Industry and neighborhoods

The Meiji period is also the time when Tokyo began its modern industrial development. There had always been industry in the city before, if only because of the great demand for manufactured products continually generated by its huge population, but it was small in scale and traditional in organization and technology level. It is said that the only large industrial site during Edo was the Ishikawajima Shipbuilding Yard built in 1849 by the Mito family in the northern part of Tsukishima, an island of reclaimed land close to the city center. Consequently, as late as 1874 the city ranked no higher than ninth in Japan in industrial production, and had an output of manufactured products that was barely one-quarter that of the leading city, Kyoto (Itakura and Takeuchi, 1980, p. 51).

All this began to change with the onset of the Meiji reforms, as both the number of factories and the scale of operations, as well as the variety of products made in the city, were greatly increased. While the new government also invested heavily in the industrial development of other cities and numerous rural locations (eg. the fishing village of Yahata, now part of the Kitakyūshū urban agglomeration, where a giant state-owned steel mill was built), there was considerable favoritism extended to the capital (Smith T.C., 1973; Allinson 1975; 1978). This is seen in the examples of several model factories built by the government in various sections of Tokyo that employed imported technical advisors and equipment: a paper processing plant in Ōji; a cement factory in Fukagawa; a glass plant in Shinagawa; a huge spinning mill in Senju; and the Government Printing Bureau in Takinogawa (Yazaki, 1968, p. 352). As a result of such construction, and because of the private investment in factory production that followed, Tokyo was quickly transformed into a paramount concentration of heavy industry: so much so that by the time of the pre-war industrial build-up of the 1930s, the city ranked as far and away Japan's prime manufacturing center.

We can identify several reasons why there was especially heavy investment in industry in Tokyo in particular. As was the case with the Rokumeikan and the Ginza Brick Quarter, new factory technology was, in part, another front along which the new government endeavored to make Tokyo into a showpiece city. The goal was to impress foreigners and Japanese alike with the city's modernity, and to demonstrate that Japan could keep pace with the fashions and useful technologies that were advancing in other countries. Secondly, as the headquarters of nearly all the most powerful private financial enterprises in Japan, such as the Mitsui and Mitsubishi *zaibatsu*, the city had the largest concentration of investment capital in the country and was a natural location for spending. So, too, the city was made into the nation's leading center of higher education, with Tokyo University, founded in 1869, being given the lead in studying foreign technologies and advancing industrial know-how in Japan. Finally, we can point to some geographical advantages of the city: its good harbor, urban rivers and ample flat land, the undeveloped space in the surrounding Kantō Plain for urban expansion, and the intermediate situation of the city within Japan between the established population centers to the west and frontier lands in the northern Honshū and Hokkaido.

The first 'industrial revolution' neighborhood of Tokyo was the section of *shitamachi* at the lower reaches of the Sumida. Now part of an oversized CBD, this area had previously been a concentration of traditional crafts such as carpenters, plasterers, barrel-makers, stonemasons, metalworkers, tailors and roof thatchers. In early Meiji, it changed to embrace various new industries such as the making of shoes and clogs, carts, rickshaws, bricks, roofing tiles, Western-style clothing, and, before long, electric motors (Yazaki, 1968, p. 353). Almost all these enterprises involved larger production facilities than the previously dominant 'home shops'. Many of their products were put on display at an Industrial Exhibition that opened in Ueno under government sponsorship in 1878 both to disseminate information about the latest technologies and to enlarge the domestic market for new products. As industry expanded, more factories were built further upstream along the Sumida, in the deltaic flatland between the Sumida and Ara Rivers that is today's Sumida and Kōtō Wards, as well as along the banks of the Arakawa itself. The Senju district was especially important. It became a major industrial rail corridor, and included among other notable plants the Senju Spinning Mill (1879) with as many as 25,000 employees by the turn of the century (a record size for the city), the Tokyo Cardboard Company (1886), the Senju Mill of the Ōji Paper Company (1888) and a large facility of the Tokyo Gas Company (1893) (Yazaki, 1976, p. 351).

A second important industrial area developed in the 1890s to 1910 period along the Tokyo Bay waterfront. It is called Keihin, a word that can be translated as 'metropolitan harbor'; it is written in Chinese characters that combine pieces of the words 'Tokyo' and 'Yokohama'. The area stretches along a reclaimed shoreline between these two cities for approximately 40 kilometers. In contrast to eastern Tokyo (i.e. the Sumida River area), Keihin was (and still is) particularly oriented to heavy industries that require imported raw materials. The most notable examples include steel milling, machinery manufacture and various kinds of chemical industries. The sizable heavy industrial city of Kawasaki, developed in the early part of the present century on the site of a highway station town between Shinagawa and Yokohama near the mouth of the Tama River in what is now Kanagawa Prefecture, is near the center of this belt and represents its industrial character. Some of the most important large industrial facilities there were the Kawasaki Salt Plant built in 1907, Tokyo Electric Company, Nihon Gramophone Company, Meiji Sugar Company, Nihon Steel Tube Company and the Tokyo Wire Company (Yazaki, 1968, pp. 465–6).

One of the key factors in the rapid rise of Keihin as an industrial region is the excellent harbor at Yokohama. Port facilities for foreign trade were opened there shortly after the first contact with Admiral Perry, and were then enlarged and improved during the Meiji period to make the city the nation's pre-eminent deepwater port. The Keihin area also benefited from the opening in 1910 of a shipping canal between Tokyo and Yokohama, as well as from a dense network of rail connections between docking facilities and the industrial precincts of Tokyo's waterfront. So, too, rail lines were extended inland from Yokohama to new industrial centers in the Tama region of Tokyo such as Tachikawa, Fuchū and Fussa. The growth of these centers was especially intense later, well after the Meiji period, during the industrial build-up of the 1920s and 1930s. Because of outstanding infrastructure, and because it is part of such a huge concentration of population, Keihin continues to be one of the biggest centers of industrial production in Japan.

As in other cities, industrialization had a profound impact on urban population growth and neighborhoods. Tokyo, always a crowded city, swelled as never before in the last decades of the nineteenth century and early twentieth, expanding rapidly in all directions. It more than recovered the population losses that had taken place earlier when *sankin kōtai* ended, and grew in numbers to record proportions by the early twentieth century. From an estimated less than 500,000 inhabitants in the 1860s–1870s, the city reached one million by the 1890s, a second million by 1907, and more than three million by 1920 (Ishizuka and Ishida, 1988, p. 14; H.D. Smith II, 1979, pp 50–1). The main reason was a massive influx of young migrants who poured in from a poor, overcrowded countryside to seek work. This was the case even though there was also considerable rural-based industrialization during this time in Japan, a fact that provided local factory employment opportunities in some regions and kept overall rates of urban growth slower than, say, in the United States (Allinson, 1978, p. 449). Thus, Tokyo (and to a lesser extent Osaka) was an unusually powerful magnet for migrants from the countryside. In 1907, for example, perhaps the height of the industrialization-urbanization process, fully one-half of the the city's two million residents were arrivals from outside (Ishizuka and Ishida, 1988, p. 14).

The physical expression of this influx was new neighborhoods at the city's edge, radial expansion of the city along highways and rail corridors that extended beyond built-up limits, and enormous increases in density in existing districts. Some neighborhoods became especially overcrowded, degenerating into unsanitary slums. This was especially true for several of the neighborhoods that had sprung up among the factories along the east bank of the Sumida. However, the worst conditions were said to be in three neighborhoods famous during the Edo period as goverment dumping grounds for freed convicts, beggars, drifters and Japan's 'untouchable classes,' the so-called *eta* and *hinin*: Yotsuya Samegabashi to the west of the city center; Shiba Shin'amichō to the south; and Shitaya Man'nenchō to the north (Taira, 1969, p. 157). During Meiji, these 'three great ghettoes' (*sandai hinminkutsu*) became refuges for the most destitute migrants to the city, and for thousands of city residents who were unemployed or seriously underemployed as 'trifling crafstmen', occasional construction workers or street performers (Ishizuka and Ishida, 1988, p. 14).

The literary response to the living conditions of industrial era slums in Tokyo was not as strong it was in the West where, for example, Dickens, Engels, Booth and Mayhew wrote passionately about the dark underside of English cities. There were, however, several notable journalistic exposés. The most important of these was by Yokoyama Gennosuke, published in 1899 with supporting statistics as *Nihon no kasō shakai* ('Japan's Lower Classes') and then reprinted in 1949 and 1958 as a classic study of the three worst neighborhoods in Tokyo (H.D. Smith II, 1979, pp. 85–6). The author is said to have been so shocked by what he encountered in each of these districts that he claimed to 'rub his eyes twice' to make sure that he wasn't seeing things (Taira, 1969, p. 157). Thousands of people jammed into dilapidated tenements called *nagaya* that extended back in long rows from narrow, unpaved alleys. The rooms, allocated one per large family, were tiny and measured only four and a half or six *tatami* mats in total (approximately 9 x 9, or 9 x 12 feet, respectively) (Yazaki, 1968, p. 366). Toilets, actually privies, were shared, and there was no water except for polluted communal wells. What is more, all three areas were infested by flies, rats and other pests, and suffered deadly epidemics of cholera, tuberculosis and other diseases. In the fashion of the Meiji period, when things Western were so quickly adopted in Japan, these neighborhoods, previously referred to as *hinminkutsu* ('caves of the poor people'), came to be called *suramu*, a modern addition to the Japanese language derived from a pronunciation of the word 'slum' (H. D. Smith II, 1979, p. 86.)

Before the cataclysm

In addition to the slums, there were many other urban problems in Tokyo during the years immediately before and after the turn of the century. Some of the others included a great flood in 1910 that covered the whole northern part of *shitamachi*, angry riots in 1918 over the high price of rice, and severe overcrowding and environmental degradation in just about every section of the metropolitan area. There were especially urgent problems regarding waste disposal. As Seidensticker described the sewage problem, Tokyo had grown so large by late Meiji that distances between the center of the city and farms on the urban periphery exceeded the daily ranges of the all-important night-soil carts that had always made their scheduled rounds. This meant that houses and businesses in the center found they could no longer sell their excrement, even if it was the more highly prized product of wealthy individuals with nutritious diets; instead they had to pay to have it hauled away, often, it emerged, by contracters who would simply dump the loads somewhere else in the city. There were similar problems with garbage disposal. Because household waste material accumulated too quickly to be carted away, Tokyo developed a pervasive bad smell from the burning carried out within city limits (Seidensticker, 1983, pp. 282–3).

However, despite such drawbacks, the last decades of Meiji and all but the last years of the short reign of the next emperor, the Taishō Emperor (1912–26), were generally a high period in the life of Tokyo. Until the crash that came suddenly on 1 September 1923, the city quickly grew in population, profited from two war booms during which industrial production was greatly expanded, and invested heavily in a new urban infrastructure that ranged from a dense network of commuter train and electric trolley lines, to ambitious flood control projects along the Sumida, to increasing numbers of large, western-style office structures, called *biru* after 1917 because of the pronunciation of the loan word 'building', in an ever more impressive downtown. A major symbol of the times was the opening of Tokyo Station in 1914, the new central station for the city that replaced the one at Shimbashi. In keeping with the craze for things borrowed, its design was patterned after the main station in Amsterdam. Other highlights of the period included numerous new opportunities for public entertainment, new technologies such as the electric light, elevators and telephones, new fashions in dress and other endeavors, and a brief period of societal openness and political reform during World War I called the 'Taishō Democracy'.

There were two districts in Tokyo that were especially revealing of the times. One was Ginza, far and away the most modern and most Westernized section of the city. The other was Asakusa. The former was famous for its department stores and its many new shops selling all the latest imported goods and new domestic products (Table 3.2), a majestic new *kabuki* theater, and great crowds of *mo-bo* and *mo-ga* ('modern boys' and 'modern girls'), many of them from affluent families in the hilly sections west of the city center, who gathered there. Theirs was the practice called *Gim-bura*, 'killing time' or 'strolling in Ginza'. They were attracted equally by the glitter of the main streets and the romance of the small side streets lined with sophisticated cafés and trendy shops. The main intersection, now called Ginza Crossing, was especially busy. Its dominant landmark was a big clock imported from Switzerland and displayed in a two-story tower atop the Hattori Watch Company building, the predecessor of today's Seiko Corporation (Figure 3.7).[4]

[4] There is still a clock in a two-story tower at the same intersection. However, the building that it graces is a newer (1932) structure, now the Wakō department store, and the clock is actually a Seiko quartz model (Waley, 1988b, p. 7).

Table 3.2 Specialty stores in Ginza, 1910

Name of Store	Specialties
Aoki Kutsu-kaban-ten	shoes and brief cases
Itōya Bunbōguten	stationery and office supplies
Jūjiya Gakkiten	musical instruments
Tamaya Tokeiten	watches and clocks
Kintarō Ganguten	toys
Satō Hōshokuten	jewelry
Kondō Shoten	books
Panya Kimura Sōhōnten	breads and cakes
Kyōbunkan Shoseikan	books, including Christian books
Mikimoto Shinjuten	cultured pearls
Yamano Gakkiten	musical instruments
Kurimoto Undōguten	sporting goods
Cafe Lion	coffee house and restaurant
Sekiguchi Yōhinten	haberdashery
Sano Tabiten	Japanese socks
Daimaruya Gofukuten	dry goods
Shogetsu Yōshōkuten	Western-style restaurant
Cafe Tiger	coffee house and restaurant
Mazuda Lamp Ginzaten	electrical lighting equipment
Morinaga Candy Store	confections
Kikusui Nagai Tabakoten	pipe and tobacco supplies
Takahashi Stekkiten	walking sticks

Source: Yazaki, 1968, p. 441.

In contrast to Ginza, Asakusa was more of a traditional stronghold and a gathering place for the ordinary people of the city. In Seidensticker's words, it 'is where the masses went to do what the masses of Edo had been wont to do, find performances to view and thereby ruin themselves' (1983, p. 267). The place continued as a center of *kabuki*, although this was somewhat less the attraction than it was before; it was also a mecca for the popular new motion picture theaters and music houses. There were also plenty of places for roistering and lechering (Seidensticker, 1983, p. 267). The main symbols of Asakusa were its great temple, which remains even today as an unbroken link to the past, and the *Ryōunkaku*, the '12-story pavilion'[5]. Built in 1890, this was Tokyo's first skyscraper and the first building in Japan to have an elevator (to the eighth floor only). There were shops, theaters, bars and restaurants on every floor, and three observation levels at the top affording a splendid view of the city. A marvelous print by Ichiju Kunimasa, showing the full length of the building as well as some fanciful kites, parachutists and balloonists, clearly reflects that it was mainly a pavilion of pleasure (Collcutt, Jansen and Kumakura, 1988, p. 197). Unfortunately, the good times there would be short-lived, and the tower would soon become identified as one of the most enduring images of a great disaster.

[5] This building was also called the *Junikai*, 'the 12-story'.

Figure 3.7 The main intersection of Ginza in the 27th year of Meiji (1895). The building with the clock tower is the former headquarters of the Hattori Seiko Corporation, the watch company. The site is now the Wako Department Store. Note the congestion of trolley cars, and the combination of Western and Japanese dress the pedestrians are wearing. (Courtesy of the Public Relations Department, Seiko Corporation)

The Great Kantō Earthquake

All the routines that had come to characterize Tokyo, as well as several tens of thousands of lives, came to a violent end with the disaster that began precisely 'one minute and fifteen and four-tenths seconds before noon' on 1 September 1923 (Seidensticker, 1983, p. 3). This was the instant of the sudden mighty jolt of the earth beneath the city, measuring an astonishing 7.8 to 7.9 on the Japanese scale, referred to as the Great Kantō Earthquake (*Kantō Daishinsai*). There was another tremendous shock about 24 hours later and several hundred minor aftershocks in the following days. The epicenter was in Sagami Bay, southwest of the city, close to the opening of Tokyo Bay, and there was extensive damage over a wide area covering parts of seven prefectures – Tokyo, Kanagawa, Chiba, Ibaraki, Saitama, Yamanashi and Shizuoka. The Tokyo-Yokohama conurbation was especially badly shaken. The worst damage was in the Kōtō section of Tokyo, between the mouths of the Ara and Sumida rivers, where

Figure 3.8 Remains of the Twelve Stories building in Asakusa after the Great Kantō Earthquake. (Asahi Company)

the soil is very soft alluvium. In this area, nearly 30 per cent of all houses were destroyed by one of the two major tremors. Also lost in the quake was the Twelve Stories at Asakusa, which snapped in spectacular fashion just above the eighth floor, tumbling to the street below (Figure 3.8).

There was even greater destruction from the fires that broke out immediately after the earthquakes (Figure 3.9). The noonhour timing was particularly unfortunate, because residents had been tending charcoal or wood fires for cooking; the extreme violence of the first shock scattered embers that ignited numerous houses. The official count has it that 134 separate blazes broke out in the city and then raged out of control for up to three days. The reason that things were so bad was that much of Tokyo (and downtown Yokohama) was, as always in its history, a densely packed tinderbox of wooden buildings, and because flames could be easily fanned by the day's unusually heavy breezes. Fire-fighting and rescue were made especially difficult because many water mains and fire hydrants had been ruptured by the quake, and because communications of all kinds were seriously disrupted. With so much aflame, the air above the city became intensely hot and unstable, which then created firestorms swept by winds of 70 to 80 kilometers per hour. Even worse, several cyclones or tornadoes

Figure 3.9 Devastation from the earthquake and fire near Marunouchi in the Tokyo CBD after the Great Kantō Earthquake. (Asahi Company)

developed in downtown Tokyo. These were especially deadly, because they were drawn by the presence of oxygen to the same open spaces in the city where much of the populace had sought refuge from the flames. One cyclone passed over the unprotected grounds of the Military Clothing Depot in the Honjo area, across the Sumida River in the heavily devastated Kōtō ward and suffocated approximately 40,000 people. A series of large oil paintings in Cenotaph Hall, a memorial building on the precise site and a haunting bronze sculpture of children in flight recall this tragedy in gory detail.

It is not possible to know the exact extent of the damage or the total loss of life. The generally accepted estimates report that, all told, 104,619 people died or were missing as a result of this disaster, and an additional 52,074 were injured. Of the dead and missing, 91,995 were from the densely built-up areas of Tokyo and Yokohama. The statistics also show that 73 per cent of the houses in Tokyo were damaged and 63 per cent were completely destroyed. Less than one per cent of the worst damage was from the tremor itself, as it was fire that brought the most ruin to both cities. The value of property damage is estimated to have been in the range of several billion yen. Insurance policies generally excluded damage from earthquakes (and the fires they started), so it became the burden of individuals and the government to finance almost all the rebuilding (Stanley, 1983, p. 66). However, insurance companies made 'sympathy payments' of some ten per cent of the value of policies to many businesses and households, because the government insisted that the companies had a 'moral obligation' to pay what they could (Busch, 1962, pp. 159–60.)

The suddenness of the disaster and its terrible magnitude resulted in considerable confusion among the population in the days that followed. There was some ill-timed disarray in government to begin with, because the Prime Minister had died unexpectedly just a week before the fateful day. Furthermore, some particularly foul rumors began to circulate among the citizenry. One was that some unnamed country in the West had developed an earthquake machine and was experimenting on Japan. Fortunately, this idea was contained before any violence was taken against Westerners. However, Korean residents of the city were not so lucky. They were an especially despised minority, mostly because of the long history of conflict between the two nations, and suffered frequent displays of bigotry in Japan on this account (Lee and DeVos, 1981). Soon after the earthquake, completely unfounded reports began to multiply that it was actually Koreans, and not flying embers, who were setting fires throughout the city, and that they were also poisoning water sources. Because police services were badly disrupted, it was difficult to counteract these stories; citizens formed vigilante groups for protection against the supposed malefactors. This led to numerous atrocities and a toll of several thousand Koreans murdered by angry mobs. One method the mobs used to identify Koreans, who are generally physically indistinguishable from Japanese, was to have suspects pronounce the common Japanese syllabary, 'ba, bi, bu, be, bo'. When the sounds of b's were given as p's, the person was marked as a foreigner and was often killed on the spot (Busch, 1962, p. 109). To protect the immigrants, police had to establish a special barracks outside the city to house approximately 10,000 individuals.

Rebuilding the city

The task of rebuilding Tokyo was put in the charge of Gōtō Shimpei, a former mayor of the city and an important national political figure. He had long advocated grand plans to redesign Tokyo to make it more modern and efficient; and as mayor he had established the Tokyo Institute for Municipal Research to guide him. In keeping with the drive for enlightenment that characterized the times, he was especially interested in learning the latest 'scientific methods' relating to city planning and public administration. His principal advisor was an American scholar he had befriended, Charles Austin Beard, who had started a similar institute in New York City. In 1921, after some study and comparison with New York, Gōtō proposed a massive, 800 million yen project for Tokyo that came to be called 'the big kerchief' because it covered so many aspects of the city. Among other improvements, it would pave and widen streets, expand the water supply as well as electric and gas services, improve the harbor and other waterways, build parks, schools, municipal buildings, public halls and other public structures, and provide a wide range of new social services to the citizens. The cost, however, was seen by critics as prohibitive: it was equivalent to nearly one-half of the total *national* budget and more than six times the annual city budget. The plan was never adopted.

The aftermath of the earthquake was a second chance for this rebuilding. An imperial proclamation less than two weeks after the disaster put to rest any ideas emerging among numerous commentators that the capital should be moved to a safer site, and got reconstruction started (Hayase, 1974, p. 195):

Tokyo is the capital of our imperial nation, and it is the axis for the political and economic life of the nation. It is also the source of the nation's culture, to which all Japanese citizens have to look. Despite the destruction of the city by the unexpected disaster, it has not lost its position as the capital of the nation. We must plan not only for the recovery of the old capital but also for future improvement.

Accordingly, Gōtō, now in command of the 'Board of Reconstruction of the Capital City', sent a telegram to Beard in New York: *Earthquake fire destroyed greater part of Tokyo. Thoroughgoing reconstruction needed. Please come immediately, even for a short stay.* The response came right back: *Lay out new streets, forbid building without street lines, unify railway stations.* (Hayase, 1974, p. 196).

However, once again the matter of cost got in the way. Because it was estimated that rebuilding Tokyo according to the Gōtō-Beard plan would require a sum that was three times the national budget, politicians began to resist the idea and withheld funds. There was also opposition from some influential landowners, who feared correctly that they stood to lose some of their accumulated holdings for use by public projects. As a result, only a few elements of the total scheme were actually put in: some trunk roads such as Showa-dōri and Taishō-dōri; grid-pattern streets in the Kōtō area and in the downtown around Marunouchi; and some new parks (eg. Hama-chō Park on the Sumida River near the downtown business district, and Sumida Park on the riverbank not far from the temple center at Asakusa). Otherwise, Tokyo built itself up again pretty much as it was before. It still looked more like Edo than the attractive sections of New York that urban reformers preferred, and because of the hasty reconstruction, it 'remained outdated, with narrow streets, slum areas, open sewers, and many other urban maladies' (Hayase, 1974, p. 199).

There were, however, some other changes that came to Tokyo after the 1923 disaster, which were not necessarily directly a part of the Gōtō-Beard plan. One was an increase in the amount of land given to heavy industry. This was especially the case in the Keihin area, which expanded along the shore of Tokyo Bay from Chiba Prefecture to far south of Yokohama, and in Tokyo's western (i.e. Tama) and northern (Saitama Prefecture) suburbs and outlying towns. A large part of this was related to the build-up of heavy industry in Japan that marked the pre-World War II period. For example, the growth of armaments-related industries, especially aircraft, had much to do with the rapid growth during the 1930s of Musashino, Tanashi, and Mitaka in the Tama district.

A second change was geographical expansion of the urbanized area not related to industrial expansion. An important stimulus was the earthquake itself which drove survivors to safer ground away from the congested center of the city. So, too, Tokyoites were pushed from the center by reconstruction activity. Thousands of households were displaced from older neighborhoods by the straightening and widening of streets that took place in the city during the late 1920s. This was done amid numerous angry protests and demonstrations by homeowners and businesses who considered themselves to be inadequately compensated for their land (Ishizuka and Ishida, 1988, p. 20). Still another factor behind suburbanization was the growth in the city's transportation network. There were new rail lines and highways that made distant lands more accessible and, from 1927, with the opening of a 14 kilometer-long subway line under the heart of the city (the Ginza Line), fast travel to and through the center of Tokyo itself became possible.

A major beneficiary of post-earthquake urban expansion was Shinjuku, a rail interchange on the west side of the city that exploded in growth to become a major urban nucleus. Some of the department stores from Ginza relocated there immediately after the disaster, as did various other shops and institutions. So, too, there was great growth in the after-dark entertainment industry. As a result, by 1930 Shinjuku rivaled Ginza with as many as 200 coffee shops employing some 2,000 waitresses and such popular new theaters as Teito-za and the Moulin Rouge (Waley, 1988a, p. 14). The nearby business center of Shibuya also grew quickly after the earthquake (Mitsuoka, 1989). Its advantages included a stategic station on the National Railways line, good connections by road and later by rail to western suburbs and to the center of Yokohama, and (after 1939) status as the western terminus of the Ginza Line.

One of the consequences of suburban growth after the earthquake was that the city's boundaries had to be redrawn. This was done in 1932. Instead of 15 wards covering a small area huddled around the Imperial Palace and the CBD, the limits of Tokyo were enlarged about five-fold when the city annexed 82 adjacent towns and villages in five nearby counties (*gun*). The new territory was reorganized into 20 new wards, bringing the total number of wards to 35. The limits of this area are fairly consistent with what is now thought of as the 'City of Tokyo' (as opposed to today's 'Tokyo Metropolis' or *Tokyo-to*). However, there was yet another redrawing of boundaries within this zone in 1947, with the result that the 'city' part of Tokyo Metropolis now has only 23 wards.

The air raids of 1945

No sooner had Tokyo begun to settle back into normal routines than the national leadership led the country to war. This brought on a second disaster, even more widespread and deadly than the first – the bombing of the city by US forces, Japan's main adversary in World War II. The first raid in April 1942 was by a squadron of 16 B25s from the carrier *USS Hornet* and did comparatively little damage. However, the raids by B29s near the end of the war in the winter of 1944–5 were devastating. There were 102 attacks in all, mostly against military targets and strategic industrial facilities, but they also inflicted grave damage to the nearby residential neighborhoods. The planes came so often to Tokyo during this period that residents began to refer to them as *okyakusama* ('honored guests'), 'regular mail', and 'Lord B' (Daniels, 1975, p. 121). By the time the raids ended in the spring, the death toll had reached more than 100,000 and almost the entire city was in ruins (Figures 3.10 and 3.11). The count of casualties would have been even worse had not much of the population evacuated the city as the tempo of bombings increased.

The worst attack took place the night of 9–10 March 1945. It reflected a change in military strategy by the Americans, and, like the bombing of Hiroshima and Nagasaki some months later, was intended to hasten Japan's surrender by creating mass carnage among the populace. Instead of the high explosive bombs previously used to demolish individual structures, this attack was designed to set fire to the city and to have the flames spread widely. It was carried out by 334 B29 Superfortress bombers loaded to the maximum of six tons each with napalm and a new incendiary device containing magnesium and jellied gasoline. The principal target was Asakusa Ward, an overcrowded *shitamachi* area of wooden houses, narrow streets and a very high roof density, but many other areas (including the Imperial Palace compound which had supposedly been off limits) were also struck. In the three hours between midnight and approximately three a.m., 700,000 bombs fell on the city (Guillain, 1981, p. 188). The result was an 'almost surrealist masterpiece of flame and agony reminiscent of Bosch, Bacon or Goya in their most tormented works', and more than 77,000 civilian deaths on that single night (Daniels, 1975, p. 125). Over 276,000 buildings were destroyed. This attack has the unhappy distinction of being the most destructive single bombing mission with non-atomic weapons in history.

Post-war reconstruction

With the end of the war, Japan was thoroughly defeated, both physically and psychologically, and faced an extremely difficult rebuilding challenge. All the largest cities except Kyoto were in ruins, there were severe shortages of food, housing and other necessities, the economy was devastated and at a standstill and the spirit of the people was all but broken. In the words of the Japanese press, it was a situation of 'one hundred million people in a state of trauma' (Morris-Suzuki, 1985, p. 196). The fact that the country was able to recover so completely and so quickly, and to become an exceedingly prosperous nation with a high standard of living so soon after

Figure 3.10 Central Tokyo after the air raids of 1945. Nihombashi is in the foreground, while the background is Kōtō Ward across the Sumida River. (Asahi Company)

Figure 3.11 Taking a bath near the ruins of Ōtsuka Station, Toshima Ward, after the bombing of March 1945. (Asahi Company).

its crushing collapse, is one of the great modern-day miracles. It is primarily a tribute to the energies and determination of its citizenry, and a happy outcome for Japan of American generosity and of various enlightened policies of the US Occupation following the hostilities.

The story of Japan's rebuilding is discussed in many excellent sources (eg. Burks, 1984; Kawai, 1960; Kosai, 1986; Reischauer, 1977; Storry, 1960; Uchino, 1978) and need not be repeated. However, we might observe that the changes that came to Japanese society during its reconstruction were just as revolutionary, if not more so, as those of the Meiji Restoration. The centerpiece was a new constitution, drafted somewhat hurriedly by the Americans but still in force by popular will more than 40 years later, that transformed the nation into a parliamentary democracy. It entrusted sovereign power to the people, made the emperor, who earlier had renounced claims to divinity, a completely powerless symbol of Japanese unity, and provided for a 30-article Bill of Rights guaranteeing basic human freedoms and outlawing most forms of social discrimination. Moreover, the country was demilitarized; responsibilities for defense were taken on by the United States. Other changes included the weakening of the powerful *zaibatsu* economic concerns so that industry and other business activity could be decentralized; radical land reforms that allowed tenant farmers to become owners; the enhancement of powers for labor unions; and, for the first time in Japan, the enfranchisement of women and the extension to them of basic legal rights. Japan also came to be heavily culturally influenced by Americans. As Reischauer described it: 'the disillusioned and demoralized Japanese, instead of reacting to the army of occupation and its leader with the normal sullen resentment of a defeated people, regarded the Americans as guides to a new and better day' (Reischauer, 1977, p. 105).

In the course of reconstruction, various cities in Japan built memorials to their bombed victims. In some, the memorial includes a remnant or more of a bombed-out building or other structure as a permanent reminder of the destruction caused by war. The best, most moving example is Peace Memorial Park and the A-Bomb Dome in Hiroshima through which a thoughtful Japanese friend once gave me an unforgettable tour. Tokyo, however, has nothing of the sort. In still another way that the city reveals itself to be different, it built no special landmark to its terrible ordeal, nor did it retain anything from the ruins for the sake of history. This does not mean that the carnage has been forgotten, because it has not. Instead, it reflects the fact that Tokyo is single-minded at looking forward and not back. As soon as it could, the city returned to business as usual on fully 100 per cent of its land. The only exception was to append some modest exhibits about the bombing to the Cenotaph Hall memorial for the victims of the 1923 earthquake. This building, as I have already described, is rather unassuming. Its outstanding feature, however, is that the curves of the roof line take on a form suggesting a large bird with spread wings about to take off in flight (Enbutsu, 1984, p. 185).

And take off is exactly what Tokyo did, as for the second time in less than a quarter-century it embarked on a fast, thorough rebuilding. Immediately there was the Herculean task of clearing away the cinders and broken concrete and making room for the city to grow. Because of a shortage of trucks and fuel, only some of the rubble could be hauled to landfill in Tokyo Bay. Much of it was piled into the canals, most of which were soon covered over forever. In this way, a distinguishing aspect of old Edo was to all but disappear. Just as fast, rudimentary huts sprang up where they could; street stalls came into business to offer food, drink, and other necessities. Because of the widespread shortages of almost everything, and because the rationing system rarely permitted adequate supplies of necessities, black markets sprang up at every gathering point in the city and every station along commuter lines. They specialized in illegally acquired foreign products, most notably from the supply rooms of the Occupation, as well as in food brought in from the countryside by 'runners' (*katsugiya*) who circumvented both rationing laws and the police. As reported by Seidensticker (1990, pp. 153–4), there were an estimated 60,000 black-market stalls in Tokyo at the start of 1946. This number testifies to the terrible misery of the time and the desperation of honest men and women to make a living.

Some of the post-war black markets merit special mention, either because of their unusually large size, or because they have survived, albeit in altered form, to the present day. Perhaps the most famous is a place called Ameyayokochō, a narrow alley lined with vendors' stalls strung out beneath an elevated railroad right-of-way south of Ueno Station. During the worst shortages, the market was a lifeline of food supplies from the farming hinterland reached by trains to Ueno, as well as a steady supply of products of various kinds from the United States, especially sweets. This explains the name *ameya*, a pun on both the word 'American' and the Japanese word for 'sweet'[6]. As rationing began to be abandoned in the 1950s, Ameyayokochō changed its functions and now sells a variety of products at discount, ranging from fresh seafood to golfing supplies (see Chapter 5) (Figure 3.12). However, there is still something of a black market there, as some shops are known to specialize in easily transported foreign goods that Japanese travellers bring from abroad without paying import fees (Seidensticker, 1990, pp. 152–3). Other famous black markets were at Shinjuku, Ginza and Ikebukuro. Bits and pieces of the one near Shinjuku Station's West Exit survive as a cluster of tiny eating and drinking stalls widely called 'Piss Alley' (*Shombenyokochō*). Still another black market, the one at Akihabara between Ueno and the CBD, was based on the collection of scrap electrical equipment, and eventually evolved into the world-renowned electronics emporium specializing in the latest products by Japan's great manufacturers that it is today.

[6] 'The *yokochō*' part of 'Ameyayokocho' means alley.

Figure 3.12 Ameyayokochō in the rain. Today the street specializes in the sale of fresh fish and other food products, but during the years immediately after World War II it was one of the city's leading black markets.

There was less chance after the war than there was after the earthquake to beautify the city in its reconstruction, or to introduce much improved urban design. One element of this problem was unprecedented population pressure. The number of residents of Tokyo (i.e. the ward area), which had declined during the war years by some four million persons largely because of evacuations to protect against air raids, swelled from a low of 2.78 million in 1945 to 5.38 million in 1950 and then 6.96 million in 1955. By 1960 the population had grown to 8.31 million (Ishizuka and Ishida, 1988, pp. 26–7). The arrivals included returned evacuees, soldiers back from their duties, repatriated Japanese nationals from lost colonies, and thousands upon thousands of desperate job seekers from impoverished prefectures and devastated cities. There were also thousands of US personnel from the headquarters of the Occupation and their dependents, all of whom made disproportionate demands for housing, office space and other land (Wildes, 1954, pp. 260–8). Thus, when the first public housing units were constructed in 1948 on what was previously military land, there were some 300 applicants for every available opening (Seidensticker, 1990, p. 160). What is more, these and other housing units built after the war were small and poor quality: both were problems that would persist in Tokyo for many years. In the same vein, the intense crowding in the city meant there was little chance to improve its poor record for park space. Always too few in numbers, the park situation actually worsened in the immediate post-war years as some parks, most notably Asakusa Park, actually disappeared to make way for urbanization. In fact, because of the unusually great demand for land in Tokyo, as well as because of the scarcity of food, there was a period of three years between 1946 and 1949 when Shinobazu Pond in Ueno Park, long one of the city's most picturesque settings, was drained to make ground for crop production.

Before long, however, economic conditions in Japan would improve, and Tokyo would recover more fully from the defeat. This was seen first at the bayfront, where revitalization was stirred simultaneously by the rise of export-oriented manufacturing and the re-establishment of much of the heavy industry lost to the bombing, and in the CBD, where company offices, financial institutions, newspapers and other media, as well as other commercial concerns, came to life by the early 1950s. This was especially the case in Marunouchi, the no-nonsense office district close to Tokyo Station that replaced Nihombashi after the war as the nation's principal management center. Ironically, it was another war, the Korean War (1950–53), that provided a key spark for this by opening opportunities for Japan to expand manufacturing and international trade by servicing military procurement contracts. Other ingredients for recovery, all of them more fundamental than the accident of a nearby war, and of much longer impact, included the dedicated work and sacrifices by the citizenry, substantial technological innovation in manufacturing, and high rates of investment and reinvestment by government and business alike in export-related industries.

As the recovery of Tokyo advanced, the city returned to an earlier trend established in the wake of the 1923 disaster – a westward shift in its own development. This had begun as a movement to the higher ground of *yamanote* to escape the fires of the old city, and was regenerated in the post-war period as a dominant pattern of growth associated with suburbanization and with plans for the deconcentration of the metropolitan center. Instead of having a uni-nodal urban form focusing exclusively on the CBD, Tokyo began to be more polycentric, emphasizing new commercial districts at the urban periphery. These were particularly important on the fast-growing west side of the city, where crossroads at Shinjuku, Shibuya and Ikebukuro were transformed from local centers into major regional sub-centers that would compete with the CBD in offices, retailing, entertainment and other functions. The word that entered the vocabulary to describe them, *fukutoshin*, means 'secondary heart of the city' (Seidensticker, 1990, p. 212). Especially after the hurried reconstruction of Marunouchi and other central office districts, a new heart was seen as necessary because of thrombosis in the CBD brought on by too many commuters on too little ground. A multi-nodal arrangement of commercial districts in and around Tokyo continues to be a major goal of metropolitan planning; the three sub-centers named here (but most especially Shinjuku) are indeed vital new centers in the life of the city.

Of all the many structures built in Tokyo during the post-war years, one stood out specifically as a monument to the reconstruction itself. This was Tokyo Tower, the instantly famous landmark opened to considerable fanfare in late 1958 in the emerging west side to signal the city's successful rise from the ashes, as well as its new 'international' outlook. While the official purpose of the Tower had to do with transmission and reception of communication waves, its greater role was simply to stand tall and be seen. Its height, 333 meters, was a calculated 33 meters taller than the Eiffel Tower was at that time,[7] and its form, although not exactly the same, was quite enough like that of the structure in Paris to be called a copy. For the designer, Dr Naitō Tachu, an emeritus professor at Waseda University who was lovingly called Dr Steel Tower, it was a crowning achievement; it was his thirtieth tower, the biggest by far, and a chance to apply his avocation to an important patriotic goal. With the opening of the Tower, which took place on Christmas Eve exactly ten years and a day after the war crimes' hanging in Tokyo of General Tōjō and other defeated military leaders, Japan could present itself around the globe as a repentant nation that was fast rebuilding and desirous of being in touch with other advanced nations during this electronic age, rather than isolated from them. As in the Meiji period, when copying of Western building styles was the vogue, this particular message abroad about the onset of a new era for Japan was delivered in the language of architecture. The Japanese public, starved by hard times since the war of fun and frivolity, as well as of perhaps assurances about their future, took to the Tower immediately. Despite a rather steep admission charge of 120 yen per person, there were from the start long lines at the elevators and great throngs of elbow-wielding sightseers at observation windows and coin-operated telescopes.

Tokyo Tower was but one symbol of post-Occupation progress. The formal debut of the new Japan into the family of friendly nations, and the public introduction of its reborn capital city, is generally ascribed to a later event: Tokyo's hosting of the 1964 Summer Olympics. Obviously, this was something that required enormous preparations and for which many key parts of the city had to be specially dressed. The need for Japan to put on a good show was all the more important given that the 1964 Games were, in a way, a substitute for the 1940 Olympics – Games that had also been awarded to Tokyo but which, for obvious reasons, never took place. Thus, the international spectacle of 1964 was a special stimulus for Tokyo to get on with its job of reconstruction, as well as a marvelous opportunity for the city to attract national monies to fund municipal projects. The city's single-mindedness at preparing for the Games is seen in the fact that the governor of *Tokyo-to*, Azuma Ryūtarō, elected in 1959 at the start of the pre-Olympics rush and in office until after the Games ended, was also chairman of the Japan Olymics Committee.

[7] The Eiffel Tower was 300 meters high until 1959, when the addition of a radio antenna increased the height to 320 meters.

Perhaps to emphasize the demilitarization of Japan after the war and the resurgence of the country as a peaceful nation, most of the sporting events were concentrated on land appropriated from the army. Specifically, the main site of the Olympics was originally the Yoyogi drilling ground of the Japanese army, and after that a main base of operations for the US Occupation. It was that part of the west side of the city between Shibuya and Shinjuku (but more closely identified with the former), and close to the sacred shrine to the Emperor Meiji, that the Americans had renamed Washington Heights. At the request of the Japanese government, the land was repatriated in time to construct several of the key Olympics facilities on the site. The biggest part of Washington Heights became an athletes' village. These were temporary quarters, but were generally thought of as more than adequate and well-planned. After the games the land would become Yoyogi Park, a welcome addition to a city that sorely lacked public recreation space.

The most spectacular permanent structure from the Olympics, and still the principal landmark of the Olympic years, was a facility that stood across from the village and hosted swimming competitions, ice sports and basketball. This is the National Gymnasium complex, which is actually two adjacent buildings, designed by Tange Kenzō, a man of many landmarks who would have inordinate influence on the shape of Tokyo from reconstruction in the 1950s to current projects at the start of the 1990s. What caused the greatest international notice for this particular facility was its amazing roofline. In the case of the larger building, it was a giant swirl, and more of a spiral for the other building, and it stood tall amid the landscaping as, simultaneously, a great show of traditional Japanese design motifs (including a hint of Mt Fuji) and a triumph of modern architecture (Figure 3.13). The fact that the larger building leaked rain is beside the point!

In addition to the games facilities themselves, several neighborhoods in the area where the Olympics were concentrated were dressed up especially for the event, and were then transformed still more by the visitors, both foreign and Japanese, who traipsed through them. An important example is the area called Harajuku just city-side of the Washington Heights Olympics sites. The main street, called Omote Sandō because of its role as an approach to the Meiji Shrine, was widened and made into an especially attractive, tree-lined boulevard. Tokyoites began referring to it as their Champs Élysées, even though there is no resemblance except perhaps in the look of the trees (Waley, 1984, p. 430). The businesses that set up along it sold souvenirs of Japan to tourists from abroad, and Western products to Japanese who came to the area to see the Westerners. It was not long before this street, and the Harajuku area generally, replaced Ginza (and before that, Tsukiji) as Japan's principal reception center for foreigners and foreign fashions. Young Japanese have been especially attracted to this district, and continue to congregate there to show off their dress and Western affectations, and to browse stores for the latest foreign fashions

Figure 3.13 The National Gymnasium by Tange Kenzō and Inokashira-dōri, one of the new boulevards put in for the Olympics.

(see Chapter 5). The fact that the Japanese television and movie industries established major studios on portions of the Olympics land after the Games departed added to the glamour of the area.

Many other parts of the city, and not necessarily only those at the Olympics doorstep, were also spruced up in time for the Games. One important project on the east side of the city was developed to improve water quality on the Sumida River. The river was so polluted with sewage and other wastes that it stank, until a special water channel was dug to flush it clean just in time for the arrival of Olympics visitors. Elsewhere, there were new, international hotels, particularly in the area of the CBD close to the Imperial Palace, some new parks and public gardens, an impressive National Museum for Ueno Park, and in several locations some hasty bulldozing of slums and the construction in their place of ferro-concrete apartment complexes. In a clean-up of a different kind, vagrants and beggars were removed from parts of the city where they were most likely to be noticed, and sent off to institutions or other exile (Seidensticker, 1990, p. 235).

Transportation projects of various kinds received extra attention. They included several other so-called 'Olympics thoroughfares' (greatly widened and straightened streets) in addition to Omote Sandō. Wherever they were built, their cost was tremendously high because of the large number of streetside homes and businesses that had to relocated and compensated. Aoyama-*dōri*, a trendy commercial avenue between the vicinity of the

Imperial Palace and the popular business center at Shibuya, is a prime example. So, too, Tokyo's first expressways were built during the pre-Olympics rush. The highways that cut through the heart of the city were put on pillars above ground level, and followed the snaking courses of old canals and moats for at least parts of their routes. The subway system was also much enlarged. Highlights included the the Marunouchi Subway Line connecting the Shinjuku and Ikebukuro sub-centers with the the CBD at Ginza, a new station at Ginza, and various other new lines north, west and east of the center. All these improvements, but especially the subways connecting residential areas with the urban center, were intended to give lasting benefit to the city over and beyond service to Olympics crowds.

There were two other transportation projects that stood out from all the rest. One was the Haneda Monorail Line, which was seen as being 'state-of-the-art' in intra-urban transportation technology; the other was the Shinkansen, called the 'bullet train' in English because of the shape of the lead car, state-of-the-art in inter-urban rail travel. The former extended from the Hamamatsuchō Station on the Yamanote Loop Line near the CBD to what was then the city's principal airport, and still provides, as it did on its opening day less than a month before the start of the Games, a quick, quiet and fairly-priced ride into the city. The first Shinkansen line, named the Tōkaidō Line, also dates to just before the visitors arrived; it connected Tokyo Station with Japan's second city, Osaka, over 500 kilometers away, in about three hours. The trains high speed – in excess of 200 kilometers per hour – the remarkable frequency of its schedule – departures approximately every seven minutes – and its incredible record of punctuality have become well-known around the world, and have been often cited by international observers since the Olympics as evidence of Japanese efficiency and technological know-how (Figure 3.14).

Urban problems

Tokyo had achieved much by rebuilding itself in time for the Olympics. However, there was also another side to the reconstruction story, one that detracted from the city's overall record and emphasized the many urban problems that also characterized the city. These included environmental problems such as poor air and water quality, housing problems, traffic congestion, poor land-use planning, inadequacy of social services and urban infrastructure, and many other concerns. It is now common to describe the time around the Olympics as one during which inordinate attention was given to two goals, the rebuilding of the Japanese economy and fabricating a positive international image for Tokyo, but very little attention was paid to the needs of citizens in their neighborhoods. One of the most poignant illustrations of this was during the Olympic Games themselves, which happened to be held during an unusually dry summer, when water was severely rationed in the city. Seventeen of the 23 wards had water for only

Figure 3.14 The Shinkansen 'bullet train' and a new expressway in downtown Tokyo in 1964. (Asahi Company)

nine hours a day, and water trucks had to ply many neighborhoods to supply their basic requirements. At the same time, nearly two-thirds of residents were without sewers, and depended on *kumitoriya*, night-soil trucks, to haul away their wastes (Seidensticker, 1990, pp. 233–4).

There were many other prominent symbols of things that went wrong. What observers from abroad picked up on most, and what has since perhaps become everybody's leading example of the way in which Tokyo can be unpleasant, is the unbelievably high levels of crowding on the city's trains and subways. From the time of pre-Olympics publicity (and even continuing to some extent today), newsreels and magazine photographers from around the world showed the great crush of Tokyo commuters, jammed inside trains like canned sardines, and pushed in even tighter by white-gloved platform attendants. It was a scene so alien to outsiders that they could not help but gasp when they saw it, and perhaps even be a little amused by the seeming impossibility of so many human beings in such small spaces. The new train and subways lines, each opened with some fanfare and grand promises about commuter relief, couldn't keep up with the demand and themselves were overcrowded from day one. Thus for Tokyoites the rail system became, literally, a hell of a way to get to work: the faces of commuters told this story in no uncertain terms (Figure 3.15).

Figure 3.15 Crowding on to a train during the morning rush hour, Shinjuku Station, 1975. (Asahi Company)

So, too, there was amazement from abroad and dissatisfaction from within about the sorry state of housing. As late as 1968, fully 834,000 households in the city (28.1 per cent of the total) were living in substandard accommodation, and 1,017,000 households (34.2 per cent) considered themselves badly housed. The most common complaint was lack of space. For example, 45 per cent of all families, not just those who voiced complaints in the survey, were in tenements that typically had shared toilets and kitchens, and that left only 10 square meters of private living space (Hall, 1984, pp. 186–7). More specifically, 176,700 families (6 per cent) had less than two *tatami* mats (3.3 square meters) per person, and 702,400 families (24 per cent) had less than three mats (4.95 square meters) per capita (Tokyo Metropolitan Government, 1972a, p. 23). Moreover, because of the high cost of land and rapid population growth, the trend of housing construction offered little hope for improvement. Forty-seven per cent of housing units built in Tokyo between 1961 and 1965 had less than 29 square meters. This compared to 42.0 per cent of units built between 1956 and 1960, 32.7 per cent of units built between 1945 and 1955, and 21.7 per cent built in pre-war days (Tokyo Metropolitan Govern-

Figure 3.16 The fight between radical students and police to control Yasuda Hall, Tokyo University, January 1969. (Asahi Company.)

ment, 1972a, p. 19). It is because of such extreme levels of overcrowding that, much to the dismay of the proud Japanese, the term 'rabbit hutches' was applied by Western observers to Tokyo's housing – and then stuck. The facts that these houses were often made of cheap materials and were fire hazards added to the problems.

It is largely because of the existence of serious problems that Tokyo entered another phase of its development shortly after the Olympics ended. The patience of the populace about their living conditions was wearing thin, and citizens were increasingly anxious to finish the time of post-war sacrifices and enjoy the fruits of their labors. Among other things, they demanded what was then called, tongue in cheek, *sansu no jingi*, the three divine symbols of the imperial throne: television, washing machines and refrigerators (Tokyo Metropolitan Government, 1972a, pp. 14–15). Their anger boiled over during the summer after the Olympics when a great plague of flies descended on the east side of the city from a poorly managed garbage dump, and gave 'last straw' proof that citizens and their neighborhoods were being ignored in plans for the city (see Chapter 6). There was also growing resentment about the continuing U.S. military presence in the city, even after the official end of the Occupation, and popular demands that bases and other American facilities (a total of 21.3 million square meters in *Tokyo-to* in 1969) be released to ease the shortage of space. The unrest of the times is also seen in the student riots at several university campuses in Tokyo and other cities. The violent struggles between students and police to control Yasuda Hall of Tokyo University in 1968 to early 1969 are especially noteworthy. Long a bastion of power and privilege, this particular university had become a symbol of inattentive authority in Japan, and was beseiged by large numbers of increasingly radical students (Figure 3.16).

Azuma Ryūtarō, the Olympics Governor, read the signs clearly and did not bother to stand for re-election after the Games. The 1967 balloting elected a 'people-first' coalition of socialists and communists headed by Minobe Ryōkichi, the university professor turned governor, and sent Tokyo off on a new course. We shall pick this story up later, in Chapter 6, when discussing the history of city planning. For now, let us leave it that Tokyo, rebuilt after the war but badly flawed as an environment for living, embarks in 1967 on a continuing program of building and still more building, but with considerably more attention to the quality of the outcome. The socialists stayed in office to work on this until the election of 1979, when the present Governor, Suzuki Shunichi, a Liberal Democratic Party member with a different approach to government, was first elected. However, even though the change of régimes was itself the cause of many important shifts in the details of Tokyo development, attention to building a better city for living was never diminished.

4
Contemporary Tokyo

Contemporary Tokyo: Introduction

In all its history Tokyo has never stayed still for long, but has changed with every need and opportunity. Ieyasu, the first Edo shogun, took one look at the city that Ōta Dōkan had built and immediately began to rearrange it from top to bottom. He put in a new castle, realigned the flow of rivers, cut down Kanda Mountain and proceeded to fill in the marshes and parts of the bay. His successors continued the work, reclaimed still more land, expanded the city in new directions and rebuilt its established districts time and again after every destructive fire or flood. Under the Meiji Emperor, a whole new face (and a new name too) was given to the city, as the nation's isolation ended and foreign fashions and building styles became the rage in the capital. The Taishō Emperor saw it all burn in 1923 in the Great Kantō Earthquake. Then, just as soon as the city had been substantially rebuilt, there was the disaster of war and the fire-bombing of 1945. Tokyo rose from those ashes, too, and in 1964 showed itself off to the world as a place of remarkable resilience and energy, and as a city that wanted to be counted among the élite of global urban centers. It did not win many points for beauty as the world looked on during those Olympics, but it proved to everyone that it was workaholic and that it would build whatever was needed for the city to advance its goals.

Now, almost exactly 400 years after Ieyasu's arrival in the city, Tokyo has reached the top of the world economically and is changing once again. This time the rebuilding is by choice rather than after some calamity, but it is as complete and far-reaching as any undertaking that has ever been done in the city before. It involves a huge range of projects, both private and public, that in various ways are intended to improve the quality of living in Tokyo and/or facilitate the needs of its important businesses, lavishing upon the city a completely new look. While most of the publicity about the construction boom focuses on the Central Business District, which is being extensively redeveloped to enchance Tokyo's status as a world leader in finance and trade, the transformations also extend in one form or another into every residential neighborhood, commercial center and industrial zone in the rest of the city and all its suburbs. To emphasize the immense scale of what is going on, and to highlight the city's exceptionally transitory nature, the rebuilding can be described as a thorough reconstruction of Tokyo – the third reconstruction (after 1923 and 1945) in less than a century (Haberman, 1987).

To put this into a wider urban context, there are certain parallels between the scope of changes taking place in Tokyo today, and the top-to-bottom rebuildings that took place in other global urban centers when they reached their economic primes. The New York City built up by Robert Moses over much of the first half of the present century, and the reconstructed Paris of Baron Haussmann in the latter half of the 19th century are the two best modern examples. In both cases, as well as in Victorian London and several notable great cities from centuries in the more distant past, the rebuilding programs emphasized the construction of monumental urban centers, facilitated urban expansion into outlying areas, radically improved transportation and infrastructure for water, sanitation and utilities, and provided for greatly enhanced open spaces in the city and other urban beautification. In this chapter, we shall see that all this and more is true for contemporary Tokyo. However, there are distinctive twists deriving from Japan's unique culture, from Tokyo's exorbitantly high land costs and from other important differences. We shall begin by discussing some of the most important social and economic trends in Tokyo that underlie urban reconstruction, trends I have grouped under four headings: (1) population redistribution; (2) aging of the population; (3) economic shifts; and (4) 'internationalization.'

Socio-economic patterns

Some of the best lessons about contemporary Tokyo can be learned from its trains and subways. This is especially so in the mornings, between 7:00 and 10:00 or so, when the commuter crush is at its peak, and one experiences through every sense the huge, crowded, busy and routinized city Tokyo has become. It's the same thing every morning, the elemental Tokyo story: thousands and thousands and thousands of commuters, workers and students alike, crowd on to the *nobori densha* (in-bound trains) for the long ride to the center – a ride like no other city can offer.

The conditions are what legends are made of. A train pulls up to the platform at the station near where you live, already so full that faces are pressed against the inside glass of the sliding doors, and the ends of coats and book bags that didn't quite make it in protrude through the openings. Several hundred or more of your neighbors are waiting to board. They crowd the platform, itself nearly a quarter of a mile long to correspond to the length of a nine or ten car train, and have arranged themselves in separate groups of 20 or more every few feet where a door will open. The train stops, the doors slide apart, and virtually no one gets off! Almost everyone is going to the same place you are, to the center of Tokyo. In the few seconds during which the train stops, you and a score or more other new riders at your door press inside, backs first so as to not confront anyone directly, and force the doorway standers further in. To do this, you gain leverage for arms from the walls inside the train just above the door and for legs from the edge of the platform. White-gloved platform attendants push in the last passengers just as the doors come together. Two or three minutes later the scene is repeated at the next station, and it is you who are pressed by a score or more new riders with leverage from the doorway and the force of a new set of platform attendants. At the same time, another crowd of riders has already gathered at the station you just left, and is hearing the loud-speaker announcement of the arrival of the next *nobori densha*, barely three minutes after your train departed. By the time one of these trains reaches an interchange station near the center such as Shinjuku or Shibuya, it is filled to nearly three times its capacity, and has a total of 4,000–5,000 passengers.

For the majority of commuters the ride is an hour or more, and often involves transferring to a second or even third train. The most jammed stretches of the ride, such as that described above based on my daily experiences with the famous Chūō Line along which I now live,[1] are almost intolerable: it's hot, you can hardly move a muscle, even if you are being jabbed by an umbrella or a briefcase, and the pressure on your body is sometimes so great it is hard to breathe. It is even worse if the person who is pressed against you happens to smell. You close your eyes, concentrate on private thoughts or on the Walkman, and suffer. Once I saw a man who had been lifted out of one of his shoes by the press of the crowd, and who had the most awful time trying to retrieve it during the frantic moment that the door was open at the next station. On another occasion, when the train lurched unexpectedly as it switched tracks, I saw a woman bump face first against the man in front of her, a total stranger, and leave a lipstick mark on his white shirt that reproduced remarkably faithfully the shape of her lips.

All of this is preface to what I consider to be the most important cluster of facts about the layout of Tokyo and how it functions. Despite its complexity, the city is essentially two zones: (1) the center where people work and also go shopping or for various types of entertainment; and (2) the periphery, where increasing proportions of Tokyoites have their homes and community life. The center is huge, perhaps the most overgrown business district in the world, and is getting bigger. It expands into surrounding neighborhoods, and changes Tokyo ever more into the classic 'hole' in the 'urban donut' – a center devoid of residential population. We

---

[1] I have moved since writing Chapter 1.

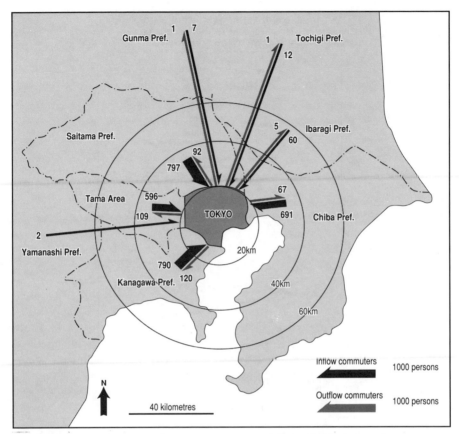

Figure 4.1 Distribution of commuters to and from Tokyo's ward area, 1985

note, for example, that the ratio between so-called 'day-time' and 'night-time' population in Chiyoda Ward is 1,999:1 (1,009,291 persons versus 50,493), and that in Chūō Ward it is 868:1 (693,960: 79,936) (*Tokyo Statistical Yearbook, 1987*, pp. 84–5). Concomitantly, the periphery expands further and further into the distance. What binds the two together is the long train rides (and to a much lesser extent commuting by car and other means). I think that Figure 4.1, a map of commuting flows in the Tokyo metropolis, is the essential cartographic representation of contemporary Tokyo. Figure 4.2, a chart using the exact words of Tokyo planners to describe levels of crowding on morning trains, is an extremely revealing indicator of what many Tokyoites must endure on a daily basis. Clearly, the situation I illustrated in Figure 3.15, the photograph of painful over-crowding on a commuter train loading up at Shinjuku Station in 1974, has not improved much and is still routine in Tokyo. At the risk of overkill, I emphasize this with Figure 4.3, my own recent photograph of Shinjuku Station.

101

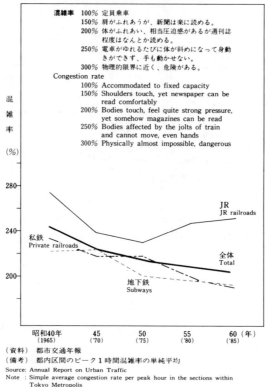

ラッシュ時の混雑率の推移（都内主要区間）
Changes of Percentage of Rush-hour Congestion
(Major Sections within Tokyo Metropolis)

Figure 4.2 Changes in rush hour congestion, 1970–1985. (Tokyo Metropolitan Government, 1988, p. 74)

Population redistribution

The population explosion that had characterized the post-World War II period is over, and the population growth rate in *Tokyo-to* as a whole has stabilized. What is now changing is the distribution of population. As the preface above suggests, the dominant trend is an emptying of the center of the metropolis of permanent residents and extremely rapid rates of growth at the edges. Some of the detailed figures are shown in Table 4.1.

Let us look first at overall figures for *Tokyo-to*. We see that the rate of population increase has declined steadily with every decade since 1950; it is now at a very low level. Between 1950 and 1960 the population in *Tokyo-to* grew by 47.6 per cent from 6,278,000 to 9,684,000, but the rate of growth slowed to 17.8 per cent in the 1960s, 1.8 per cent in the 1970s, and only about +0.5 per cent during the 1980s (1980 to 1988). Thus, in contrast to the 1950s, when the population exploded by some 3.4 million

Figure 4.3 Morning rush hour at Shinjuku Station, 1990

inhabitants, the net number of new residents in *Tokyo-to* as a whole during the first eight years of the 1980s was only about one-tenth of that. In fact, in recent years there have been slight decreases in population registered for *Tokyo-to*, such as between the census counts of 1975 and 1980 when the population dropped from 11,764,000 to 11,618,000.

The greatest declines are in the central wards. The three innermost wards of the metropolis, Chiyoda, Chūō and Minato Wards, an area that roughly corresponds to the CBD, have been losing residents since early this century and now have a total that is much less than one-half of what it was in 1920 during a peak census count of 818,000. So, too, the old *shitamachi* wards of the city (by this definition, Arakawa, Bunkyō, Kōtō, Sumida and Taitō Wards) have dropped significantly. Their peak census year was 1940, when the total was 2,011,000, but there have been steady declines since then (except for the immediate post-war rush to the city) to a level of 1,182,000 in the 1985 census.

Another inner ring of wards, the 'sub-central wards' just beyond the CBD and the *shitamachi* area, has also lost numbers, in this case from a peak in 1965 of 3,824,000 to 3,266,000 in the latest census. Thus, the overall total for the 23 wards comprising the historic boundary of Tokyo City has also dropped. The peak was in 1965, when 8,894,000 people lived there, but now the total has fallen by more than half a million to less than 8,355,000 (1985).

The contrast is with all the rest of the Tokyo metropolitan area: i.e. the

Tama region of *Tokyo-to* and all the neighboring prefectures. The Tama area has grown more than ten-fold since 1920 (from 340,000 to 3,474,000 in 1985) and now has about 30 per cent of the total population of the Tokyo government unit. Kanagawa, Chiba and Saitama Prefectures have also grown in spectacular fashion. We see, from Table 4.1 that in each of these three cases (as well as the Tama area) the population more than doubled in the 25 years between 1960 and the 1985 census. The result is a rapid overall growth for the Greater Tokyo Metropolitan Area as a whole (now more than 30 million), and ever-larger fractions of this total to be outside the *Tokyo-to* unit. In the early part of the century what is now *Tokyo-to* comprised about one-half of the population of the four-prefecture metropolitan area (eg. 48.1 per cent of the total in 1920; 57.7 per cent in 1940), but this dropped to 39.1 per cent in the 1985 census and an estimated 38.5 per cent in 1988. What all this means, in the context of the 'third rebuilding of Tokyo', is our principal topic in this chapter: its tremendous expansion of housing, commercial centers, and employment places at the edges of the metropolis, and the redevelopment of land uses in the center.

Aging of the population

Because of declining birth rates, increased longevity, and to a lesser extent the reduced numbers of young migrants to the city, the population of *Tokyo-to* is older on the average than ever before. This is related to the aging of Japan overall: a trend that is also evident in many other advanced societies. According to official statistics, *Tokyo-to* now has more than double the percentage of its total population aged 65 years or older than it did just a quarter of a century ago (9.4 per cent in 1987 versus 4.0 per cent in 1962). The average age of the population increased at the same time: from 28.6 years to 34.2 years for males and from 30.0 years to 36.5 years for females. The flip side of this is that the younger age groups have declined in proportion: between 1962 and 1987 persons aged 0–14 decreased in *Tokyo-to* from 23.5 per cent of the total population to 17.3 per cent. I have summarized these and related statistics in Table 4.2. These trends are expected to continue, such that by the year 2025 as many as one in four of all residents in Tokyo will be aged 65 or older. The population pyramid below (Figure 4.4) illustrates the rapid change in age composition expected in *Tokyo-to* between 1985 and the year 2000.

There are distinct geographical patterns to the aging of the population within *Tokyo-to*. This, too, is a familiar pattern in urban areas in advanced societies: the center, particularly the older neighborhoods with declining population totals, tends to have higher proportions of elderly residents; the periphery, especially those areas that have grown recently as bedroom suburbs of the central city, tend to have greater proportions of young families with children (Knox, 1982, pp. 74–100). Thus, the 23-ward area as a whole has 9.5 per cent of its population aged 65 or older (as opposed

Table 4.1 Population trends in the Tokyo metropolitan region, 1920–1988 (thousands)

	1920	1940	1960	1980	1985	1988[a]	% change 1960–1988
23-Ward Area	3,359	6,777	8,311	8,350	8,355	8,343[b]	0.4
Central Wards[c]	818	767	545	339	325	303[b]	−44.4
Shitamachi[d]	1,418	2,011	1,546	1,181	1,182	1,174[b]	−24.1
Subcentral[e]	911	2,831	3,535	3,314	3,266	3,320[b]	−8.7
Outer Wards[f]	212	1,168	2,585	3,516	3,582	3,547[b]	37.2
Rest of *Tokyo-to*	340	570	1,373	3,268	3,474	3,581[b]	160.8
TOKYO-TO TOTAL	3,699	7,347	9,684	11,618	11,829	11,924	23.1
Chiba Prefecture	1,336	1,588	2,306	4,735	5,148	5,327	131.0
Kanagawa Prefecture	1,323	2,183	3,443	6,924	7,432	7,677	123.0
Saitama Prefecture	1,320	1,608	2,431	5,420	5,864	6,078	150.0
CAPITAL REGION TOTAL	7,678	12,726	17,864	28,697	30,273	31,006	73.6
23 Wards as % of Capital Region	43.7	53.2	46.5	29.1	27.6	26.9	–
Tokyo-to as % of Capital Region	48.1	57.7	54.2	40.5	39.1	38.5	–

a 1988 figures are official estimates. The years 1920–1985 are census years.
b These figures are for December, 1987.
c Chiyoda, Chūō and Minato wards.
d Arakawa, Bunkyō, Kōtō, Sumida and Taitō wards.
e Katsushika, Kita, Meguro, Nakano, Ōta, Shibuya, Shinagawa, Shinjuku and Toshima wards.
f Adachi, Edogawa, Itabashi, Nerima, Setagaya and Suginami wards.
Source: Fujū, 1987, p 13; various census sources.

Table 4.2 Population composition by age group, *Tokyo-to*, 1962–1987. (per cent of total population)

	1962	1967	1972	1977	1982	1987
0–14 years old	23.5	20.6	21.8	22.3	20.5	17.3
15–64 years old	72.5	74.7	72.7	71.0	71.4	73.4
65 years and older	4.0	4.7	5.5	6.8	8.2	9.4

Source: Tokyo Metropolitan Government, 1987a, p. 22.

to the 8.9 per cent for *Tokyo-to* mentioned above), and the CBD wards and historic *shitamachi* wards are older still, generally having between 12.0 and 15.0 per cent of their populations aged 65 or more. In the Tama area, by contrast, the percentages of elderly residents are generally in the 7.0 to 10.0 per cent range. Table 4.3 compares a selection of wards in Tokyo and cities and towns in the Tama district according to age composition.

Table 4.3 Age structure comparison, selected wards in Tokyo and cities (*shi*) in the Tama Area, 1988

	0–14 years	15–64 years	65 years+	Total
CBD and shitamachi wards				
Chūō Ward	15.5	70.7	13.8	100.0
Taitō Ward	13.5	71.7	14.8	100.0
Sumida Ward	15.5	72.4	12.0	100.0
Arakawa Ward	14.6	72.5	12.9	100.0
Western wards (*yamanote* and west)				
Meguro Ward	14.0	74.5	11.6	100.0
Shibuya Ward	12.8	76.0	11.2	100.0
Setagaya Ward	14.6	75.1	10.2	100.0
Suginami Ward	13.9	75.1	11.1	100.0
Towns in Tama District				
Hachiōji	19.8	72.1	8.1	100.0
Tachikawa	18.9	72.3	8.6	100.0
Musashino	16.0	73.5	10.5	100.0
Mitaka	16.0	74.5	9.4	100.0
Fuchū	18.1	74.0	8.1	100.0
Chōfu	17.1	75.1	7.8	100.0
Komae	16.0	76.0	8.0	100.0
Machida	19.9	73.0	7.1	100.0

Source: Tokyo Statistical Yearbook, 1978, pp. 40–1.

Economic shifts

One of the most important aspects for understanding the current rebuilding of Tokyo is to think of it as investment in Japan's capital city by government and big business, in a remarkably smooth-working partnership, which makes sure the economic successes of the country will continue in the future. There are no punches pulled about this at all. There are especially large ambitions for Tokyo in the area of international trade and finance; the rebuilding of the city is part and parcel of a plan to assure that Tokyo achieves as high a place as possible among world leaders. One goal is to attract multinational companies to open in Tokyo and use the city as their main base for East Asia or Pacific Rim operations. This is to compete against Hong Kong, Singapore and other fast-rising capitals in the region, and to take over some of the trade Hong Kong would lose if the 1997 changeover in government fails to work out for business. Even more, it is hoped that Tokyo can surpass New York and London in international finance and stock dealings, and that the city will be the next century's undisputed number-one global financial center. Tange Kenzō, one of the leading architects for the city's rebuilding, was quoted not long ago in *The New York Times* as saying: 'Paris is a symbol of the 19th century . . . Manhattan may be the symbol of the 20th century. If we can succeed in our plans, Tokyo could become the model for the 21st century' (Haberman, 1987, p. 14).

A major objective of the rebuilding is to provide more space for offices for the growing number of companies, both Japanese and foreign, that concentrate in Tokyo. Because it is the overwhelming city of choice and business necessity for any firm that does business in Japan, vacancy rates for offices in Tokyo are extremely low (typically 0.2–0.3 per cent in recent years). So, too, rental prices have been exorbitantly high (Table 4.4). It is not uncommon, to pay as much as 55,000–65,000 yen per tsubo (3.3 square meters) each month for office space in Ōtemachi, Marunouchi and other desirable sections of the center (*Nihon Keizai Shimbun*, 21 February 1988). Moreover, most offices are notoriously crowded and working conditions in them, as measured by space per employee, standards of office decor, personal privacy and other amenity indicators are almost always substantially inferior to those in rival cities abroad. Consequently, some of the most important and visible aspects of the Tokyo that is now emerging include the redevelopment of existing commercial districts, most notably the CBD, to make room for new office towers that are taller and more comfortably equipped than those they replace, as well as the redevelopment of non-commercial districts to permit expansion of space for offices and related land uses (Figure 4.5).

Closely related to this is the structural shift taking place in Tokyo's economy: that of declining emphasis on manufacturing and increased attention on the services sector. This is part of a more general shift of the national economy to post-industrial economic foundations, as well as a

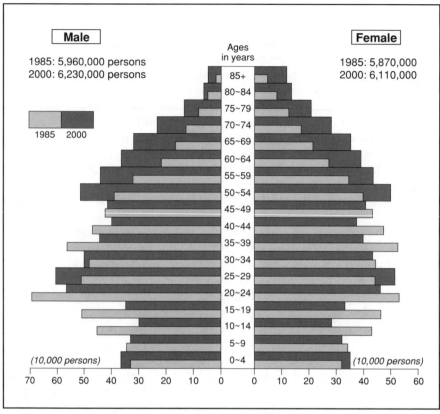

Figure 4.4 Population by age and sex, *Tokyo-to*, 1985 and 2000

shift within Tokyo specifically away from large factories. The latter has been a city objective since the late 1950s when regulations were put into effect restricting expansion of most industrial sites within the 23 wards and encouraging the relocation of factories to outlying 'satellite' cities in the Tama area and neighboring prefectures. This was to reduce urban pollution levels, to cut down on traffic and to foster economic growth in outlying sections of the metropolis. In many cases, it also paved the way for the redevelopment of industrial sites for new offices, hotels, commercial centres and in some cases, for large high-rise housing estates. Many of the most impressive of these changes have taken place in and near the CBD, at the inner-most reaches of Tokyo Bay, the lower stretches of the Sumida River and in the newly-fashionable neighborhoods of Tokyo's west side.

We can see the outlines of this economic shift by looking first at the three gross categories: primary industries, secondary industries and tertiary industries. The first two of these have declined markedly in recent decades, while the tertiary category has grown. In 1950 primary industries (eg. farming, fishing, forestry) accounted for 6.4 per cent of all employment in *Tokyo-to*; secondary industries (mostly manufacturing and related employment) were 37.1 per cent, and tertiary industries (eg. offices, commercial

Table 4.4 Comparative office rents, Tokyo and other cities, November 1989. (annual occupancy costs per square foot; US dollars)

Tokyo	159
London City	139
London (West End)	116
Hong Kong	100
Paris	69
Sydney	56
Zurich	51
New York	51
Toronto	47
Madrid	47
Washington	47
Moscow	47
Singapore	45

Source: Colliers International/taken from Davies et al., 1990, p. 14.

establishments, education and other services) accounted for 56.2 per cent. By 1970, the primary category had dropped to only 0.9 per cent of the total, the secondary category increased somewhat to 38.2 per cent because of the post-war push for economic growth, while the third category grew to 60.7 per cent. The most recent census (1985) shows even greater growth in tertiary industry, now 69.8 per cent of the total, and declines in the other two, particularly in the secondary category which dropped to 29.3 per cent after programs to relocate industry and rebuild key factory sites had begun. A projection for 1995 shows further declines in primary and secondary industries (0.5 per cent and 27.2 per cent of the total, respectively), and more gain in tertiary employment (72.3 per cent of the total) (Tokyo Metropolitan Government, 1987a, p. 24 and 1990a, p. 3).

More detailed patterns are shown in Table 4.5. This breaks the economy into 11 major industrial groups, using both the number of employees in each group and the number of establishments as measures of economic activity. The total economy of *Tokyo-to* is clearly growing. The total number of employees increased from 6.7 million in 1972 to almost 8.0 million in 1986, while the number of business establishments grew from 643,973 to 797,483. The fastest-growing sectors include services (eg. education, medicine and various business services), finance and insurance, and the wholesale and retail trade. The latter includes the great many shops of all kinds found in Tokyo, as well as the city's thousands of eating and drinking places, and accounts for 45.3 per cent of all business establishments. On the other hand, declines are registered for the primary industries and manufacturing. In manufacturing this is especially evident in terms of the numbers of employees. As Table 4.6 indicates, the number of factory jobs in *Tokyo-to* declined by almost 300,000 between 1972 and 1986, and the percentage of the total workforce employed in this category has slipped from 27.5 per cent to 20.7 per cent. However, manufacturing is still

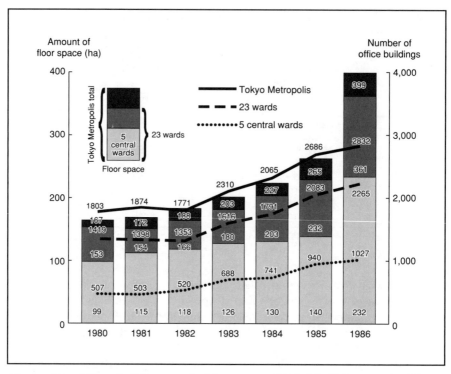

Figure 4.5 Office buildings and office space, 1980–86, *Tokyo-to*, the 23 wards, and five central wards. (*Tokyo-to*, 1989, p. 88)

extremely important in the Tokyo economy, and in terms of gross municipal product (a measure that is not illustrated in the table), it ranks number one in the city at 12,825.2 billion yen (1986 figure; 21.9 per cent of the total) (Tokyo Metropolitan Government, 1990b, p. 46). The major specialities of the manufacturing sector in Tokyo are illustrated in Figure 4.6.

Perhaps the most striking feature of Tokyo's manufacturing sector is that it is comprised very heavily of tiny factories. According to statistics for 1985, 46.4 per cent of all manufacturing plants in the city employed only one to three people, and an additional 35.8 per cent employed between four and nine workers. What is more, the number of small manufacturing companies is increasing rather than decreasing. This indicates that the erosion in manufacturing shown in gross statistics involves mainly large and medium-sized firms. Other statistics show that a great many of these companies have relocated to the seven prefectures of the Kantō region outside *Tokyo-to*. Of the industries in Tokyo, the largest category is printing and publishing. It is comprised mainly of small firms and accounts for

Table 4.5 Economic structure of *Tokyo-to*, 1972–1986

sector	Number of Employees						Number of Establishments					
	1972 number	%	1978 number	%	1986 number	%	1972 number	%	1978 number	%	1986 number	%
Agriculture, forestry and fisheries	10,501	0.2	11,889	0.2	10,609	0.1	767	0.1	938	0.1	1,029	0.1
Mining	7,862	0.1	6,473	0.1	6,509	0.1	203	0.0	170	0.0	185	0.0
Construction	487,358	7.3	549,493	7.7	561,516	7.1	37,493	5.8	45,636	6.1	49,111	6.2
Manufacturing	1,849,743	27.5	1,631,372	22.8	1,644,835	20.7	119,852	18.6	125,080	16.8	127,338	16.0
Utilities	34,494	0.5	37,735	0.5	39,522	0.5	692	0.1	603	0.1	612	0.1
Transport and Communication	482,892	7.2	521,122	7.3	538,521	6.8	14,341	2.2	18,450	2.5	27,508	3.4
Wholesale and Retail Trade*	2,028,915	30.2	2,241,628	31.3	2,608,705	32.8	301,119	46.8	342,650	46.1	361,416	45.3
Finance and Insurance	319,342	4.8	380,157	5.3	407,307	5.1	7,767	1.2	9,666	1.3	12,141	1.5
Real Estate	111,206	1.7	139,661	1.9	174,314	2.2	32,686	5.1	43,958	5.9	44,364	5.6
Services	1,177,305	17.5	1,422,898	19.9	1,901,783	23.9	127,065	19.7	154,026	20.7	181,193	22.7
Government (not elsewhere classified)	208,026	3.1	225,332	3.1	220,592	2.8	1,988	0.3	2,072	0.3	2,121	0.2
TOTAL	6,717,644	100.0	7,167,810	100.0	7,956,726	100.0	643,973	100.0	743,249	100.0	797,483	100.0

* includes eating and drinking places.

Source: *Tokyo Statistical Yearbook*, 1987, pp. 98–101.

111

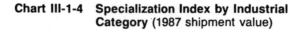

Chart III-1-4 Specialization Index by Industrial Category (1987 shipment value)

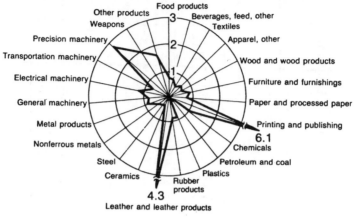

Source: Tokyo Metropolitan Government, Bureau of General Affairs, *Tokyo Manufacturing Industry*.

Figure 4.6 Industrial specialization in Tokyo, 1987. (Tokyo Metropolitan Government, 1990b, p. 47)

20.3 per cent of all factories in *Tokyo-to*, 21.6 per cent of all workers in manufacturing and 23.7 per cent of the value of finished products. Other important categories are leather and leather products, precision machinery (eg. cameras and lenses) and electrical machinery (Tokyo Metropolitan Government, 1990b, pp. 46–9).

There is also a strong traditional crafts industry in Tokyo. It is concentrated largely in the eastern part of the city, particularly in the *shitamachi* wards, as well as in some of the offshore islands of *Tokyo-to* (eg. Ōshima and Hachijōjima), and has suffered long-term declines in both numbers of employees and of firms. However, recently it has been targeted by economic planners as an industry that should be preserved in the city and given 'a second chance in the limelight' (Tokyo Metropolitan Government, 1990b, p. 48.) Table 4.6 lists the largest of Tokyo's traditional crafts industries.

Internationalization

We can also understand the current rebuilding of Tokyo as one facet of what is being called 'internationalization' or *kokusaika*. This is a common buzzword in Japan these days, and seems to refer simultaneously to a number of different things: (1) the increasing influence Japan has achieved among the nations of the world; (2) the increased facility many Japanese have today with foreign ways and languages; and (3) the growing presence

Table 4.6 Traditional crafts industries in Tokyo, 1988 (50 companies or more)

Craft (Ymillion)	Companies	Employees	Production value
		Production Status	
Murayama Ōshima pongee	73	849	1,091
Yellow hachijō silk	95	104	115
Tokyo-style silver utensils	200	252	3,000
Tokyo-style hand-printed silk	280	760	2,600
Edo lacquerware	90	615	8,600
Edo tortoiseshell works	144	420	4,500
Tokyo-style Buddhist altars	74	208	980
Tokyo-style picture frames	60	186	1,080
Edo ivory carvings	65	377	8,250
Edo cabinet work	50	110	630
Edo cut glass	104	514	1,274
Edo embroidery	74	273	730
Edo wood carving	76	115	550
Edo metal carving	57	63	148

Source: Tokyo Metropolitan Government, 1990b, p. 49.

on Japanese soil of foreigners and foreign companies. In our context, the word refers especially to still another aspect of internationalization: (4) the rebuilding of Tokyo to make it more comfortable and appealing to foreigners, particularly those with high-level business or diplomatic credentials. A key part of this is the construction of office buildings and other infrastructure to enhance Tokyo's standing as a leading international business center. We see these goals explicitly expressed in the current official development plan for the city – *The 2nd Long-Term Plan for the Tokyo Metropolis*. Under a heading called 'Correct Approach to Internationalization' the document dictates, among other things, that 'Tokyo should be made a comfortable and friendly city for both foreign visitors and foreign residents', and that 'it is important to make Tokyo a safe, beautiful, comfortable and dignified city by increasing and improving parks, roads and other facilities, and shaping a tasteful cityscape'. All this, we are informed, is 'required in order to make Tokyo a truly international city that can lead the world in keeping up with the progress of internationalization' (Tokyo Metropolitan Government, 1987b, pp. 21–2).

There is nothing particularly new in all this. The Japanese have long been extremely sensitive to what foreigners say about their country, and have felt particularly aggrieved by any unfavorable comparisons of how they live and work. This has been true since that day in 1853 when Commodore Perry's 'black ships' anchored near Tokyo in Sagami Bay and began meddling in internal affairs; it continues to be true today. Time and again I am reminded by experience that even the smallest unfavorable comments about Japan or Tokyo from a foreigner can be irksome to the Japanese, even when those comments are but a small part of a larger complimentary evaluation. During Meiji, the leaders of Japan responded to the foreign presence with an aggressive internationalization push that gave certain sections of Tokyo an exaggerated Western veneer. I think that today, too, in response to the complaints that foreigners most often make about Tokyo – high prices for everything from rent to a cup of coffee, chronic traffic jams, non-stop crowds and typically small, somewhat primitive housing units – there are calculated efforts to put on a different face. Developers have responded most energetically. Seeing an opportunity for profit, they have built great numbers of Western-style houses and condominiums close to modern office districts and international embassies, several new Western hotels and various other facilities (especially shopping) designed to cater to the foreigner market as well as to the Japanese with 'international' tastes.

The push to be international can be applied to virtually every aspect of the urban scene, including the most mundane. If I may be a bit irreverent, I can quote one example from a fringe area of city planning I had never considered before, that of toilet planning. Alerted by an intriguing notice in a newspaper, I once attended a day-long conference in Tokyo (and a field trip the next day) called the International Toilet Forum. Sponsored by the Japan Toilet Association, a group that represents manufacturers of toilets and related equipment, it had as its purpose an evaluation of public toilet facilities in Tokyo and other Japanese urban areas from the standpoint of the comfort of foreigners. There were sessions entitled 'Looking at Our International Cities – Tokyo, Yokohama, Nara, Kyoto, Kobe – from Toilets' and 'Future Toilet Policies from an International Viewpoint', as well as a featured address by an architectural critic, Kawazoe Noboru, called 'Urban Planning – From the Toilet'. There was an amazing late afternoon session: 12 foreigners representing 12 different countries (including every one of the world's inhabited continents) giving testimonials called 'My Experiences with Toilets' in which they compared public facilities in Japan with those back home (Figure 4.7). Everyone was perfectly serious, and I had the feeling that I was the only person among the 300–400 attendees who wanted to laugh. All the Japanese listeners, it seemed, were thoroughly professional and totally dedicated to the issue, behaving as if they were on some sort of sacred mission to contribute to the internationalization of their country's capital.

The business center

Nearly 2.3 million commuters arrive each working day in the three central wards of Tokyo (Chūō, Chiyoda and Minato) that correspond to the Central Business District and its fringes (Table 4.7). This is probably the largest daily flow of people in the world, and speaks of the immense

Figure 4.7 Panellists at the 1988 International Toilet Forum discussing 'My Experiences with Toilets' from an international perspective

importance of the Tokyo CBD as a place of employment, shopping and many other activities, as well as of its considerable geographical extent and high levels of crowding. There are no agreed-upon boundaries to the CBD because the limits would vary according to the definitions one would use. However, the core of the area is well-known and easy to identify: it is the same district at the foot of the Imperial Palace where over 350 years ago, when Edo Castle stood there, the city's first merchants set up a fish market near the boat landing at Nihombashi. For our purposes, we can say that the CBD extends in all directions from this core to cover the area between the Imperial Palace grounds to the west, the mixed residential, commercial and light-industrial quarters of Kanda to the north, the banks of the Sumida River and its mouth at Tokyo Bay to the east and southeast, a zone of industry, warehouses and transportation facilities near Tokyo Bay a little further to the southeast, and the higher grounds and loftier status neighborhoods of *yamanote* to the west, not far from Tokyo Tower. This is an area of some five or six square kilometers, and consists of several distinctive sub-districts, each with its own personality, physical appearance and special role in the overall CBD economy. We shall first discuss those areas in the core of the CDB and then the areas of CBD expansion (Figure 4.8).

Table 4.7 Daytime/night-time population and daily population inflow/outflow, *Tokyo-to* and selected parts, 1 October 1985

	Day population	Night population	Day population index*	Daily incoming population	Daily outgoing population
Chiyoda Ward	1,009,291	50,493	1,999	970,333	11,535
Chūō Ward	693,960	79,936	868	631,479	17,455
Minato Ward	819,495	192,615	425	682,161	55,281
TOTAL, THREE CENTRAL WARDS	2,522,752	323,044	781	2,283,973	84,271
20 Remaining Wards	8,435,426	8,023,665	105	742,783	331,016
TOTAL, 23 WARDS	10,958,178	8,346,709	131	3,026,756	415,287
All *shi* and *gun*	3,005,672	3,439,190	87	292,047	725,565
All islands	33,799	33,587	101	266	14
TOTAL, *TOKYO-TO*	13,997,649	11,819,486	118	2,602,840	424,677

* Day population index = (Day population ÷ Night population) × 100

Data are based on the population census. Day population refers to night population (*dejure* population) plus inflow of commuters and persons attending school from other places minus outflow of commuters and persons attending school to other places. Persons of unknown age are excluded.

Source: Tokyo Statistical Yearbook, 1987, pp. 84–5.

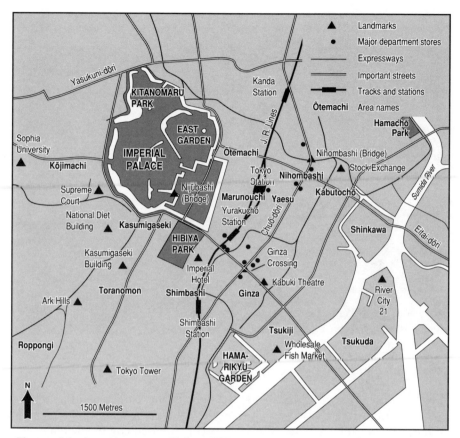

Figure 4.8 Location map, Tokyo CBD

The CBD Core

The center of the CBD, both geographically and symbolically, is Tokyo Station. This is the ornate, red-brick train facility built over eight years during late Meiji and early Taisho, and completed in 1914 to be a landmark of the city's new modernity. It sits stategically between the Marunouchi office district developed 100 years ago by the Mitsubishi company on empty land next to the palace, and the retailing core of the city, where the great department stores were born, in Nihombashi, Kyōbashi and Ginza. The station is far and away the busiest disgorger of commuters among the many other train and subway stations in the center, and is often shown by foreign (and domestic) news correspondents as the backdrop for reports about Japan's economy and its 'modern army of office samurai' on its way to work in surrounding high-rises. Some 2,500 trains stop there each day and nearly 700,000 passengers pass through its turnstiles. In fact, we can say that Tokyo Station is now the center of Japan because it is the hub of

117

Figure 4.9 The Marunouchi office district as seen from the walls and moats of the Imperial Palace

the *shinkansen* network, the high-speed bullet trains connecting the capital city with almost all the largest cities in the country. A substantial fraction of the early morning activity comes from Tokyo-based company employees and government bureaucrats who pass through the station to board high-speed trains (one leaves every few minutes during peak times) for a day of meetings in Nagoya, Osaka, Kobe or some other regional center.

Marunouchi is Tokyo's premier office district (Figure 4.9). It is right at the main exits of Tokyo Station, stretching between the track corridor on the one side and the Imperial Palace grounds on the other. It derives much of its prestige, as well as its exceedingly high rents, from this centrality. The Mitsubishi Company (actually, *group* of companies) is still the prime landowner, and sets the tone for this district both in terms of physical design and rhythms of activity. The 'Londontown' plan of a century ago did not survive the 1923 earthquake-fire and the area has since been redeveloped. Much of the present landscape dates to the time of post-war reconstruction. The overall design is a no-nonsense setting where the important work of big companies can continue without needless distractions. The streets are laid out in an orderly grid, and the blocks are covered from end to end with big office buildings that are functional, but almost totally without adornment. There aren't even many restaurants or drinking places – highly unusual for a crowded commercial area in restaurant-rich Tokyo – except for company cafés in some of the buildings, and numerous smaller establishments tucked away in the basement levels to serve 'set breakfasts' and 'set lunches' to workers on the run.

A walk through Marunouchi reveals its single-minded dedication to work. The day starts early, in part to overlap with the workday in New York and other overseas locations, and extends well into the evening. The first commuters begin to emerge from Tokyo Station and other nearby stations as early as 6:00am. By 7:00am, the pedestrian traffic has become a steady march. The subterranean passages connecting stations with work-places fill with dress-alike men (dark suit, dark tie, white shirt, trench coat in bad weather) carrying briefcases and with smaller numbers of women, resounding with footsteps. Almost no one speaks. It is a fast, silent march, through the passageways, up the stairs to street level, down the block and into the buildings. Once inside, most of the women, 'office ladies' or *OL's* as they are called, change into company uniforms. We see them on the sidewalks throughout the day, often in pairs, as they emerge from buildings to run errands. The buildings themselves – the Marunouchi Building, the New Marunouchi (*Shin Marunouchi*) Building, the Marunouchi Center Building, the Mitsubishi Building, the Mitsubishi Heavy Industries Building, the Mitsubishi Electric Building, the Mitsubishi Shōji ('commercial') Build-ing, the Mitsubishi Bank Building, as well as the government buildings for *Tokyo-to*, the Central Post Office, and numerous other banks, insurance companies and other corporate enterprises – all reflect the sameness. Except for Mitsubishi Bank, which is a new tower twice as high as the rest (24 stories), they are trim and level, because of the restrictions on building height; most are made of similar materials arranged in similar ways on the façades. Perhaps it is in Marunouchi that the old Japanese maxim about human behavior, now a cliché among foreign observers of the country, that the nail that sticks out higher than the rest is the one that gets hammered down first, is most clearly reflected in the landscape.

The other side of Tokyo Station, the Yaesu Exit, is somewhat different. There is still the silent, morning procession to work, the long working days, and a lot of rather drab architecture, but there is also more individuality in the design of buildings, a considerable mixture of land uses and plenty of distractions from neons, billboards and other calls to attention. The non-office land-uses include a multi-level department store, (Daimaru), built into this remodeled side of the station, and a big underground shopping mall that sprawls in labyrinthine fashion between the station and its more distant exits some blocks away. However, Yaesu is still big business first. This is heralded by a large digital clock high up on a bank building across the street from the station. It outlines a map of the world, and gives up-to-the-minute quotations for the price of the yen in the New York and London markets.

Just to the north of Tokyo Station is Ōtemachi. Named after the nearby Ōte Gate of the Imperial Palace-Edo Castle, the area is part a spillover of offices from overcrowded Marunouchi and part an alternative to Marunou-chi's conformism. It is generally newer than Marunouchi and a number of its office buildings are taller. This area, too, has an impressive list of tenants. Among others, there are the head offices of Fuji Bank and Sanwa Bank, the Yomiuri Newspaper publishers, Sankei Newspapers, Nihon Keizai Newspapers, the global communications giant NTT, Nippon Steel and the Mitsui Mutual Life Insurance Company. There are also several other large banks in the area. Government offices include the Immigration Bureau, the Publications Center and Tokyo's International Post Office. Sometimes observers note physical similarities between Otemachi and the office tower sections of Midtown Manhattan, but with lower buildings. A statue of Shibusawa Ei'ichi (1840–1931), who founded more than 500 companies before retiring in 1916 and is acknowledged as Japan's guiding light in its transition to capitalist economics, stands in a small park near the Nippon Steel headquarters and reflects the area's orientation to business.

Still another major concentration of economic power is Nihombashi, just across an old, narrow canal, the Nihombashi River, from Ōtemachi and northeast of Tokyo Station. This was the heart of commerce in old Edo, where the city's first financial houses and early department stores originated. The blocks closest to the canal, near a place where some of the stone wall of Edo Castle can still be seen, is given to some of the biggest banks. The Bank of Japan, the nation's central bank, is the most imposing structure. One part of it, on the site of Tokugawa Ieyasu's gold mint, is a massive stone building designed in neoclassical style dating to the 1890s; the other part is a modern high-rise faced with stone and built to look like a fortress. Across the street is the high-rise headquarters of the Bank of Tokyo. The Industrial Bank of Japan and the Yasuda Bank and Trust Company, also in impressive buildings, are across the canal where Nihombashi borders Yaesu. The center of Nihombashi is still the domain of the Mitsui financial empire, the old rival to the Mitsubishi interests. The headquarters of the Mitsui Bank (recently reorganized as the Taiyo Kobe Mitsui Bank) and the flagship store of the Mitsukoshi Department Store chain are there, side-by-side on the main street. Both are elegant structures in the classic European style that was popular in Tokyo during late Meiji, and are strong examples of the persistence of tradition in Tokyo's fast-changing CBD.

The Tokyo Stock Exchange, obviously another major center of economic influence, is a sub-section of Nihombashi called Kabutochō. It is down-canal from the core of Nihombashi, and somewhat removed from Tokyo Station (about 20 minutes' walk away) and its adjacent office districts. It developed there because the port was once nearby, and because it was closer to the city's Grain Exchange and warehouses with grain and other commodities. The Stock Exchange is surrounded by numerous securities companies and related establishments, many of which spill over into neighboring Kayabachō; it has emerged as the nucleus of still another important subdistrict of the CBD, oriented to finance. The area has been an especially active zone for office building construction in recent years, partly because land costs have been a cut or two lower than closer to the center, and

Figure 4.10 Miyuki-dōri in Ginza

partly because of an influx of new companies that arrived after the Tokyo Stock Exchange began accepting its first foreign members early in 1986.

The main street of Nihombashi is Chūō-dōri. Its length from the Mitsui buildings in Nihombashi to Shimbashi (about 2.5 kilometers) is the principal retailing spine of the CBD. It extends along a major trolley corridor that shaped the district nearly 100 years ago (look again at Figure 3.6), and is anchored at either end by clusters of department stores at stations of the Ginza Subway Line, the city's first underground. The Nihombashi end (Mitsukoshimae and Nihombashi Stations) has, in addition to the main Mitsukoshi Store, the flagship stores for the Tōkyū and the Takashimaya chains, while the Ginza-Shimbashi end (Ginza Station) has, among others, Matsuya, Matsuzakaya, Wako and a major branch of Mitsukoshi. In between and on the side streets are many other stores, restaurants and other business establishments. On most Sundays, the principal shopping day in Japan, Chūō-dōri is closed to vehicles and becomes a long pedestrian mall. A side street called Miyuki-dōri is especially fashionable (Figure 4.10). Other side streets specialize in the popular nightclubs for which inner Tokyo (eg. Ginza) is well known. All of them are quite expensive. The Ginza retailing district has expanded in recent times (since the 1960s) along Harumi-dōri, a busy street running perpendicular to Chūō-dōri in the direction of Hibiya and Yūrakuchō. The area near the track corridor leading to Tokyo Station, long the city's leading center for moviegoing and theaters, has three huge, new department stores in gleaming high-rise towers.

Not far away, now on the south side of the Imperial Place grounds and about 20 minutes' walk southwest from Tokyo Station, is the national capital district. It covers most of Nagatachō and Kasumigaseki. Because it is an area of former *daimyō* estates, and because of the monumental nature of many of its buildings, it is much less crowded than the CBD and has some greenery and open spaces. The largest is Hibiya Park, downtown Tokyo's 'Central Park' or 'Hyde Park', and a pleasant buffer between the business core of the city and the government buildings. The National Diet Building (*Kokkai-Gijidō*) is the centerpiece of this district. It is an imposing gray granite structure built in a Prussian style and embellished on top with a rather ill-proportioned ziggurat. The site is a low hill overlooking the palace grounds and the other government buildings: the Prime Minister's Office, the headquarters of various ministries, court buildings, offices for members of the Diet, the National Diet Library and many others. Because of the large numbers of government buildings, their substantial proportions, and the atmosphere of workaday hustle and bustle, it is all a rather impress-ive scene. In total, the message that Tokyo is a substantial center of power and a strong capital is well-conveyed.

CBD expansion

We can identify several special areas within Tokyo's three central wards that are leading edges of CBD expansion. One is the city's waterfront, where Tokyo Bay reaches closest to the heart of the city and the Sumida River has a major distributary. This is a large district of industries, warehouses and docking facilities on reclaimed land, and includes several close-in off-shore islands, loosely connected peninsulas and sections of 'mainland'. Various parts of it are now being transformed for the expansion of offices, hotels and other uses related to the CBD. The best examples, seen clearly from Tokyo Tower, are the World Trade Center building, a tall office tower and trade show facility adjacent to an important rail corridor in a district called Hamamatsuchō, and the Tōshiba Building, world head-quarters for the giant electronics firm on a former manufacturing site nearby. Today, these two buildings appear as somewhat lone towers in a still largely industrial area. However, there are grand schemes to transform the entire waterfront near them into an especially important part of an expanded CBD.

So, too, the CBD bank of the lower reaches of the Sumida River is another zone of CBD expansion. A major target there is the Shinkawa area, long a district of *sake* wholesalers, other warehouses, small stores and old wooden houses. However, nearness to the Stock Exchange area of Kabutochō, combined with lower land costs and the presence of larger development sites (because of the warehouses), has caused an office building boom that promises quickly to incorporate this neighborhood into the main part of the CBD. Riverfront sites are most desirable and have been taken by the biggest companies for the tallest buildings. The Sumitomo Twin Building, a 24-story and a 21-story office complex constructed by the Sumitomo Warehouse Company, a member of the huge Sumitomo financial group, is the most imposing (Satō, 1988). The same pattern is true in the neighboring riverfront district, Hakozakichō. There, the biggest builder has been the IBM Corporation, which has its headquarters for Asian/Pacific operations on the river in a new (1989) 25-story tower. The IBM Building is also distinguished for having one of the best (and there are precious few) public promenades at the waterfront of central Tokyo.

Similar land-use transition, in which warehousing, transportation facilities and industry are replaced by CBD land uses, is also seen in other areas of central Tokyo. An area called Shiodome, for example, close to Ginza and Shimbashi, is slated for conversion to a sizable cluster of office towers, hotels, high-rise residences and shopping centers – a 'new town in town'. The opportunity comes from a 26-hectare rail freight distribution center that is being displaced further out (Tange, 1987, pp. 28–31; Yada, 1989a, pp. 33–6). Similarly, parts of the Shiba area near the waterfront to the southwest of the center, long known as a center of manufacturing in Tokyo, especially of electronics products, are being converted to offices and related land uses. Just like the Tōshiba Corporation has done with its office tower near the waterfront, another electronics giant, NEC, has recently completed a landmark headquarters high-rise (43 stories; distinctive shape) on a formerly industrial site.

Another direction for CBD expansion is north into Kanda. This has been an area of small shops, artisans, craftsmen and residences, as well as a district of colleges and university campus built during the enlightenment programs of the Meiji. Its nearness to the center, convenience to train and subway lines, and higher prestige compared to changing industrial districts, has drawn a flood of builders in recent years, and changed some sections, into high- and mid-rise boom-towns seemingly overnight, particularly along arterial streets (eg. Yasukuni-dōri) and near important train stations (eg. Ochanomizu). There are no showpiece high-rises that stand out alone as in the previous examples; instead, there are multi-story buildings just about everywhere, and the rooflines of the entire district seem to be rising from one and two stories to seven, eight, ten, twelve or more, almost in unison. Many different kinds of businesses are involved, but printing and publishing is a leading staple in Kanda.

However, the most spectacular growth is reserved for the west side of the CBD, south of the Imperial Palace. This includes several districts contiguous to the CBD or the adjacent government center such as Akasaka, Toranomon, Uchisaiwaichō and Shimbashi and Nishi-Shimbashi, as well as some districts that are a little further afield from the CBD but expanding so rapidly with high-rise commerce that they are likely soon to coalesce with the center. Examples from this category include Roppongi, Aoyama,

Shibuya, Shinagawa and Shinjuku. Already, the major roads such as Aoyama-dori and Shinjuku-dori connecting the CBD with what are supposed to be outlying commercial subcenters (eg. Shibuya and Shinjuku, respectively) are lined along most of their courses with tall office buildings. Moreover, major intersections and subway stops such as Aoyama-Itchōme, which has the Aoyama Twin office towers and the high-rise headquarters of the Honda Corporation, one of the most attractive new buildings in the city, are mini-CBDs in themselves. Consequently, it is not difficult to imagine that in the not-too-distant future, the whole west side of Tokyo within the Yamanote Loop (and all areas within the loop north, south and east of the center) will become part of one super-enormous business center. If this happens, it would be about as big as the entire city was during the height of the Tokugawa era, when Edo was the most populous urban center in the world!

There are several reasons why CBD growth is especially active toward the west. One is that the west is the principal direction of *yamanote*, the higher ground and higher prestige zone that has been a feature of the city since early Edo times. As a result it has been the direction of quickest expansion of Tokyo as a whole. Most of its better suburbs are to the west, as are most of the giant new commercial sub-centers, largest and busiest nightlife districts, and centers of fashion and many popular trends. Secondly, the west side of Tokyo is where most of the city's foreign embassies and consulates are located (often on grounds that were once feudal estates), and where the majority of foreign diplomats, foreign business executives and other highly placed foreigners in Tokyo reside. Consequently, this is where Tokyo shows its international side the most, and where many of the foreign firms doing business in Japan have been drawn. For the same reason, the west is where most of the city's large international hotels (as opposed to the smaller 'business hotels' that are more typical in Japanese city centers) have chosen to locate. Finally, I note a true down-to-earth advantage of the west: it is more stable geologically than the delta lands and reclaimed flats east and south of the center, and therefore more desirable for the construction of tall buildings.

The Toranomon area, a fast-developing office district adjacent to Kasumigaseki, presents a fascinating, albeit somewhat idiosyncratic, case study of CBD expansion. Until recently, the area was a neighborhood of homes, shops and small businesses, a great many of which were owned by the same families who have inhabited the land for generations. This was a typical pattern for inner-city Tokyo. However, in recent years Toranomon has undergone an almost total transformation, and it is now one of the hottest office rental markets in Tokyo. Peter Popham, whose book *Tokyo: The City at the End of the World* I introduced as being one of my favorites, describes this change as being largely the doing of the Mori Building Company and its octogenarian founder and president, Mori Taikichirō, now the third largest landowner in Japan (after the Mitsubishi and the Mitsui interests) (Popham, 1985, pp. 73–84).

The son of a rice dealer, Mori was born and raised in Toranomon, and took upon himself a personal mission to transform the area. In an exceptional interview with Popham, he explained he saw long ago that 'the ordinary old Japan could not survive, it would be defeated by the advanced nations, so we had to struggle to achieve rapid Westernization'. Therefore, he began acquiring property from his neighbors and 'Westernizing' it by converting it to offices. His first building, *Mori Biru 1* (Mori Building) was completed in 1955. Now there are over 50 'Mori Birus' in and near Toranomon, most of them identified by numbers in the sequence of construction. From our perch in Tokyo Tower, where we conducted an introductory reconnaissance of the city we can see the words 'Mori Biru 40', 'Mori Biru 35' and 'Mori Biru 37' (in Japanese), among other Mori numbers, high up on the buildings in Toranomon that face us. This naming system was adopted because there is a custom among many Japanese families to give children names indicating the order of birth (Ichirō, Jirō, Saburō, etc.), and because Mori looks upon his buildings as if they were his children (Popham, 1985, p. 74).

One of Mori's most recent offspring is the grand-scale project called Ark Hills, so-named because it is where Akasaka, Roppongi and Kasumigaseki come together. It is different from the other Mori developments because it is a complex of several buildings rather than just one. It was Mori-san himself who proclaimed this place in advertising to be 'Where Tokyo is Headed' (Figure 4.11). What makes Ark Hills special is that it is a mixed-use development: in addition to the office towers and hotel, there are private residences in three of the high-rises and various 'community facilities'. According to the publicity, this is to stimulate a reversal of the depopulation of inner Tokyo – a depopulation with which Mori himself had much to do. In Toranomon, for example, in the past decade alone, the number of residents has slipped from 4,838 in 1980, to 4,111 in 1985, and then to 3,231 in 1989. How this depopulation was accomplished and how it has affected established neighborhoods will be our topic soon. For now, we turn to the flip side of CBD growth in Tokyo – the expansion of residential areas well beyond the center.

The residential ring

There is a place alongside the commuter rail tracks near Shinjuku Station, the three-million-passengers-a-day commuter hub on the city's west side, that signifies much to me about how population distribution patterns are evolving in the Tokyo Metropolis. It is a sizable ground, much larger than any of the other land parcels in this highly congested vicinity, stretching for nearly 400 meters along the tracks and 50 to 100 meters deep. Until recently, it was a rail freight yard, but the site has now been redeveloped, albeit temporarily, for use as a 'model home park'. It is one of several

ARK
IT'S WHERE TOKYO IS HEADED.

It's an architectural complex in total harmony with its environment. Built on a grand scale to meet human needs. And it will redefine architecture in Tokyo.

Akasaka/Roppongi City Redevelopment Project Specifications:
Total Ground Area: 56,000 sq.m
Total Floor Area: 360,000 sq.m
Facilities will include: Offices, Hotel, Residences, Concert Hall, Television Studio, Parking Space and much more.

Opening spring 1986

森ビル
MORI BUILDING
President: Taikichiro Mori

5-1, Toranomon 3-chome, Minato-ku, Tokyo
Phone: (03) 433-2211

REDEFINING ARCHITECTURE FOR THE 21st CENTURY
Urban Redevelopment. Office and Apartment Buildings.
Hotels and Resort Facilities. Cultural and Commercial Environments.

Figure 4.11 An advertisement for the Ark Hills development in the Akasaka-Roppongi-Kasumigaseki area of Tokyo. (Courtesy of the Mori Building Company)

such facilities in Tokyo,[2] and gives potential house-buyers a chance to comparison-shop in one location. In this instance, some of the nation's biggest housing developers, Misawa Home, Mitsui Home, Seibu House and others, have put up a total of 27 beautiful and in some cases remarkably luxurious, suburban-style single houses, as well as some appropriate front-yard landscaping, along either side of a new street that parallels the tracks. Especially at weekends, when families have time to spend together, people come to inspect the houses and perhaps place an order with one of the sales agents. No one actually buys exactly what is on display, because the models are too expensive for most budgets and most houses too big for typical lots in and around Tokyo. What is actually sold are scaled-down versions of dream houses to some people, and dreams for a future house to others.

The market for new housing in and around Tokyo is huge. According to one source, the current official housing plan for the Tokyo Metropolis, the demand for new and rebuilt residential units during the 15 years between 1986 and 2000 will be approximately 2.3 million houses (Tokyo

---

[2] Another model home park temporarily occupies the large redevelopment site at Shiodome in the CBD, mentioned earlier.

Metropolitan Government, 1987b, p. 195). There are many reasons for this. A sizable fraction of the metropolitan population, especially in the 23 wards section of Tokyo, is generally poorly housed and anxious for improvement. Surveys show that about one-third of the 23-ward population is 'dissatisfied to some extent' with where they live, and that an additional 8.6 per cent is 'very dissatisfied' (Tokyo Metropolitan Government, 1988, p. 48). Most complaints are about neighborhood crowding and cramped residential quarters (Tokyo Municipal News, Summer, 1988, p. 8). Furthermore, the fact that this is a time of considerable prosperity in Japan has raised people's expectations of housing and redefined their standards. So, too, demand for housing has been stimulated by the demographic structure of the population, which now has a disproportionate share of young households with dwelling needs that change with marriage, divorce, the birth of children, changes in employment and many other factors.

The specific location of the Shinjuku Rail-City Housing Display Grounds, being at trackside at a busy mass-transit interchange between the business-oriented heart of the city and its largest sector of residential suburbs, reflects good marketing strategy. Because the site is visible from the passing trains, it reminds commuters as they travel to and from work about a financial objective many of them hold. This marketing message is reinforced by advertisements for real estate posted in the trains themselves, in ads in the newspapers and magazines that train riders always seem to be reading, and on the backs of the small tissue packets one is always being handed near train station exits and in busy commercial centers. There are also plenty of leaflets about houses for sale stuffed each day in residential mail boxes, especially in apartment buildings and overcrowded condominiums (*manshon*) where young working people are known to live (Figure 4.12). Indeed, it is as if there were some sort of massive propaganda machine at work, repeatedly encouraging the metropolis's laborers to toil on and promising them the imminent reward of a dream house. In one specific ad, a train-car poster promoting a particular single-family housing development in suburban Saitama Prefecture, an adorable little girl, about four years old, in a very comfortable domestic setting and holding a kitten, says sweetly to her *sarariman* (salaryman) father: '*otōsan gambare*' – 'keep it up daddy, give it your best' (Nussbaum, 1985, p. 81).

For most *otōsan* (as well as for home buyers who are not fathers), the greatest hurdle to homeownership is the price of land (Table 4.8). This is a problem probably found in every country with private ownership of land, but in Tokyo it seems to be most severe. Prices are so high that just about everyone who does not already own a piece of Tokyo is priced out of the market, and has to resign him- or herself to continue to exist in a tiny apartment or, with luck, to moving to either a modest *manshon* some distance away or to a very inconveniently located single house far in the boonies. The extent of this problem is seen in Figure 4.13. It is a schematic map based on one that appeared, luckily for me, along with 11 full pages

Figure 4.12 An advertisement for a house for sale on the Ōme Line in the western suburbs of Tokyo. (From a circular left in the author's home mailbox)

of related data in the *Asahi Shinbun,* a widely read daily newspaper, on the day I was writing this paragraph; it shows the geographical distribution of current prices for one square meter of residential land over a broad, 60-kilometer radius around Tokyo. Inner-ring areas, particularly such popular districts as Roppongi and Shibuya, are shown to be outrageously expensive – 6,790,000 yen per square meter in the case of the former. Prices decrease with distance from the center, the rate of decrease varying with direction

Table 4.8 Average land prices in *Tokyo-to* by use, 1989 (1,000 yen per square meter)

	Residential	Commercial	Quasi-industrial	Industrial
Central 3 wards	6,241.2	15,079.9	4,764.0	–
Ward Area	1,275.5	7,859.9	1,363.8	776.9
Tama Area	474.4	1,975.7	440.9	710.2
Tokyo-to	853.5	6,678.6	1,175.0	721.8

Source: Tokyo Metropolitan Government, 1990a, p. 93.

(the west is most expensive) and with the particular train line, but even in the 30–40 kilometer ring, prices of over 500,000 yen per square meter are not uncommon. This too is outrageously expensive. Not until one gets beyond 40 kilometers from the center, or even 50 kilometers, do prices fall to below 200,000 yen. Even this is expensive, much more than the average for any city in Japan outside the Tokyo area except Osaka (*Asahi Shinbun*, 23 March 1990, p. 1).

It hardly makes sense to translate these figures to specific prices for houses, because the prices skyrocket so dramatically, and vary again with with distance, always expressed as 'numbers of minutes' from a given train station. Convenient walking distance is most expensive, followed in order by bicycle distance and feeder-bus distance. Nevertheless, as a round-numbers illustration, consider that a modest single house on a small lot close to the center (eg. within the Yamanote Loop) is certain to exceed the yen equivalent of two million US dollars; that a similar house in a middle-distance suburb (eg. nearly one hour away by train) is, say, one million dollars; and that an unspectacular spread almost two hours away is, say, $500,000. This last amount translates to over 20 years salary for an average breadwinner. Even 'a nothing-special flat out among the power lines' can be prohibitive: say, 10 or 15 years of breadwinning (Kauffman, 1988, p. 78). So if a piece of real estate is possible at all, or even a circumscribed volume of air in a multi-story condominium, it usually takes considerable savings, a long-term mortgage and generous help from relatives or friends (Nussbaum, 1985).

It is because the cost of land is so high that the great majority of sales made at the Shinjuku Rail-City Housing Display Grounds, and places like it, are made to people who already own property and who intend to replace an older house on that site with a new one. This is another important dimension of 'the third rebuilding of Tokyo', and accounts for much of the construction activity that one sees around the city. One aspect of this is, very simply, people who want to improve their living conditions by having a house that is larger, more modern or better tailored for changing household needs. Many others erect a structure that accomodates two generations of the same family. It is common for parents to assist their adult children who are priced out of the land market by combining resources with them and replacing their old house with one they can share. This dovetails with traditional patterns of multi-generational living in Japan, so that there is nothing particularly new about this concept. What changes is the increased extent to which multi-generation living is forced on Tokyo families by land costs. There are also novel architectural designs blending the traditional house with layouts that increase privacy and appeal to modern tastes. High-tech houses that are loaded with the newest appliances and electronic gadgetry are especially popular. One of my favorites was to see a 360-degree body-drying blower to be used when you step out of the *ofuro*, the Japanese-style bath.

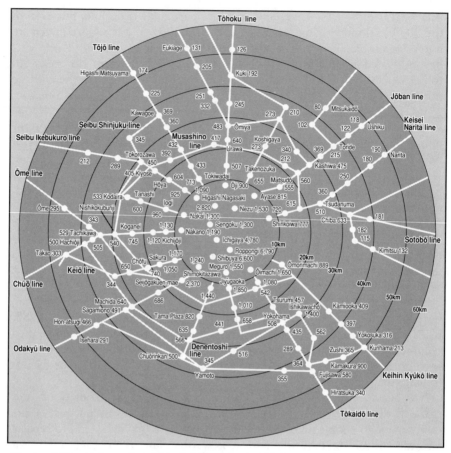

Figure 4.13 Value of residential land in the Tokyo area by distance from the city center and commuter line, 1990

Types of suburban development

It would be wrong to think of the residential ring around central Tokyo as being nothing more than bedroom communities, or to assume that all places there are the same. As in any other large metropolitan area, the broad zone surrounding the main city is extremely diverse and contains many types of areas, both residential and other. Because the previous paragraphs concentrated exclusively on new, single-family housing, it is necessary now to present a more balanced account of the urbanized ring around Tokyo and to show a fuller range of the kinds of places found there and the various forces that shaped them.

Suburban expansion in the Tokyo area is not new: it has been going on in one form or another for more than a century. Even during Edo (before 1868), new districts were continually being added to the edge of the city, be it on reclaimed land close to the center near the bay or in the form of 'ribbon urbanization' along some of the highways leading from the city to the provinces. With the coming of railroads in the 1880s and 1890s suburban expansion increased. The first train line to be used by commuters was the Chūō Line (the 'central' or 'middle' line), due west of the city. It was developed by private interests in the 1880s primarily to link Tokyo with Yamanashi, a provincial city about 90 kilometers away. Starting in 1889 it stopped at four stations in the farmlands on the west side of Tokyo (Hachiōji, Tachikawa, Kokubunji and Sakai), eventually changing the settlements there into populous commuter centers. Other early lines were the Ōme Line, built in 1894 to connect Tachikawa with Ōme in the western mountains; the Seibu Ikebukuro Line (1915), originally an industrial corridor for hauling limestone and silk, but now a key commuter link through western suburbs north of the Chūō Line; and the Keiō Line (mid-1910s) that runs from Shinjuku to Hachiōji, Fuchū, Chōfu and other settlements south of the Chūō corridor (Allinson, 1979, pp. 22–3).

However, because of poor scheduling and considerable distances between stops, service was slow in the first years and the pace of suburban growth unimpressive, at least until 1923. The Great Kantō Earthquake began to change all this. Its disaster chased residents and businesses alike from the heart of the city and stimulated public demands for improved access to the periphery. As a result, other train lines were soon extended west, southwest, northwest, north and east of the city, and the number of stations and the frequency of trains increased. The urbanized area began to expand more quickly than ever before, especially to the west and southwest where the most ambitious transportation projects were located; what was once a tight urban cluster started to transform itself into a sprawling metropolis of sizable proportions. This is seen in Figure 4.14, a map illustrating the expansion of the built-up area of Tokyo during different periods.

The laying of commuter rail lines to the suburbs was largely the initiative of private companies. The most successful saw opportunities for profit not only in train fares, but also in land sales and housing development along the tracks that they extended, in retailing at the entrances to train stations, as well as in various other related enterprises. In the manner of entrepreneurial land speculators at the edge of cities in numerous Western countries, company founders bought up farmland and forests beyond the urbanized area in advance of transportation, laid tracks and built stations, and developed housing sub-divisions and entire new towns for a growing metropolitan population. The largest enterprises went so far as to build giant department stores at terminal stations close to the central wards of Tokyo (eg. at Shinjuku, Shibuya, Ikebukuro and Ueno), branch stores at key commuter stations along their tracks, and chains of supermarkets covering every point where there was growing settlement. Because of severe central-city housing shortages, their advertising messages to move to the suburbs were well-received by Tokyoites, many of whom were eager to live in fresh surroundings where they could have ample room and cheaper accommo-

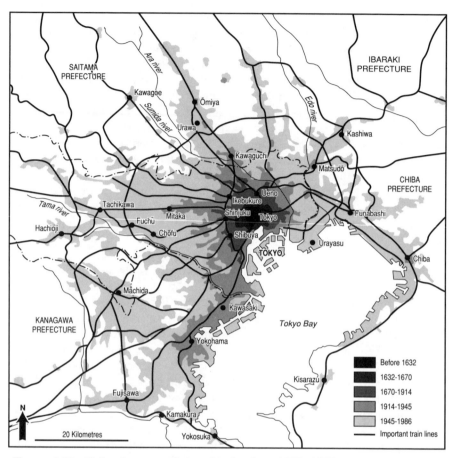

Figure 4.14 Tokyo's expanding urbanization, 1632–1986

dation. 'To the suburbs where cosmoses bloom' was one of the popular advertising phrases of the 1930s (Ishizuka and Ishida, 1988, p. 22).

Perhaps the most successful of the giant companies born in this way was the Seibu Group. Founded in the mid–1910s by Tsutsumi Yasujirō (1889–1964), a remarkably entrepreneurial migrant to Tokyo from a farm in Shiga Prefecture, the company grew quickly from a few small investments into a huge, highly diversified concern spanning real estate and railroad holdings, hotels, golf courses, ski resorts, the Seibu department stores and supermarkets empire, amusement parks, consumer credit and insurance firms, the championship Seibu Lions baseball team and stadium, and many other ventures. It is now divided among two feuding sons, the younger of whom, Yoshiaki, was said by *Forbes* magazine (27 July 1987) to be the richest man in the world. His personal fortune, estimated at over $21 billion, includes 220,000 square meters of land in Tokyo and 150 million square meters nationwide, the Seibu Railway system in Tokyo's western suburbs and elsewhere, 30 golf courses, 30 ski resorts and almost 60 Prince hotels (Nagaharu, 1988, p. 193). The company has had an especially great impact on the development of the commercial sub-center at Ikebukuro, where it has the world's largest department store, and on a broad sector of Tokyo's west side and western suburbs reached by the Seibu Ikebukuro Line, the Seibu Shinjuku and other Seibu lines. A similar concern, although without a baseball team and some of the other kinds of Seibu holdings, is the Tōkyū Corporation. Its focus is Shibuya, a train-station commercial center in which the company owns several department stores, and from which it (or its predecessors) extended train lines to Yokohama and to western suburbs (the Den'en-Toshi Line and the Inokashira Line) and developed extensive residential areas where once there were just farms or hills. Den'en-chofu, a planned 'garden city' type of community built in 1922 at a stop on the Tōkyū Tōyoko ('Tokyo-Yokohama') line, is an especially well-known example.

Still another powerful force behind suburban growth, in addition to the transportation/land development firms, was industry. The plentiful undeveloped land surrounding Tokyo was ideal for the demanding space requirements of large factories, particularly once a rail network was extended connecting likely factory sites with port facilities. An example from the west side of Tokyo is an industrial corridor that grew up along the Nambu Line, a freight carrier that opened in 1929 between Tachikawa in Tokyo's Tama district and the port of Yokohama. Some of the important industries that developed there were electrical equipment in Koganei and Mitaka, aircraft manufacturing in Fussa and Tachikawa, and precision instruments, heavy machinery, photographic film and electrical equipment in Hino. The suburban area grew still more during the late 1930s, after the government declared that new factories producing war material should be situated away from the center of Tokyo but within a a 20-mile radius. Thus, the town of Fuchū attracted Nihon Sēkō, a firm that would begin production of tanks in 1940; Musashino, a town on the Chūō Line, became the largest site for the Nakajima Aircraft Corporation's manufacture of military planes and plane engines (Allinson, 1979, pp. 55–7). In each of these cases, housing was developed close to the factory for the workers, so that each of these towns (as well as several others north and east of the central city) is properly classified as a self-contained urban center, with its own employment base, in addition to being a bedroom appendage for commuters to central Tokyo.

Thus, there are several different kinds of suburban communities surrounding Tokyo. Some resemble central cities and have busy commercial centers at the train stations that serve them, industrial districts stretched out along the tracks and local river, and large tracts of cheaper housing nearby called *danchi*. Some of these are provided by employers for their workers, and others by government, for example, local government or the national Japan Housing Corporation (JHC). Typically, the *danchi* are planned clusters of drab multi-story apartments, identical except for an

Figure 4.15 Apartments and other dwellings along commuter tracks in the suburbs. The picture was taken near Machida on the Odakyū Line, Kanagawa Prefecture

identifying number painted in black high up on a grey concrete wall, and all with tiny units described as having 'privacy provided by lock, steel door and private bath' (Honjō, 1975, p. 378). JHC's *danchi* are especially numerous, both inside the 23 wards and in Tama and the suburban prefectures. Their scale is often several thousand units at one site, which often happens to be a less accessible place where land is cheaper, and therefore generally includes some minimum of community facilities such as shopping, schools and recreation areas. While not attractive physically, such public housing units have been extremely important in providing secure shelter for hundreds of thousands of Tokyoites in the face of an overall short supply of housing, rapid metropolitan population growth and high prices on the open market (Figure 4.15).

Other suburbs are known for their institutions. There are several places where college and university campuses have been relocated from the 23 wards and where dormitory students make up sizable parts of the population. Hachiōji, a town in the western foothills nearly 30 kilometers from the center of Tokyo that was designated for this purpose by Tokyo Metropolitan Government, is a good example. Other college towns (*gakuen toshi*) were developed by businesses as as part of their real-estate promotions, such as Kunitachi, to the west of Tokyo. Developed originally by the Seibu empire as a planned community with spacious, regular-sized lots, it grew because of its focus on Hitosubashi University, one of the nation's largest (Allinson, 1979, p. 54). Still other towns are known as exclusive suburbs for the rich. Den'en-chōfu, a planned garden city associated with the Tōkyū Corporation, is a prime example. Sometimes called 'Japan's Beverly Hills', it is an area of stately single houses, beautiful gardens and private clubs, and a fine commercial district with fashionable boutiques and expensive restaurants. It is arranged spatially in a distinctive pattern formed by ginko-shaded streets emanating like wheel spokes from a European-style central train station (Chapman, 1987).

Still another type of suburb is the planned new town, important in Tokyo planning since the 1960s. It combines public and private investment to construct self-contained new cities that include commercial, educational and other urban functions with a range of housing choices at designated sites outside the central city. The largest of these is Tama New Town, a project started in 1965 in the Tama Hills area west of Tokyo's 23-ward zone by Tokyo Metropolitan Government and two public corporations, the Urban Development Public Corporation and the Tokyo Metropolitan Housing Supply Public Corporation. It covers over 2,200 hectares and has over 101,000 residents. When finished in a few years' time, it is expected to house more than 300,000 individuals and to be one of the most important sub-centers in the metropolitan area. A fuller discussion of Tama New Town and other planned centers in the suburban ring is given in Chapter Six.

Exurban settlement

As in many large metropolitan districts, the greater Tokyo area has a zone of dispersed housing and other scattered urban land lying well beyond the city and its ring of crowded suburbs. This area is sometimes called exurbia; typically it consists, among other land uses, of outlying suburban housing developments, second homes, small satellite towns built around a particular local industry or resource, and isolated country houses owned by long-distance commuters who exchange travel time and convenience to the urban center for privacy and environmental amenities. This is a good place for me to say a few words about distant reaches of exurban Tokyo that are growing with urban commuters and functioning more and more like integral parts of the city.

Perhaps the most noticeable areas of exurban residences are in the foot-hills and mountainous areas lying beyond the limits of the Kantō Plain. This includes the Oku-Tama ('deep' or 'distant' Tama) area beyond Hachiōji, Akigawa and Ōme cities, where the Chūō and Keiō Lines, and the Seibu-Haijima and Ōme Lines, push deep into narrow valleys between steep wooded hills; as well as mountainous areas of the several prefectures that encircle Tokyo and its suburbs. The direction of Mt Fuji, the slopes of which are west of of Kanagawa Prefecture's high ground at the boundary between Shizuoka and Yamanashi Prefectures and too far to commute from regularly, is especially popular. For many of the regular riders, the outer limits for commuting are marked by express station stops in the centers of such towns as Odawara, an historic castle town in Kanagawa Prefecture about 75 kilometers from central Tokyo that is both on the shore of Sagami Bay and at the entry to the mountainous Fuji-Hakone-Izu National Park complex, and Enzan, Yamanashi and Kōfu, all of which are in Yamanashi Prefecture 90–100 kilometers from central Tokyo. So, too, there are distant commuters to the center of the city from the hills and beautiful shorelines of the Chiba Peninsula, and to both Tokyo and Yokohama from the scenic hills and shoreline towns on the Miura Peninsula between Tokyo and Sagami Bays. Picturesque tourist towns on the north shore of Sagami Bay such as Enoshima and Kamakura (both in Kanagawa Prefecture) also have special appeal. Kamakura, for example, is distinctive as an ancient capital city replete with famous temples and historic sites set amid green hills with spectacular views of the bay and its beaches.

The social context of such long-distance commuting begins with the gigantic extent of Tokyo itself, and its great crowding, high land costs and other characteristics. For many households the economic calculation is quite simple: pay more in time and train fares to live far from Tokyo, but in return gain considerably in both the cost of housing and in the cost of time and travel to weekend amenities. Over the years I lived in Tokyo, I met many people, both Japanese and foreigners, who reside at such places as Odawara or Atami (on Sagami Bay on the Izu Peninsula) and commute to Tokyo, and who explain that the train ride of two hours or so is actually an advantage: they get a seat all the way in, and can use the time spent on the train to sleep or read for their jobs or for pleasure. Some friends of mine who are professors, journalists and artists, and whose schedules do not require five or six days per week at an office, have been particularly enthusiastic about such arrangements. This is especially so when gloating over having a spacious study in their homes or private gardens that would have been completely unattainable in the land market of Tokyo. Another variation on this is to keep two addresses: a main home at the distant outskirts of Tokyo for living, and a room or small apartment in the city for those days when being 'on the job' is most important.

I am certain that the attraction of distant edges of the Tokyo metropolis will increase in the future as the city continues to grow outward, and as the nature of work continues to evolve in Japan to emphasize white-collar occupations and new freedoms from the office. For many people this is a welcome development: it allows not only for an escape from urban ills, but also for residence in settings that are especially highly prized in Japanese culture: mountainous backdrops, views of Mt Fuji, rocky shorelines, tall stands of cypress or other trees, and productive paddy fields, orchards, tea plantations and other rural scenes. On the other hand, this is also a case of a city that is already thought to be too big becoming even bigger, and yet another example of where urbanization paves over the countryside. So it is not surprising there are often complaints from rural towns that the city is overtaking them, that there is too much growth in their direction, too fast. A specific example I was able to follow was the 'green revolt' against a 920-unit housing complex for US military personnel in the hills above Zushi, a 'surf-suburb' close to Kamakura (Tracey, 1985).

The squeeze on inner-city neighborhoods

We can now return from the suburbs to the 23 wards of Tokyo to see a third major dimension of present-day urban development in the city. (The first two were redevelopment and expansion of the CBD and expansion of the residential ring around the city.) We can call this the intensification of land use in established neighborhoods close to the center of the city. Because of high land costs and expanding commercial functions, there is unprecedented pressure to put every available parcel to intensive use, no matter how small or awkwardly situated, and to build as many stories to a structure as regulations allow. Everywhere one looks in the neighborhoods surrounding the CBD, there is redevelopment: older houses are giving way to new; single-family structures are yielding to multi-family buildings and apartments; small 'ma-and-pa' stores are replaced by commercial chains and shopping centers; busier streets are coming to be lined ever more with high-rises and non-stop ribbons of slow-moving traffic. Open space, always at a premium in Tokyo, is even more scarce. A view from any high place, be it Tokyo Tower, the Sunshine 60 observation level in Ikebukuro, or the private windows of a friend's company high up in the Aoyama Twin office complex in the super-high-rent *yamanote* area west of the CBD, confirms this again and again (Figure 4.16).

For the residents of these neighborhoods this means a tremendous change in their surroundings and living patterns. In some sections of the city, particularly those directly in the path of CBD expansion or the expansion of other business districts, residential displacement by commercial uses has been almost total. We saw this in Toranomon, where only a few small pockets of single houses remain, and where population decline has been extremely steep since the 1970s and 1980s when the neighborhood became a prime target for office development. In other areas a little more distant from the CBD, residential land-uses remain in place, but under conditions of much higher density. Long-term residents of these neighborhoods often complain about too much crowding, too many new stranger-neighbors, the demise of old neighborhood shops and other businesses and their replacement by impersonal chain stores, increased traffic and noise, high rental prices, and about the many inconveniences brought on by non-stop construction activity in their midst. This is seen in surveys by the Tokyo Metropolitan Government. One recent study of citizens' opinions reported that the ten most common complaints among residents in the central wards about their neighborhoods were, in descending order:

Figure 4.16 The view south across Minato Ward as seen from the Aoyama Twin office complex. The picture was taken in 1986 and shows the Ark Hills complex still under construction. Tokyo Tower is to the right. The crowding typifies the 23-ward area

1 too many people
2 too much traffic
3 small living quarters without private gardens
4 high costs of housing and other necessities
5 scarcity of greenery
6 'clear blue or starry skies can't be seen'
7 noise and vibrations because of traffic and construction
8 rush-hour congestion;
9 pollution of rivers, the sea and the atmosphere
10 lack of playgrounds for children.[3]

A perfectly good example of all this is the neighborhood in a corner of Shibuya Ward where I used to live. It is a mix of old and new, of residential and non-residential uses just down the street from the bustling high-rise center of Shinjuku. Our house there was where my daughter's bedroom was illuminated by the neon from the Denny's restaurant across the street, where we could reach from the window and almost touch a neighbor's

[3] This is from a poll conducted in November 1987 of 3,000 men and women aged 20 and over. Results were reported in *Tokyo Municipal News* (Vol. 38, No. 2, 1988, p. 8), but were not broken down by where in Tokyo the respondents lived. Information about the special problems of living in the inner-most wards comes from the Tokyo Metropolitan Government, 1987b, especially pp. 71–5.

house, and where everything shook whenever a truck or a bus passed on the nearby street. A visit a year later reveals some of the changes. Our house is still there, but a small parking lot for six cars that was nearby, where children used to play during the day, is now six stories of steel skeleton draped in a blue cloth – a new building under construction; a small vacant lot that was tucked without street frontage behind a neighbor's house now has an oversized new house on it; several of the single houses on the street behind us and on a parallel street nearby are gone, replaced by condominium structures of the *manshon* type that have just opened for trade; and a little candy shop that my children liked is gone, too, replaced ironically by the offices of an American chocolate bar distributor. Everywhere, there is more of a feeling of being closed in – perceptibly more so than ever before. There is less sky to see because of the high-rises; so many of the vacant spaces have been filled in that everything seems to be packed even more closely together. The twin towers of new City Hall, now nearing completion, have risen far above all the other buildings and loom into view to the east as giant reminders that big-Tokyo begins just down the street and that, in comparison, the old neighborhood is quite insignificant.

There are many ways in which developers from outside a neighborhood can acquire the parcels they need for construction of the high density buildings they favor. They can offer homeowners and other landowners high prices for their holdings, fully confident that the money they spend will be returned with profit from high rents or sales of condominium units. They can also be assured that within certain guidelines set down in the building codes of Tokyo and individual wards, there will usually be little red tape to delay the fast completion of a building project, and that once finished there will be plenty of takers in space-starved Tokyo for the residences, offices or commercial units that are made available. Secondly, developers can (and do) wait for owners of desirable parcels to die so they can aquire the land from heirs. The key is a stiff inheritance tax, equal in many cases to more than 50 per cent of the value of the land and due in cash within one year. Especially in an inflated land market, this pretty much forces the heirs to part with their inherited land or to develop it themselves at high density. The tax, which seems to exist primarily to stimulate land development, can be so onerous that from time to time it leads heirs to commit suicide. Some of the biggest developers in the city are said to keep an eye on the age and health of owners of the real estate they want, so they can be ready to make an offer when the time comes. Still another mechanism, similar in its effect to the inheritance tax, is the *koteishisan*, the fixed property tax. Owners find that because of rising land values and encroachment by high-rent land uses, their tax assessments go up faster than their ability to pay; they are therefore sometimes forced to seek relief by selling their land to a builder.

There is at least one other force to be mentioned at this point as a major stimulus to the rampant land development that has been taking place in Tokyo's close-in neighborhoods: the activities of persons called *jiageya*.

The word is translated literally as 'land raisers', and refers to a special category of real-estate agents and land speculators who are especially adept at acquiring hard-to-get parcels for inner-city construction projects. Part businessman and part gangster, they number in their hundreds and comb the 'hot' neighborhoods of the city in search of older homes and small shops to buy, so the land can be converted to *manshon* or office buildings. In doing so, they prey on the misfortunes of the landowners who are caught in a bind by inheritance and property taxes, and employ a variety of tactics, both legal and illegal, to convince owners to part with land they would otherwise prefer to keep. This ranges from harassment, such as repeated telephone calls and personal visits, to various levels of threats and intimidation. In the worst cases, when an owner has been stubborn about keeping the land or holding out for an especially high price, *jiageya* have resorted to arson and violence. One occasionally reads stories in the press or sees 'human interest' pieces on the TV news about homeowners who fight back, either alone or in small organized groups of angry neighbors, attempting to stem the tide of high-density development around them (Gill, 1990). A typical result of such confrontations is that the person holding out is sooner or later surrounded by incompatible new construction, and becomes isolated both physically and socially in her or his own neighborhood (Figure 4.17).

However, one should not assume that the redevelopment of Tokyo's residential neighborhoods is only the work of outsiders. The inhabitants of the neighborhoods themselves are very much a part of this, and often make use of opportunities of their own to upgrade their properties and perhaps to derive some rental income. For many people, the increased value of their land provides a fund to borrow against for this purpose. The aging owner of a tiny neighborhood convenience shop, down the block from the newly opened high-rise that is the campus of the university where I work, is a case in point. Seeing an opportunity for himself in the change that nearly 2,000 students on his street represented, he demolished his shop and old-fashioned house, and built in their place a six-story, tile-faced building that from the outside is pretty much like any other mid-rise proliferating all over Tokyo. Its specific design, however, is tailor-made for the local situation: the street level is where the owner parks his car and maintains several vending machines for students to put money in; floors two to five are classrooms for rent to our overcrowded school (only two rooms per floor on this tiny parcel); the top floor is for his own residence, now much better-equipped and more comfortable than the drafty wooden house he had before. Some of the other neighbors are not particularly happy to see this, because they would have preferred to keep the area as a quiet district of single houses. However, they accept the higher density as the ineluctable trend of Tokyo and an inevitable consequence of being in a close-in location, as people all over the city have learned to do.

Another example of indigenous redevelopment, but one with a different twist, concerns my former neighbors, Tamura-san, the *tatami* maker, and

Figure 4.17 A neighborhood of tightly-packed single houses is giving way to the construction of mid-rise apartments and *manshon*, seen at the top left. The tall chimney in the center marks the neighborhood's *sentō*, the public bath house. This is Aoyama in Minato Ward

his family. In the year since my family and I moved away, the Tamuras have torn down the old building that housed their workshop and residence, and replaced it with a substantially bigger structure that typifies in still other ways the new Tokyo. It is a bright, clean building covered with the same highly practical, washable white-brick tile that now covers so many other new buildings. It is made entirely of standardized parts (same doors, same windows, same balcony railings, same rain gutters) that are seen all over the city and come from builders' catalogues. The street floor is still a workshop, but now with air-conditioning and a better parking space for the pickup truck, and the family lives on the floor above. A rooftop deck provides additional space, for laundry drying and childrens' play. To make it all affordable, there is a third floor to the building as well, one floor more than the old house. It is rented to friends, but after a few years it might be where one of the Tamura children will live after marriage. Thus, the new house is a multi-generational building, similar in concept to those we saw earlier at the Shinjuku Rail-City Housing Display Grounds, and is of the type designed to solve the housing problems of young people in an over-priced city. Moreover, it will help to keep the family in place on the same land it has occupied for more than half a century.

Finally there are certain neighborhoods in the belt between the the city's commercial core and the residential ring that are exceptions, at least in part, to the intensification of land use experienced almost everywhere else. These are the super-rich areas that have had the power to exclude, at least from some streets, encroachment by taller buildings, incompatible land uses and hastily made *manshon*. There are no huge expanses of such territories, only bits and pieces among other nicer districts, especially in certain sections of Minato Ward, Shibuya Ward and other areas of the old *yamanote* district. In some cases fine old houses remain, but more typically the landscape is of large modern houses along quiet, tree-lined streets, and private gardens that show just a little from behind the seclusion of walls and impressive gates. Some of the houses, for example some that have been pointed out to me in Jingūmae and Minami-Aoyama near the trendy Omote Sandō area, belong to movie stars and popular singers. Others are where rich industrialists, financiers, land developers, politicians and others at the top of Japan's economic hierarchy live. One commonly sees black Nissan Presidents, Japan's limousine of choice, on these streets and on the streets of other nearby high-status districts.

Certain sections of this 'rich side of town' are known for their large populations of foreigners, especially highly placed business executives, ambassadors, top diplomats and other VIPs. This is particularly true for Hiroo and Minami Azabu in Minato Ward, both areas with numerous embassies and foreign diplomatic missions that are sometimes referred to as gilded ghettos for foreigners. In addition to the large single houses in these neighborhoods, there are also numerous fancy, Western-style apartments called *homat*. These are multi-story buildings developed especially to meet the residential needs of the city's growing number of foreigners with generous housing allowances from the embassies or corporations that employ them. They stand out for the comparatively large number and oversized proportions of their rooms, the attractive landscaping of their grounds and monthly rents in the range of several thousands of dollars.

Historic preservation

Because of the terrible destruction that Tokyo experienced twice this century and the thorough makeover by the real-estate industry that the city is now undergoing, there is very little historic urban fabric immediately visible. Almost all the city is comparatively new, having been built since World War II; the few districts that pre-date both present-day reconstruction and the bombing tend to be only a little older. Many of the oldest intact neighborhoods in Tokyo date back only to the rebuilding that took place after the 1923 earthquake. There are only bits and pieces of the city that pre-date that tragedy, and certainly no 'old town', such as many other cities have, that would give visitors and local residents alike a feel of the 19th century or earlier city. The only place to see historic Edo is in a museum, specifically the Fukagawa Edo Museum in Kōtō Ward, where some old streets of *shitamachi* have been rebuilt for display, and in stage sets at movie and TV studios where the ubiquitous *samurai* dramas are filmed. For a look at old Japan, visitors are almost always steered to Kyoto, the historic capital purposefully spared the bombing, never to Tokyo. In fact, for many people Tokyo seems to be a city where history has been all but eradicated and that lives only in the present (Popham, 1985).

It is tempting to joke that any essay about historic preservation in Tokyo would be extremely short. However, the topic is much more complex than it seems at first, and deserves careful attention. For one thing, there are, in fact, a number of significant older structures that have somehow survived all the convulsions that have befallen the city and that are properly counted as important historic landmarks. This includes sections of the fortifications (walls and moats) of Edo Castle, several prominent temples from the Edo era (rebuilt with new materials since World War II, sometimes as a matter of course to keep them looking fresh and new), and various Meiji buildings related to government, commerce and higher education. The red-brick Tokyo Station building, completed in 1914, is a prime example of a surviving landmark. Despite recurrent attempts by developers to put up high-rises on the site, the station building stands in the middle of the CBD's financial and corporate headquarters nucleus as a rare relic of the craze for Western European architecture that gripped Japan during its time of modernization. However, because of damage from the war it is missing its upper two floors and its once-prominent cupolas. A grassroots group with the wonderfully descriptive name 'Group of Citizens Who Love the Red Brick Tokyo Station' is given much of the credit for staving off the most recent threat to the building's existence, expressed most forcefully during 1987–8 by high-risers representing, among others, the powerful Mitsubishi trust (Fujimoto, 1987).

There are also many other examples of historic preservation. In some of the older neighborhoods there is a small but discernible trend for citizens to restore old houses and shops, and to use them in preference to having new constructions. In some locations there is active support for this by the Tokyo government, which itself is becoming increasingly interested in promoting the historic ambience of specific districts. A current publication from the planning office promises that 'efforts will be made to preserve at least the facades of historical and traditional buildings as they are remodeled', and that 'Historical and Cultural Promenades will be built to link moats, shrines and temples, gardens and slopes' (Tokyo Metropolitan Government, 1990, p. 90). There are also more and more fights between citizens and developers in Tokyo about the latter's plans to demolish old structures. This is especially the case in certain sections of *shitamachi*, the old low city, that are close to an expanding CBD. For more than two years, one of the most interesting conflicts has been about plans to put in a parking lot for as many as 2,000 cars under a pond in an historic temple setting called Shinobazu Pond (Figure 4.18). The project is promoted by store owners in the nearby commercial center of Ueno, as well as by Taito

Figure 4.18 Shinobazu Pond in Ueno Park. (Courtesy of the artist, Kiritani Itsuo)

Ward, but opposed by a coalition of several citizens groups (eg. 'The Society of the Lovers of Shinobazu Pond') who argue convincingly that development will destroy the water table and do away with the currently thriving and abundant plant and animal life (Ma, 1989; Symposium Executive Committee, 1990).

A second reason for having a look at historical preservation in Tokyo is that there is a rather unsual twist to it. Because the city has learned by experience that none of its buildings can have a long life expectancy, it has adopted a perspective on historic preservation that invests little emotional stock in what is built on the surface, and instead concentrates its genuflections to history on *sites*, even if those sites are empty or covered with something new. We saw an example of this in our orientation to Tokyo when we looked at Shiba Koen, the park that contains Tokyo Tower. This is the place that, in addition to the tower, has two bowling alleys, a huge golf range and various other uses with no relevance whatsoever to the past, even though the ground is best remembered as the burial place for shoguns and the site of historic temples. Even more to the point is the Imperial Palace compound. This is the symbolic center of the city and covers more than 100 hectares, but has no castle or old palace. The emperor lives in a new (1964) building, scaled-down in size to reflect the diminished status given to the position after World War II, but the grounds around him are deeply revered for what they once represented. Not only is the area inviolate to developers, even though the world's most expensive urban land is right next door, it is extremely private and almost totally inaccessible to the public.[4]

Many other aspects of central Tokyo reflect the city's past even though the surface is all new buildings and other changes. The best example is the physical layout of the CBD and other older-developed districts. It is not just that the center is given to what little is left of the Edo Castle complex. We also see that the pattern of streets and major roads, as well as other infrastructure, has been carried over from Edo and is everywhere in evidence as the sub-stratum for today's urban form. With a little imagination, from the high perspective of Tokyo Tower, we can still make out the old clockwise spiral that characterized the shape of Edo amid today's tall buildings and car-choked streets. Most of the moats that formed the spiral have long since been paved over and the retaining walls dismantled, but there are just enough remnants in place to make it possible to extrapolate and visualize the bigger complex that existed more than two centuries ago. Moreover, if we consult a plan of old Edo as we look at the modern city, we see that expressways in the CBD and other wide roads follow the courses of former moats and canals almost exactly (Jinnai, 1988, p. 13). We can also see that certain key intersections and important bridges near the approaches to the modern CBD correspond precisely to the distribution of old gates along the outer perimeter of Edo's defensive spiral.

[4] There is more detail about the Imperial Palace compound in the next chapter.

It seems ironic that we should look for expressways and other busy roads to see the form of the old city amid central Tokyo's many thousands of new buildings. Yet that is just what we do, because the configuration of these thoroughfares follows the moats and canals that shaped Edo during the time of the shoguns. What is more, we can still see some of the old Edo waterways hidden beneath today's modern highways. In some cases, the canals of *shitamachi* have been transformed into little more than storm sewers beneath pavements, but they are there nevertheless and follow ancient courses. Better-known examples are the several 'rivers' that flow through the central city below street level within concrete embankments, and that have along their lengths above them expressways or other roads supported on thick concrete pillars. These are waterways with little light and virtually no aesthetic appeal, but they do carry away rainwater and, in some cases, provide limited transportation functions. The scene of the underside of a modern highway covering over what could otherwise be a charming central city watercourse is one of the most frequently cited examples of environmental degradation in modern Tokyo (Jinnai, 1987, pp. 26–8) and unambiguous evidence of the city's pressing lack of space. However, it is also a reminder that 'the structure of old Edo survives as the substructure of modern Tokyo', and that modernization of the city has involved little more than a substitution of one urban component for another within a stable configuration (Jinnai, 1987, p. 24).

Perhaps the most striking specific example of the survival of older aspects of Tokyo beneath the hubbub of the modern city is at Nihombashi, where the famous 'Japan Bridge' crosses an old watercourse now called the Nihombashi River. The orginal bridge, which was put up in 1603 under orders from Ieyasu, was the nucleus of Edo's first commerce and the symbolic starting point for journeys to all parts of Japan. It is long since gone. The present structure – a European Renaissance-style span erected in 1910–11 during the height of the Meiji's fascination with Western architecture – is a beautiful structure that graced the CBD in the early part of this century and blended with stately buildings that lined the river and reflected in its waters. It was repaired after damage from the 1923 Great Kantō Earthquake and the 1945 bombing, and is one of the oldest structures still standing in the CBD. However, in the early 1960s, in the rush to prepare Tokyo for the 1964 Summer Olympic Games, the Number 4 Loop Line of the Shuto Expressway was put in over the Nihombashi River, and the bridge was all but obliterated. It still carries a lot of traffic, as it is part of the busy Chūō-dōri, an important thoroughfare crossing the heart of the CBD, but in terms of view it is clearly subservient to the newer road above (Figure 4.19).

Visitors have grumbled that Nihombashi Bridge is almost impossible to photograph well because of obstructions and poor lighting; they express displeasure that authorities should have allowed such desecration of a significant landmark. The response to such critics is that the landmark *is* there, intact, and a working part of Tokyo. Nowadays, instead of fish-

Figure 4.19 The historic bridge at Nihombashi and the expressway above

mongers and *samurai* processions, the bridge is crossed by salarymen in dark business suits and office ladies in the required company uniforms, as well as by taxis and private cars. However, this in itself is a meaningful continuity: despite the time that has passed, and despite the fact that the present structure is not the original bridge, the traffic at the Nihombashi Bridge site still reflects the main business of the contemporaneous city. In this way, the bridge is another example of how, in central Tokyo, the present is played out on foundations that were laid down in the past.

Other historic preservation

Another way that the past survives in central Tokyo is through the proper names that have been given to various locations such as neighborhood-scale sub-districts, important streets and numerous train and subway stations. It might appear at first that this is a trivial detail, not substantially different from what happens in the many other cities that employ historic toponymy. But place names take on special importance in Tokyo, first because the city has an unusual lack of more tangible links to its past; and secondly because place names in Japanese are typically highly descriptive and unusually effective in conveying messages such as lessons about the past. Thus, some names in central Tokyo remind citizens about the characteristics of the natural environment before urbanization; others honor specific individuals who played significant roles in the city's early growth; while still other names recall the layout of the old city and the origins or economic functions of particular sub-sections. Examples from each of these categories are listed in Table 4.9. We can imagine, therefore, that a worker in the Tokyo CBD might commute from home on the Marunouchi ('within the circle of moats') subway line, get out at Ōtemachi Station (named after a main gate to Edo Castle) and walk a short distance along Eitaidōri (a less geographical word that means 'Eternal Ages Street' but that is also the name of an historic bridge) to an office tower on Sotoboridōri ('Outer Moat Street') in an area called Yaesu, a sub-district of the CBD named after a ship-wrecked Dutch sailor, Jan Joosten (Japanese pronounced his name 'Yayosu') who lived in Edo during the time of the first shogun.

The past is also visible in contemporary Tokyo in the design of many special 'touches' that are added to new buildings and other redevelopment sites precisely to create historic ambiance. This is something that Sugiura, a Tokyo geographer, referred to as 'the urbanization of nostalgia'. As a

Table 4.9 Selected historic place names in Central Tokyo

Chūō Ward:	
Ginza	place of the silver mint
Irifune	ship's entrance
Horidome	place where the moat ends
Kayabachō	place where miscanthus (used for roof thatch) grows
Koamichō	place for drying fishing nets
Kyōbashi	the capital bridge
Nihombashi	Japan bridge
Ningyochō	place where there are doll shops
Tsukiji	reclaimed land
Tsukudajima	an island with cultivated rice fields
Yaesu	a mutation or Yayosu, the Japanese name of the Dutch sailor Jan Joosten
Chiyoda Ward:	
Daikanchō	place where government officials live
Fujimichō	place with a view of Mt. Fuji
Kajichō	place of ironsmiths
Kasumigaseki	barrier of mist
Konyachō	place where there are dyers
Hanaokachō	place where there is a hill with flowers
Nagatachō	place where Nagata family resides
Ōtemachi	the place in front of Ōte gate to Edo Castle
Minato Ward:	
Akasaka-Mitsuke	'red slope watchtower' or 'approach to the castle'
Aoyama	taken from a family name of a *samurai* who lived there
Azabu	a combination of 'flax' (*asa*) and 'cloth' (*bu*)
Enokizakachō	place with a slope planted with hackberry
Ipponmatsu	one big pine tree
Roppongi	six trees
Toranomon	tiger gate

Figure 4.20 The police box at Sukiyabashi Crossing. The Seibu Department Store is in the background

specific example, he described a current trend to incorporate homey, country-style restaurants, often clearly associated with one of the mountain provinces in Japan and sometimes having thatched roofs and other 'authentic' decor, into the bowels of giant office towers and other megastructures. This is to create a 'world of make-believe . . . right underneath the concrete jungle', to remind modern Tokyoites of their rural or small-town origins and give them an escape, albeit if only for an occasional meal like mother's, from the fast-changing, giant metropolis in which they work. He counted 343 such restaurants listed in telephone directories, more than one-half of them in the CBD and most of the rest in other parts of inner Tokyo with extensive redevelopment (Sugiura, 1987, quotation from p. 14).

Another example of new urban landscaping that recalls the past is the core of Ginza. An area of several blocks has recently been redecorated in a fashion suggesting themes from both the famous Ginza Brick Quarter and the high-life in the CBD during the Taishō era: simulated historic street lamps, brick sidewalk pavements and street signs, and rows of willow trees along the side streets. In addition, some of the police boxes (kōban) in the area have been refurbished in historic-looking fashion. They are made of brick and have the same Victorian-style design that was popular along the main street of this business district during the Meiji. In fact, there are at least two police boxes shaped like the cupolas lost in 1945 to Tokyo Station. The same is also true for public toilets in this neighborhood.

An especially well-known police box at the busy Sukiyabashi Crossing between Ginza and Yūrakuchō is a well-known and much photographed example (Figure 4.20). While it is an extremely tiny building in comparison to the modern megastructures of steel, glass and neon that surround it – the huge Hankyū and Yurakuchō Seibu Department Stores, the Sony Building and others – it occupies a prime site in this setting and is just as much a landmark as the other buildings. There is something extremely telling about its relative proportions and its spatial relationships: the historic building, such as it is, is small and clearly inferior to the main business of Ginza (which is selling). But it is in the middle, and all the other buildings, big and impressive as they are, have to gather around it to compete for the passing pedestrians. This is elemental Tokyo: huge, new, showy and rich, but underneath is a nucleus, however small, that in one way or another binds what is on the surface to the past.

5
Epitome districts

Epitome districts: an introduction

Tokyo is so many different places, each with its own distinctive character, that it is impossible to cover all the city within the scope of one book. The best one can do is to write at least something about the most important places, and to be representative in making choices about which of all the other landmarks, neighborhoods, commercial centers and other types of places in the city to include. For this, I find the concept of 'epitome districts' to be extremely useful (See *Close-Up: How to Read the American City*, by Grady Clay). As the dictionary meaning of 'epitome' suggests, such districts are where 'one can see the bigger place in compression or in miniature'. In Clay's words, they are the 'special places in cities [that] carry huge layers of symbols [and] that have the capacity to pack up emotions, energy, or history into a small space' (Clay, 1973. p.38).

This chapter introduces a succession of epitome districts of different kinds in the Tokyo Metropolis. They are the places I need to write about in order to be representative and reasonably complete about the city. Some of them have already been introduced in the earlier chapters, but now require more detail; others will be mentioned for the first time. We begin with (1) the Imperial Palace, the traditional center of Tokyo epitomizing traditional and unchanging aspects of the city; and then cover, in order: (2) Shinjuku center, the emerging new center of business and municipal politics in Tokyo; (3) Shibuya and several nearby districts on Tokyo's west side that represent the youth and vigor of the city, as well as its considerable material wealth and proclivity for fun; (4) selected parts of the Sumida River wards, where we can see Tokyo hard at work behind the scenes, and where play is much more in line with traditional Japanese cultural patterns than in the trendy west side; (5) Sanya, a slum neighborhood somewhat hidden away in Tokyo and something of a secret that many Japanese prefer not to mention; and (6) a selection of 'suburban' localities in the the Tama district of Tokyo that collectively represent newer forms of living and working in the metropolis.

The Imperial Palace

Perhaps the most important of all the epitome districts in Tokyo is the very center of the city. This is the site where Edo Castle, the imposing fortress that accounted for the founding of the city almost exactly 400 years ago, once stood, and that is now the location of Japan's Imperial Palace. It is where we are reminded of Tokyo's history, and reflect on the persistence of tradition in the heart of an otherwise dynamic, fast-changing city. It is also one of the clearest examples of Tokyo as a unique city – a city that follows its own rules about how it should look and how its parts should be internally arranged (Figure 5.1).

The grounds of the Imperial Palace cover 110 hectares; they are much larger than required for just the emperor's residence and the Imperial Household Agency offices. Consequently, most of the land is empty, and given to forests, meadows and fields. There used to be a golf course there, too, because the previous emperor, Hirohito, took a liking to the game when he visited England as a young man in 1921, but for more than a half century it has reverted to nature and is habitat now for rabbits, pheasants

Figure 5.1 Posing for a class portrait in front of Nijūbashi, the famous bridge across a moat to the Imperial Palace

and other small creatures. Popham described this urban center as 'an enormous void . . . so vast [that] it seems to belong to a different city, perhaps a different civilization' (Popham, 1985, p. 93). The French anthropologist Roland Barthes was so astounded by this scene when he visited Tokyo more than a generation ago that he wrote it up in his now-famous book as Tokyo's 'empty center', a 'sacred nothing' around which this great and unusual city turns (Barthes, 1982, pp. 30–2).

Such a sizable undeveloped area would be remarkable in the center of any city, but there are a number of things that make this particular tract especially amazing. There is the incredible contrast between the emptiness of the palace grounds and the super crowded Central Business District immediately next door. This contrast is more profound than in other cities, even the case of Manhattan and Central Park, because in Tokyo the emptiness of the core is emptier and the crowdedness of the CBD is more crowded. There is simply no other place like this in the world. From Tokyo Tower, it appears like a huge dark-green island of trees and other vegetation (and a little bit of roof belonging to the emperor's residence) that sits idly amid a dense sea of high-rises and traffic that completely engulfs it. The two seem to have absolutely nothing to do with one another. There are no clear connections between them, such as by road, and no evidence of any movements by people or traffic. In fact, we see that the palace grounds are surrounded by walls and moats that as barriers are just as effective today as they were in the age of the shoguns more than a century ago. There is also an additional barrier in the form of a wide (nearly 100 meters), desolate plain of coarse gravel between the palace area and the main part of the CBD. It is usually unbearably hot in summer and bitterly cold and unprotected from the winds in winter, and is one of the most unpleasant places I have ever experienced. It is supposed to be a refuge from fire for CBD workers in the event of a disaster, but the more evident effect is to isolate the palace even more from the city, increasing the distance between the two environments.

The second characteristic that makes the Imperial Palace area highly unusual is that it is so intensely private. In most urban settings, the center is a highly public space where people gather for business or enjoyment or some other common function. In central Tokyo, however, the largest tract of land is reserved for the exclusive use of one man and his family; the public is almost totally excluded. The only exceptions are one section of the palace compound (the East Garden) that has been made accessible since 1968, and another area (Kitanomaru Park, where palace guards once lived) that has some museums and a pleasant picnic ground, open since 1969. Otherwise, the compound is completely closed. However, on two days each year, the day after New Year's Day and the emperor's birthday, the public is permitted to enter a portion of the preserve for a few minutes at a time and under the tightest security. I went in 1985, along with tens of thousands of Japanese and a sprinkling of other foreigners, and received New Year's

Figure 5.2 Looking over the vast, empty space that is the heart of Tokyo from the observation windows at the Kasumigaseki Building

greetings from Emperor Hirohito (or the Shōwa Emperor as he was renamed after he passed away.)

Another detail about the unusually private nature of the site is that there are not even many good places at the top of tall buildings nearby for visitors to get a good peek behind the walls. The only place of this kind that is listed in the guidebooks is the Kasumigaseki Building a few blocks to the south. It has a low-key observation level on the 36th floor that gives a panorama of the city and a view of roof-tops within the palace compound (Figure 5.2).[1] Office building workers in Marunouchi and other central districts can look out of their windows to see the palace, but I am told it is considered extremely impolite to peer too intensely into this private compound, so people rarely do. Moreover, out of respect for the privacy of the imperial family, the palace building is not often shown in photographs or on television, even when there is front-page news about the emperor.

Such deference is all the more remarkable given that Japan has changed so much in recent times, and that the role of the emperor has been significantly redefined since the defeat of the country in World War II. The imperial system is now a glaring anachronism that makes little practical

[1] Tokyo Tower, which is located farther south from the palace than the Kasumigaseki Building, offers a partial view only, because the Kasumigaseki Building blocks all but a little bit of the imperial residence.

sense for a modern country with a mostly democratic government. But it persists nevertheless, protected in the postwar constitution of 1947 as 'the symbol of the State and of the unity of the people'. While many citizens strongly object to having an emperor at all, many others are fiercely loyal to the idea, seeing it as an essential Japanese institution (Nishibe, 1989). The great outpouring of national grief that followed the recent death of Emperor Shōwa was testament to the latter. The sadness was recorded by news media from around the world during the elaborate funeral ceremony that took place some six weeks later. However, even as the solemnities were under way, video rental shops across the country reported record levels of transactions, as hundreds of thousands (or perhaps millions) of Japanese had apparently had their fill of uninterrupted TV coverage of emperor-related events and hired something else to watch.

The Imperial Palace tract is also especially interesting because it is such an obvious impediment to what might be called 'normal' urban development. The presence of such a large, empty area in the middle of a huge metropolis ignores the powerful economic imperatives about land values and violates most accepted tenets of urban land use planning. The land is simply too expensive and the CBD too starved of building sites to allow space to be given to the residence of a single family and its associated offices. Any sizable piece of the grounds that might be put up for sale would be worth untold *billions* to developers for offices, hotels, retailing or any other spillover of downtown land use. Moreover, city planners might like the opportunity to put the tract to some more 'rational' uses that would ameliorate crowding in Tokyo and reduce the growing problems of long-distance commuting. It would also be good to improve the flow of downtown traffic. Even though the Shuto Expressway, one of Tokyo's most important highways, has a carefully measured right-of-way through the northern margin of the palace area, the imperial tract as a whole is a major obstacle for roads, rail and subway lines that focus on downtown, and the cause of considerable congestion where traffic is forced to skirt around the perimeter of old walls and moats.

Because of such problems, it must be tempting sometimes for city planners to mentally remap the center of Tokyo without including the Imperial Palace grounds, or at least substantially to reduce the size of the tract. Such a fantasy might come from the constant frustration of having so many problems to solve on so little land. But it would be a fantasy only and a fleeting one at that. The imperial land is not for sale and it is unthinkable for most people in Japan that it ever would be. While the Tokyo that surrounds this core is as changeable as any urban scene can be, the core itself always remains intact. It has been nibbled away somewhat in modern times for a highway, a musuem, and some other public uses, but as a whole the place never changes. In fact, in kind of a magical way, it is still the site of Edo Castle – even though Edo Castle has been gone for centuries. Now the tract is identified with the Imperial Palace, but there is really no 'palace' there either. The famous building that was erected during Meiji was destroyed in the 1945 war; the present structure is a modern house completed in 1964. It is an ample structure, but it is unspectacular and unassuming, not so important in itself as a building. It is the site that is sacred, even if there is not much that is built on it; it is the site that is protected as the center of Tokyo.

A Japanese friend explained some of these ideas to me with great determination and every expectation that I, like so many other foreigners, would misunderstand. In the West, we attach special reverence to important buildings and often go to great pains to preserve them through the ages and to reconstruct them faithfully if they are damaged. But I am taught this isn't done so much in Tokyo, because Tokyo is so highly changeable. Instead, there is an intangible sub-stratum from history that is fixed forever, and that provides a base for all the changes swirling around it. Consequently, a different conception of Tokyo begins to take shape. The city is not 'empty' at the center, but is instead focused on a deeply solemn place filled with history and cultural meaning. Moreover, instead of the formlessness apparent at first sight from Tokyo Tower (or from other vantage points), one begins to see a city with a strong ground plan that focuses, in a unique way, on a highly prominent center. So, too, in complement to the view that Tokyo is constantly changing and redeveloping, and always building upward and outward, one sees that Tokyo is also a city that stays very much in place, confidently holding on to its past in some rather special ways.

Shinjuku: Tokyo's new center

The Imperial Palace will probably always remain the spiritual center of Tokyo; adjacent business districts such as Marunouchi and Nihombashi will probably always be thought of as the city's traditional centers of economic power. However, Shinjuku, located five to six kilometers west of this center, has recently emerged (especially since the 1960s) as a formidable commercial nucleus in its own right, laying legitimate claims to being the new principal center of the Tokyo Metropolis. Already, Shinjuku's main train station, Shinjuku Station, is far and away the busiest station in the city (and for that matter in the world), handling more than three million passengers each day. This is in comparison to the 0.7 million who pass through Tokyo Station. Other distinctions include having most of Tokyo's tallest buildings (see Table 2.4), being the city's number-one retailing center (as measured by number of stores and value of sales), and having one of Tokyo's biggest and best-known night-time entertainment districts. Shinjuku has also recently been designated the new location for the government center of Tokyo Metropolis.[2]

[2] I became keenly aware of Shinjuku's considerable importance when I lived nearby and walked each morning past its tallest skyscrapers to Shinjuku Station to catch an out-bound train to work. My walk was always against the flow of pedestrians

The new-found centrality of Shinjuku is part and parcel of a grand strategy in Tokyo, in effect now for over 20 years, to remake the city into what planners call a 'multi-nodal metropolis'. The idea is to relieve the CBD of some of its congestion and ease the burden of commuting for long-distance train riders by stimulating the growth of commercial centers closer to where Tokyoites live. This has been particularly so at key mass-transit interchanges between the residential periphery and the center.[3] Shinjuku has been a principal beneficiary of this planning because it lies at an especially important junction of passenger rail lines: it is where several crowded commuter lines, including the Chūō ('main' or 'central') Line of the Japan Railways system and the private Keiō and Odakyū Lines, come in from the fast-growing western suburbs and intersect with both the Yamanote Loop around the city center and the city's subway system. Other reasons for favoring Shinjuku include its reputation in the city as an alternative business center (eg. it was where many of the downtown's businesses were re-established after the 1923 earthquake, as well as the site of the city's largest black market during the time of postwar shortages), and the fortuitous presence of a substantial redevelopment site close to the station (an outmoded water filtration plant) that was available for new building projects (Sode, 1987, pp. 119–70).

The principal showpiece of the new Shinjuku is a prominent cluster of about 15 high-rises, most of them around 50 stories, formally called the New Shinjuku City Center (*Shin Toshin Shinjuku*), or simply *Nishi Shinjuku*. As the name implies, it is on the west side of Shinjuku Station (*nishi* means 'west'). It is an on-going redevelopment project, publicly announced in June 1960, covering the 107 hectares of the old waterworks and several of the adjacent blocks. Its core is a carefully laid out arrangement of office towers and international hotels interspersed with straight, wide streets, sheltered pedestrian concourses and various combinations of public plazas, enclosed shopping malls, fountains, sculptures and landscapers' greenery. There is also a sizable park called Shinjuku Chūō Kōen, Shinjuku Central Park (Figure 5.3). The first high-rise building was the Keiō Plaza Hotel, completed in 1971. Other important structures include the Shinjuku Sumitomo Building, the Shinjuku Mitsui Building, the Yasuda Fire and Marine Insurance Company head office, the Shinjuku Nomura Building, the Shinjuku Center Building and the Century-Hyatt, Hilton and Washington Hotels, all opened in the 1970s and 1980s. This is the area I described in the introduction as being Tokyo's answer to Manhattan's skyline. Because it is often shown in film and television as the setting for big-city detective adventures and other dramas, and the backdrop for commercial advertising

---

on their way to their jobs and, therefore, exceedingly difficult. Every sidewalk in the vicinity of the station was a river of humanity rushing toward me, creating a din of footsteps. I always had to thread my way carefully against the relentless current to avoid collision.

[3] Other aspects of this scheme, in addition to those that concern Shinjuku specifically, are discussed in Chapter 6.

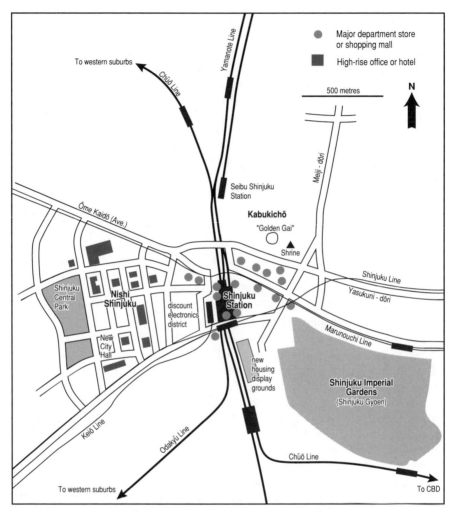

Figure 5.3 Shinjuku Center location map

for various 'urban-sophisticated' consumer products (eg. cigarettes, whis-
key and luxury cars), the Shinjuku skyline is one of the most widely
recognized places in Japan.

The New City Hall for Tokyo is scheduled to open in Nishi Shinjuku in
March 1991. The decision to relocate it to this district has been a pet
project of Governor Suzuki Shunichi, and is in itself a telling indicator of
the rising importance of the area. Its purpose is to bring the center of
government closer to the geographical center of population, and to do
away with overcrowded and exceptionally unimpressive city administration
offices in Marunouchi. The design, by Tange Kenzō, the architect who
designed the City Hall that is being abandoned (and who, therefore, has
been given a rare chance to redeem himself), promises to make the New

Figure 5.4 The familiar skyline of Shinjuku as seen from the children's playground in Shinjuku Central Park. The construction cranes in the center are from an early stage of City Hall construction

City Hall not only the number-one landmark in Nishi Shinjuku, but also an especially widely known international symbol of Tokyo itself, perhaps on the same level as Tokyo Tower. The project is on a prominent site overlooking Chūō Kōen, facing the city's sprawling western suburbs, and consists of three buildings: two massive skyscrapers with distinctive shape and texture and a lower semi-circular assembly building that opens on to a public plaza (see again Figure 1.1). The taller tower, the so-called Number One Building, will rise to 243 meters and be the tallest building in the city. Needless to say, there has been considerable hype about the New City Hall, and lots of notice that on the 400th anniversary of its founding, Tokyo will have both a new symbolic landmark and a new center. Because the New City Hall is planned as a state-of-the-art, high-technology construction, promotional literature proclaims the complex will launch Tokyo 'toward the 21st century and beyond' (Tokyo Metropolitan Government, 1989, p. 74).

The carefully arranged landscape of the redevelopment area in Nishi Shinjuku contrasts sharply with other parts of the commercial center. This is particularly so for several of the blocks closest to the station on the west side and for just about all of Shinjuku's large east side. This is where Shinjuku displays the dazzling side of Tokyo's capitalism: a world of lights and flashing neon of every shape and color; of giant billboards and multi-story advertising banners; of commercial jingles blaring non-stop from electronic loudspeakers; of hard-sell claims about 'low, low prices' from touts with megaphones; and of every type, size and fashion of store, restaurant or bar and other commercial establishment imaginable. This is Tokyo's main shopping area, now larger than Ginza and the other commercial nodes of the CBD, larger than all the other giant shopping centers scattered in all directions around the metropolis. Comparative statistics are hard to come by, but it seems that the east side of Shinjuku Station alone does more retail trade than number-two ranking Ginza (41.5 billion yen in the east side of Shinjuku Station versus 38.7 billion yen in Ginza in 1985), that Shinjuku's west side is fourth in the metropolis (25.4 billion yen), and that the two 'halves' of Shinjuku combined are pulling away from the competition and becoming ever more dominant (Fukuda, 1990, p. 21).

One of the biggest concentrations of commercial activity in Shinjuku is right at the station itself. This is a location pattern typical of several other rail-oriented business centers in Tokyo (and in other large Japanese cities, too), and stems from the tendency of huge department stores to build right in to the station buildings themselves because they also own the rail lines (Hattori, et al., 1980). In Shinjuku the specific examples are the Keiō and Odakyū Department Stores on the west side of the station. They rise several stories above track and street levels, looming like the lords and masters they are over the entire west exit area. Their rail lines, the Keiō and Odakyū Lines, extend west to the suburbs and bring commuters and shoppers directly to the entrances of the stores. Because this has been such a cushy business arrangement for them, both stores have been able to expand to nearby parcels where they have built branch stores and other types of shopping centers.

A second major concentration of commerce is the massive east side of Shinjuku Station, especially along Shinjuku-dōri, a former streetcar corridor now the main avenue from Shinjuku to the center of the city. This is the historic core of the neighborhood, the place where its business began to expand when the train station opened in 1885, and the section of Shinjuku that prospered most greatly after the 1923 earthquake because of devastation to the CBD. Descendants of some of the earliest shops are still there: eg. the famous Takano fruit parlor-cum-shopping center that grew from Takano Kichitarō's fruit stand of 1885; and the huge and equally well-known Kinokuniya book store that began about the same time as a roadside charcoal shop (Waley, 1988a, p. 14). There are also a great many newer businesses, including several of Tokyo's largest camera and electronics emporiums, and a seemingly endless array of clothing boutiques, accessory shops and other fashion outlets. The famous Mitsukoshi department store, a branch of the one on Chūō-dōri in Ginza (see Chapter 4) is also here, having come in after the earthquake. So, too, there is Isetan, a huge department store and major landowner in east Shinjuku that is across the street.

Both of these establishments have art galleries and museums on their upper floors, and are considered to be centers of high culture as well as major retailers. A large part of their routines includes cultural programming during the day, as well as opportunities for shopping for prosperous house-wives from the residential neighborhoods served by Shinjuku's train lines. On most Sundays, traditionally the busiest shopping day in Japan, Shinjuku-dōri is closed to vehicular traffic and given over to pedestrians.[4] From about noon until dinner time it is jammed with families spending their one day of the week together among the shops, with young couples and older couples, and with hordes of fashion-minded teenagers and college students.

The area close to Shinjuku Station, both west and east of the tracks, is also the site of a great many restaurants, coffee shops and other types of eating and drinking establishments. This is in response to the considerable pedestrian volume the station generates. It also reflects a natural symbiosis between these establishments and the other business functions of Shinjuku. Many of the restaurants open early and serve breakfasts to the first arrivals in Shinjuku, the so-called *asagata ningen* or 'early morning crowd'. These are people who prefer to get a jump on the day at work or who will soon be opening the stores in the surroundings, as well as those who prefer to commute before the trains overfill. It is not uncommon to see individuals in the latter group dozing behind a newspaper in a breakfast restaurant. For many other restaurants the main source of business is lunch, either to workers or those who have come to Shinjuku to shop or go to a movie in one of the local theaters. Still other places do big business delivering meals to workers who are too busy to leave their offices.[5] All over Shinjuku and other commercial centers, one sees small motorbikes specially equipped on the back with carrying devices for food, most notably for bowls of noodles. A special category of establishments, generally called *kissaten*, serves coffee or tea and daytime snacks to customers who use them as venues for business meetings or other appointments (such as those built around shopping out-ings), or for a quiet rest. There are many reasons for the popularity of *kissaten*, including overcrowding or lack of privacy in offices, and con-venience to the train stations that bring the different parties in for a business appointment or personal meeting together.

Still another category of restaurants is busiest at the end of the day when people go out for dinner and drinks. Many of them are especially set up for groups. This is because a large fraction of the trade comes from the common practice in Japan of co-workers going out together *en masse* after the office closes (Forbis, 1975, p. 75), as well as to cater to other kinds of groups (eg. reunions from schools and clubs), that come together from time to time at convenient transit centers and then go out to eat and drink.

---

[4] This is done also in Ginza and many other of the biggest shopping districts in Tokyo and other Japanese cities.
[5] I know of a McDonald's restaurant in Shinjuku that has a fax machine to take orders from workers who can't leave their offices for a meal.

Epitome districts

There is a place in front of a major exit of Shinjuku Station, the entry to a multi-level shopping center called Studio Alta, that is especially well-known as a staging area for groups (and couples, too) who arrange to meet for a night out in Shinjuku. On any given evening there may be well over 100,000 individuals enjoying the bars and restaurants of this neighborhood. The reason that so many people can fit into Shinjuku (to answer what would be a perfectly reasonable question, given the numbers involved) is that much of the restaurant business, here and elsewhere in Tokyo, is arranged vertically, often in tall, slender buildings containing nothing other than places for food and drink. Starting from two levels below ground, and then rising six, eight or even more levels above, a given building might have 20 or more eating places inside. Typically, there is a long neon sign that runs along the outside, top to bottom, listing the establishments inside floor by floor. One place in Shinjuku, a building called Ichibankan, is described in Popham's book as being typical of the new commercial architecture. It is all bars, 49 of them, on its eight floors (Popham, 1985, pp. 110–11).

Kabukichō

There is one sub-district of Shinjuku that is more popular than all the others for nightlife. This is Kabukichō, named after a *kabuki* theater that was once planned there but never built. Located a few minutes walk north and east of the station, it is itself an 'epitome district' that speaks volumes about how Tokyo works and about the intricacies of certain aspects of Japanese society. To put it simply, here is a place that is much more than just the largest and bawdiest entertainment district in the city; it is a gigantic fantasyland for adults, a total escape, if only for a few minutes or hours, for the tens of thousands who enter on a given day, from all the ills and oppressions that surround them (Nakawa et al., 1989, p. 26). It is most famous for its several hundred sex businesses: hostess clubs, strip shows, peep-show parlors, 'no-panties coffee shops', pornography shops and massage parlors the Japanese now call 'soaplands'[6]. A lot of what goes on is just downright kinky (Van Hook, 1989). Prostitution has been illegal since 1957, but it thrives in this setting nonetheless. There are also a great many 'legitimate' diversions: restaurants and bars with every kind of cuisine and decor imaginable, movie houses, bowling alleys, video arcades, *pachinko* (a type of pinball) parlors and *karaoke* clubs. They are no less important in the overall activity of the area and attract a varied clientèle that includes women, students and others, in addition to carousing salarymen. Nevertheless, for many Tokyoites, perhaps the uncounted thousands and thousands who wouldn't set foot there because of the first reputation of

[6] The massage parlors used to be called *toruko-buro* ('Turkish baths') until complaints from a Turkish student in Tokyo and the Turkish embassy led to the new name.

Kabukichō, the place is not an escape from problems at all; it is one of the problems. For them, and for some of the Westerners who have observed the scene (Levin, 1986; Pons, 1984), Kabukichō represents some of the worst of Japan: rampant exploitation of women, Japanese and foreign, as well as such widespread problems as excessive drunkenness, gambling and gangsterism.

The busiest time in Kabukichō begins at dusk when the lights go on and the streets come aglow with neon. Huge crowds of customers, just released from work or school, cross Yasukuni-dōri, the broad, traffic-choked boulevard separating the district from the main part of Shinjuku, and descend on its more than one thousand places of pleasure. They are beckoned by flashing signs of every shape and color, by tall columns of neon running the length of tall buildings and listing the names of pubs and eateries, by touts carrying signs and calling out invitations, by scantily-clad bar girls who appear in the doorways and smile at likely prospects, and by fantasy-land architecture ranging from bar and restaurant buildings shaped like medieval castles from Europe to a giant mechanical crab affixed to a seafood restaurant that claws at the attentions of passers-by. Even the Mister Donut shop, certainly one of the tamer establishments in the neighborhood, is inviting; it is a sleek post-modernist arrangement of glass and neon that is spacious and comfortable, and that fits through its decor all the glitter of the neighborhood. A special sub-section of Kabukichō, a place called Golden-gai, is a maze of some 240 tiny establishments, some no bigger than three or four bar stools, packed together in a quarter of a city block. The buildings are seedy and falling apart, and it is something of a wonder that they have not been demolished in the face of the considerable rebuilding that has gone on in the surroundings. Perhaps it is because they appear to be in imminent danger of being urban-renewed away, and because they look dangerous, like the haunts of gangsters that TV is fond of portraying, that it has become a mark of prestige in the nightlife world of Tokyo to be welcome there and to have a seat among the regulars (Kennerdell, 1988).

Still another area, the secluded far side of Kabukichō, specializes in what are called love hotels. These are establishments that rent rooms by the hour. They cater for couples on dates and furtive office romances, and for married couples who might lack privacy in small houses or apartments. They are busy not just at night, but during the day, too, especially it seems during the Sunday afternoon leisure time that is so much a part of the Japanese routine of life. The architectural design of love hotel buildings and individual guest rooms emphasizes fantasy. Themes from foreign lands and past eras (eg. fairyland castles) are especially common (Pons, 1988, pp. 404–9). Figure 5.5 shows a good example from a similar sub-district in the Ikebukuro commercial center north of Shinjuku.

The history of Kabukichō is actually quite recent. It did not emerge as an entertainment area until after World War II, when a local residents' association proposed to establish it in its plan for rebuilding after the

Figure 5.5 A fanciful love hotel near Ikebukuro Station. The photo was taken in 1986; the site has since been redeveloped. The King Kong figure in the foreground is a popular device for calling attention to particular business establishments

bombing. This was in keeping with a long-standing tradition in Tokyo for having specialized quarters for pleasure, such as Asakusa and Yoshiwara, at key locations in the city (see Chapter 3). It was supposed to have been high-class (*kaori takai*) entertainment, including the kabuki theater that was never built, but it soon turned to sex. This was, in part, to satisfy US Occupation forces who were encamped nearby, and was, in part, the doing of gangsters (*yakuza*) who moved into the area and took over many of its establishments. At the same time, its cinemas showed the first European movies in Japan (the proverbial 'art film'), helping to make Kabukichō a favorite haunt for students and intellectuals. This was especially so during the radical 1960s (Waley, 1988a, p. 15). Nowadays, the place fits a new social ecology. It sits just off the busiest commuter interchange in the metropolis, a perfect location for after-work or after-school gatherings on the way home from the city. There are other places like it in Shibuya, Ikebukuro, Ueno, and the other train-station commercial centers around the edges of the central city, but they are not nearly as big nor so raunchy. What makes Kabukichō unique is its special appeal to salarymen from nearby office districts and the commuter routes that focus on Shinjuku. The gangsters are in firm control of the sex trade, the pinball arcades and many of the other businesses: they know exactly what thousands of routine-weary men are looking for.

Shibuya, Harajuku, and Roppongi: the 'good life' in Tokyo

If Shinjuku represents the new center of Tokyo and the world of the salaryman, then several other places on the west side of Tokyo represent the high-living consumer culture that has recently invaded Japan. We see this especially among the city's younger population: its great many high-school and college students, its students in special cram schools, its recent graduates and other school leavers and its growing numbers of *shinjinrui*, a commonly used word meaning 'new breed' that describes the city's highly conspicuous class of trend-loving 'young professionals'. Shibuya, Harajuku and Roppongi are especially popular haunts. These areas are within a few minutes of each other by car or train, and along with several other neighborhoods nearby, such as Aoyama, Hiroo and Azabu, comprise an extremely fashionable section of Tokyo. This is the core of the modern-day *yamanote*, the direct descendant of the privileged side of old Edo, and the spiritual capital for the many new high-status neighborhoods that have formed in the expanding west of the city (Gekkan Akurosu, 1987). For us they give insights to some of the 'good life' that Japan, and especially its capital city, is blessed with during this time of prosperity.

Shibuya is the largest. It is about three kilometers south of Shinjuku and is a similar gigantic commercial center that is focused around a huge, desperately overcrowded train station. Shibuya Station is one of the busiest stops along the Yamanote rail loop around the center of the city. Like Shinjuku Station, it is a major transfer point for commuters between the suburbs and the CBD, and a popular destination for thousands of workers, students, shoppers and others who disembark there each day and enter the surrounding neighborhood. As is typical of large, train-station-centered commercial districts in Japan, including Shinjuku, the spatial structure of Shibuya includes various specialized sub-districts: an area of department stores and other retailing; an area of banks and office buildings (but in this instance only one building that might accurately be called an office *tower*); several specialized areas of restaurants, coffee shops and other eating and drinking places; a large night-time entertainment zone (and some smaller ones); and a quiet district of love hotels. I have described this geographical arrangement in a detailed article about this neighborhood, and have included there a schematic model of a typical layout for a commuter-oriented commercial center (Cybriwsky, 1988a, especially p. 53). Figure 5.6 is a revision that I prefer.

The sub-district of Shibuya given to retailing is especially large and, if the rate of expansion of its leading stores is any indicator, extremely profitable. Two major department-store chains dominate the trade. One is the huge Tōkyū chain; the other is Seibu. In addition to the flagship stores, which themselves are opulent multi-level consumer showcases, they have, between them, at least 15 giant branch stores within a few blocks. During a recent construction boom, the two companies averaged two large new

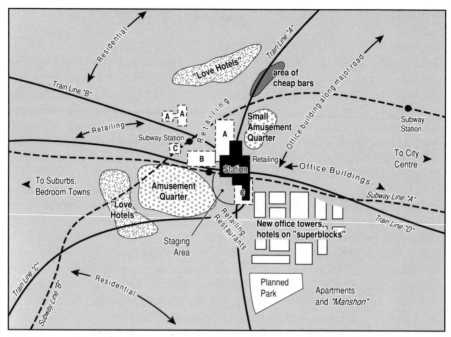

Figure 5.6 Model of typical train-station commercial district. The boxes A, B and C near the station represent department stores.

retailing buildings in Shibuya each year (Wade, 1988, p. 39). Some of the main Tōkyū holdings include fancy multi-level shopping malls, such as Tōkyū Plaza, 109, 109–2, One-oh-Nine, and One-oh-Nine–30s,[7] a large underground shopping concourse near the train station, and a huge 'do-it-yourself' and gadgets store called Tōkyū Hands. There is also a second gigantic department store, a branch, built directly into the train station. As in so many other big commercial centers in Japan, the rail lines that feed to its entrances are owned by the same parent company. These are the Tōkyū Shin-Tamagawa Line to the western suburbs and the Tōyoko Line to Yokohama. Seibu, on the other hand, which owns no Shibuya train lines (but which does own several train lines in other areas), is concentrated a bit further from the station. One of its branches, Seibu Seed, a megastructure large enough to be a flagship department store just about anywhere else, has a name that makes me picture an analogy between farm crops in the field and sprouting department stores.

What makes Shibuya particularly distinctive is that a disproportionately large fraction of users are young and apparently wealthy. According to one estimate, nearly 60 per cent of shoppers are under 30 (Mitsuoka, 1989, p. 18). They come after school or work and on their days off, in couples

[7] The unusual name for a store, 109 and its various derivations, comes from a play on the word Tōkyū: one meaning in Japanese for the sound *to* is 'ten' and for *kyū* is 'nine'.

or in groups, to shop, to hang around in the restaurants and coffee shops, and for movies, bowling, pool and many other amusements. Their numbers are so large, 100,000 or more on a typical evening, 250,000 on a busy Saturday night, and 250,000 again on Sunday afternoon, as to make this perhaps the single greatest gathering spot for high-school and college-aged youth in the world. One can't but be amazed by such numbers and the throngs they create at station exits, in the surrounding streets, in the shopping centers and in all the favorite nightspots and other establishments (Figure 5.7) Some streets, for example, the popular Spain-dōri with its many boutiques and accessory shops, get so crowded at times that they become, literally, wall-to-wall people. So, too, Hachiko Square, the sizable public plaza in front of Shibuya Station where people commonly wait near a statue of a faithful dog to meet their dates or other appointments before venturing into Shibuya, fills regularly to overflowing with thousands of arrivals (Katō, 1979; Sode, 1987). A relatively new development, one that has come in over the past two years or so and that itself reflects the increasing affluence enjoyed by younger generations, is the enormous night-time traffic jams on the streets in the vicinity of Shibuya Station because of thousands of junior and senior high-school and college students, collectively

Figure 5.7 A typical Sunday afternoon in the heart of Shibuya. The majority of shoppers are high-school and college aged. Shibuya Station and the Tōkyū Department Store are in the background

called *shibukajizoku,* who cruise around the area to show off their shiny new cars.[8]

I have spent a lot of time in Shibuya and got to know it quite well. Even so, I continue to be impressed with every visit by the enormous scale and incredible trendiness of its commercial activity, and by the obviously discretionary nature of what its many thousands of youthful shoppers spend considerable money on. I am especially astounded at the immediate attention to every new fashion in clothing and accessories one sees in Shibuya, and by the profusion of gadgets of all kinds that are for sale for the home, for recreation or travel and for countless other uses. So, too, I am impressed with the multitude of travel agencies. There is one at every turn, it seems, in every instance lined in front with tall racks of glossy brochures that promise fun in Okinawa, Hawaii, Australia, ski resorts in the Japanese Alps and other popular destinations. There are also dozens of different kinds of places to simply hang out and spend money: coffee shops, fast-food restaurants (there are more McDonald's outlets per unit area in Shibuya than anywhere else in the world) and video arcades. The conclusion one comes away with is that Japan's youth are lucky indeed, and that older generations, particularly the so-called *yake-ato no ha* ('the after the fire people') who had worked so hard and lived so austerely during the difficult postwar years, have handed over to their children and grandchildren quite a prize.[9]

If we go a short distance from Shibuya, north to the next neighborhood, Harajuku, we see even more evidence of a comfortable material existence. There, at the doorstep to the Meiji Shrine, the famous landmark memorial to the emperor whose reign is synonymous with Western influences and modernization in Japan, is yet another super-trendy area. Just as in Shibuya, some streets are as good as heaven for teeny-boppers. Takeshita-dōri is store after store with young fashions, costume jewelry and cute ('Hello Kitty!') accessories, as well as lots of hamburger and fries places and ice-cream shops. On Sundays in good weather, a broad boulevard in nearby Yoyogi Park is closed to traffic and youngsters take over completely with end-to-end rock-and-roll bands and throngs of energetic dancers moving in unison (Figure 5.8). Other sections of this district, such as along Omotes-andō-dōri, the landscaped boulevard built to make Tokyo impressive for the 1964 Olympics, rank among the top centers of high fashion in the world. There are fabulous boutiques (typically with fabulously high prices) all over this area, some in tall shopping-center buildings, others in cubby-hole shops on quiet side streets. There are also several of the most famous

[8] This is a new word and means 'casually dressed in Shibuya' ('Police Target "Shibukajizoku" Youths,' *Japan Times,* 5 March 1990, p. 2).
[9] Because I know many university students personally, I am also aware that a great many of those who hang out in Shibuya and similar places, and who wear such nice fashions, do so on the basis of their own money earned from part-time work. Moreover, even in this time of considerable prosperity in Japan, many struggle to pay expensive college fees.

Figure 5.8 The teeny-bopper rock-and-roll scene in Yoyogi Park near Harajuku Station. In good weather this is a Sunday afternoon ritual that involves thousands of youngsters

fashion designer studios and some outstanding art galleries. These are the places that you read about in shoppers' guides to Tokyo and in-flight magazines.

The nearby streets, once an unassuming residential area, are now highly desirable addresses, particularly for status-conscious young professionals. As in the other areas of Tokyo-style gentrification nearby, rents are astronomical and many of the living units small, but the surroundings boast great shops and nightspots. Partly because of its proximity to television and recording studios, this is the area where many of Japan's best-known screen personalities and music stars have chosen to live. A popular pastime for some of the many visitors who descend on Harajuku, especially on Sundays and holidays, is to try to spot a favorite actor or actress in the crowds or in a passing Mercedes or, as many teenage girls are wont to do, keep vigil in front of the home of an idolized singer. The back-street areas around Harajuku, such as the Jingūmae neighborhood, are also fine places to explore new trends in residential architecture. Even from the outside, one sees terrific examples of creative design and new ideas for the efficient use of crowded space.

Both Shibuya and Harajuku are also known for nightlife. Shibuya is especially crowded and appeals mostly to students. Its main entertainment district begins directly across the street from the station, and is entered through a symbolic gate or arch marked *Senta-dōri*, or Center Street. This is a common architectural device in urban Japan that signals passage into a world of play.[10] The entertainment district is large, almost as big as Kabukichō, and emphasizes food and drink, clubs that play popular music, concerts and movies, and the same video arcades and other amusements that stay busy during the day. As one might expect in a place where the numerical balance between students and salarymen is the reverse of that in Kabukichō, there is a lot less of the sex-for-money business in this area. However, there is just as much, if not more, public drunkenness. The going-home scene in time for the departure of the day's last trains from the station (around midnight) is especially unrestrained.

An even more famous place for nightlife is Roppongi. Located in the direction of the CBD from Shibuya and Harajuku, and not far from Tokyo Tower, this is Tokyo's premier section of trendy bars and fast-paced discos, and its liveliest district during the small hours when every other place has gone to sleep. It is an exceptionally popular haunt for some of the high-living 'glitterati' of Tokyo who can afford expensive clubs and who follow a personal time clock that departs wildly from the mainstream of the city. It is also a popular hang-out for many of the foreigners in Tokyo: well-heeled business travellers and diplomatic emissaries; the many fashion models from the US, Australia and Europe who find good work in Tokyo; US military personnel from nearby bases; and the various rock stars and other entertainers who come from abroad to perform in Japan. As such, it is something of a 'foreigners' ghetto', a sort of modern-day reincarnation of the old enclaves during Meiji where foreigners were kept and entertained. The Roppongi scene, both night and day, when the neighborhood is known for fashion boutiques, art galleries and some exceptionally nice lunch restaurants and coffee shops, is often glamorized in movies and on television. As a result, it enjoys a fashionable image among many Japanese, and is often thought of as being synonymous with the good life of the international jet set.

The other side of Tokyo

There is also an entirely different side to Tokyo. If instead of going west from the center, where most of the city's fashionable residential districts and business centers cluster and where there is the most growth, we go a short distance east or north to the vicinity of the Sumida River and its mouth, we come to what is left of *shitamachi*, Tokyo's old plebian section. It is more of a private and unassuming district than the flashy neighborhoods we have just left, but is very much alive nonetheless and fully an integral part of Tokyo. Because it has changed more slowly and taken some different directions than in other parts of the city, *shitamachi* is sometimes

[10] There is also a gate like this at a main entrance to Shinjuku's Kabukichō.

nostalgically referred to as 'the real Tokyo'. It is where many of the most traditional aspects of the city are visible, where there are fewer trappings of imported Western culture, and where an outsider in Japan, such as myself, stands out most sharply. There are also distinct contrasts in economic base, social characteristics of the Japanese population, physical conditions of the living environment and other considerations. We shall go there now not just to balance our view of the city, but also for fundamental lessons about what an important section of Tokyo is actually like. For our purposes, we can define the area to be visited as Arakawa, Taitō, Sumida and Kōtō Wards, and those portions of Chūō Ward that have not yet been incorporated into the expanded CBD.

Perhaps the most striking impression is that here is truly a part of the city given over to work. Other places are busy, too, in fact extremely so as we have seen in Marunouchi and other parts of the CBD and in the Shinjuku sub-center, but in this case much of the work is of a type that all those other centers depend on before they themselves can begin. I think of this area as being the foundation for the rest of the Tokyo economy. It is home to thousands of small and generally unheralded companies functioning at the broad base of the city's economic pyramid, supporting with their work the enterprises of big corporations above them and the routines of the city's more conspicuous districts. Among a hundred or more other distinctions, this is where many of the taxis and taxi drivers that serve the center of the city come from; the site of its largest produce market; the central place where fresh fish and other seafoods are sold and distributed; the district where many of the city's newspapers, magazines, business cards (*meishi*) and seemingly indispensible cheap comic books for commuters (*manga*) are printed; the factory zone where many of the cardboard boxes and wrapping papers are made that retailers, manufacturers and others in the city require for their businesses; and the place where a large fraction of the tissue packets are put together that advertisers press into your hands as you pass a busy train station or shopping center. There are also many warehouses and other storage facilities; wholesaling companies, transportation facilities such as bus and truck terminals, rail sidings and piers; dispatching centers for package delivery services; and a great many factories of all sizes, but mostly small.

A good example of the workaday rhythms of this area and the scale of its enterprises is seen at Tsukiji, a district in Chūō Ward at the mouth of the Sumida known for its huge fish market. Its name has been mentioned before as the site of a foreigners' compound in the 19th century. Now, however, it is *Tokyo no daidokoro*, 'Tokyo's pantry'. This is where some 14,000 restauranteurs, sushi chefs and retail fishmongers come each day to purchase their supplies of fish. They shop at one or other of 1,677 stalls, most of them tiny, family-run operations, competing fiercely for business within the confines of a centralized market the Tokyo government set up in 1935 (Bestor, 1989b, pp. 17–18). All night long, trucks with fresh seafood arrive from fishing ports all over Japan and from Narita Airport, the biggest fishing port of all, and unload their wares. Auctions start at 5:00 am. and are finished a short while later. The careful inspection of row after row of huge tuna by buyers who peer with flashlights inside deep incisions is something to see. Purchases are then taken by barrow to be cut and resold at one of the stalls, or to one of hundreds of trucks and vans that are double and triple parked to make deliveries to supermarkets and other retail outlets. Many purchasers pedal away on bicycles, headed for the sushi shops of Ginza, Shimbashi and other nearby districts with full styrofoam crates stacked one atop another and strapped precariously on the back. Much of the rest of the day is given to retailing. All told, some 65,000 people work in or visit the market each day (Bestor, 1989b, p. 18).

As we tour through the Sumida River wards, we see many other specialized districts providing important services or materials to the rest of Tokyo. Some of the most prominent examples include Kiba and Shin ('New') Kiba, two areas, one older and the other its planned replacement, of sawyers and lumberyards in Kōtō Ward; Kuramae in Taitō Ward, an area with some 300 wholesalers of toys and dolls (as well as fireworks) stretched out along a street called *gangu tonya-gai* (toy wholesale street); Bakurochō-Yokoyama, also in Taitō, Tokyo's *sen'i tonya-gai*, the principal textile wholesale street; Kappabashi (Taitō, too), a street where kitchen and restaurant supplies are sold, including the fantastic plastic replicas of everything from sushi to spaghetti to sundaes many city restaurants display in their windows as their menus; and Inarichō (Taitō Ward once again), a concentration of 50 or so shops selling Buddhist and Shinto household shrines. Not far away, but actually just within the boundaries of Chiyoda Ward, is the famous electronics wholesaling district called Akihabara. This is where tourists and natives alike descend on giant electronics emporiums for the best buys on cameras, video equipment, stereos and other products from Japan's well-known electronics and photo-equipment manufacturers. This area also has a dense maze of tight little alleyways in which electronics' parts and equipment such as wiring, transistors and various knobs, dials and circuit boards are sold. Nearby is what is left of the Kanda Market. This has been the largest wholesale produce market for the city, but it is now being relocated to modern facilities elsewhere. Its rhythms and traffic patterns are similar to those I described for Tsukiji Market.

The residential environment is also a sharp contrast with other parts of the city. It is hard to generalize, because there is a variety of neighborhoods, including several pleasant ones. However, on the whole, the housing stock of the Sumida River wards is older, lower in quality and more lacking in amenities than standards elsewhere. Greenery, open space and quiet are particularly lacking. Many neighborhoods are a mix of residential and non-residential uses; a large fraction of the population lives among factories, warehouses, parking lots, shopping streets and other non-residential neighbors. There are also many examples where people work at home. Small-scale industries such as printing shops, carpentry, metal stamping or the assembly of small parts in the front rooms of old houses that open right

Figure 5.9 One of the many thousands of small at-home workshops that comprise the broad base of Tokyo's manufacturing pyramid. This example is from Shioiri in Arakawa Ward. The proprietor is tooling small metal pieces for automobile window assemblies

on to the street are conspicuous (Figure 5.9). Many of these are family-run operations working under contract on a piecework basis for bigger companies. In some of the back streets of the Sumida area, small clusters of *nagaya* still stand. These are wooden tenement structures of a type that were once the principal dwelling form for commoners in old Edo. The original structures are all long gone, so what remains are survivors of the newer generations of these buildings, put up in the late 19th century and the early part of this century as workers' housing in factory zones. They were miserably crowded slums then, and now serve as reminders of the hard times that this part of the city has endured (Waley, 1989b).

Even some of the newer housing is not particularly attractive. I am thinking in particular about a type of multi-story apartment development called *danchi*. In the past some of these have been built by large employers to house their workers, but most of the latest projects are by the Tokyo Metropolitan Government and the Housing and Urban Development Public Corporation as part of their overall program to relieve the housing shortage for low- and moderate-income families. They are found in virtually every ward and town in the metropolis, and should not be identified solely with the Sumida area. However, *danchi* are especially numerous and visible in Kōtō Ward, particularly on newly reclaimed land close to Tokyo Bay where there are thousands of units. Some of the construction seems to be well-

Figure 5.10 The Shirage Higashi flood control project in Kōtō Ward. (Courtesy, Office of Information, Tokyo Metropolitan Government)

planned, but many other examples stand out because of the ugliness of their design, their isolation from other neighborhoods and basic facilities such as shopping and schools, and the small units inside. One public housing project in Kōtō Ward is part of a 'disaster prevention plan' for the Shirage Higashi neighborhood along the Sumida; it consists of a long row of 18 or 19 identical multi-story *danchi* arranged end-to-end and connected to each other to form an impregnable flood wall against the river (Figure 5.10).

The largest business center in the Sumida wards' area is Ueno. In many ways it is the equivalent of Shinjuku or Shibuya on the other side of the city: it has an overcrowded commuter station where several train and subway lines intersect; a busy retailing center with major department stores and the usual mix of fast-food restaurants and chain boutiques stores; a growing sub-section of banks and office buildings; a busy night-time entertainment zone; an area of love hotels, and so on. However, economically the place is also evidently a cut or two below the other centers. Like nearby Asakusa, the second biggest commercial center in the Sumida area, there is an expansive discount-shopping area reflecting both the lower income levels and higher proportions of older people among its clientèle. At Ueno, this area stretches beneath an elevated rail corridor. Instead of the overpriced trendy stores on Tokyo's west side, there are stalls with cheap imported clothing, imitations of popular brand names, discount cosmetics and toiletries, and various kinds of seconds and remainders. One street, Ameyayokochō, which runs alongside the tracks, is always especially crowded. It was one of the leading black-market centers during the desperate shortages of food and other necessities that plagued Japan after World War II; today it is a highly colorful and unusually noisy market in which sellers of fish, fruits, nuts and other foods, as well as other products such as golf clubs, shout out bargain prices and other sales pitches to passing customers.

For me, one of the clearest reminders that this part of the city differs profoundly from the more affluent west side comes from watching the passenger traffic at Ueno Station. While there are the usual commuters to the city center from outlying wards and suburbs, the station is also a major approach to Tokyo from farmlands and mountain provinces to the north and east; it counts among its many users a disproportionate number of poor job-seekers in the city, country folk on holiday, and farmers with produce to sell in city markets. In this way, Ueno Station resembles transportation centers I have seen in Third World capitals. In warm-weather months, for example, dozens of old women arrive to sell fresh vegetables directly to restaurants and other pre-arranged buyers in the city or at rented stalls in neighborhood commercial centers. They travel on early trains from Tochigi and Ibaraki prefectures and other rural locations, carrying huge baskets, bent over physically from a lifetime of hard work and dietary deficiencies. Sometimes they are called *gyōshōnin*, a generic word translated as 'itinerant peddler'. In winter, many of the passengers arriving at Ueno are seasonal laborers (mostly males), displaced from the north by ice and snow, who come to the capital to do construction work until it is time to prepare rice fields in the spring (Waley, 1984, p. 151.) Because of this, the Ueno area abounds with lower-cost hotels and rooming houses and cheap eateries. It is also one of the largest concentrations in Tokyo (and in Japan as a whole) of people who sleep in the streets. At all times of the year, there are 200 or more individuals who sleep in the corridors and stairways of the train station, in doorways, on benches and on cardboard in the bushes of Ueno Park.

That the Sumida River side of Tokyo is the lower status side of the city is clearly explained in the detailed case study of Arakawa Ward by Wagatsuma and DeVos (1980). Although they are careful to point out the charms and attractions of living in this district, as well they should, they emphasize that large parts of Arakawa Ward have negative connotations in Tokyo's public consciousness. This is particularly the case for some of the neighborhoods close to Minami Senju, an aging commercial center in eastern Arakawa on the city side of a key bridge across the Sumida. The reasons for this begin far back in the history of the district, when certain events took place that stained the reputation of the area in the thinking of pre-modern society, and that set in motion a succession of land-use decisions relating to Arakawa Ward that continue to taint the place today. As the authors refer to it, Arakawa's unkind fate has been to become 'a place of disposal'. This is particularly so in matters related to the disposal of corpses, an unavoidable task in any city and one that Arakawa has performed for Tokyo since early Edo times. There is a lot of superstition attached to this even today, so that for many Tokyoites the fact that Arakawa has the city's largest crematorium (at a site close to Machiya Station) is reason enough to be biased against the ward and its residents. It is particularly unfortunate for the ward's reputation that many people in the city, especially those from the west side, go there only for funeral services after the death of a relative or friend, and that cremation is what they think about whenever Arakawa or the Machiya neighborhood are mentioned.

The background to all this is fascinating. One of the first chapters concerns a temple near Minami Senju during the Tokugawa shogunate that came to be called the *Nagekomi-dera* ('the throw-in temple') or the *Muen-dera* ('the temple for the unrelated'). This is where the bodies of prostitutes from Yoshiwara were brought for cremation and burial. Because of a belief that a deceased prostitute would come back to haunt a person who treated her corpse with respect, the bodies were typically wrapped in straw, as was the custom for dead animals, and thrown in the yard of the temple where an already-tainted caste of workers would take over. Some people remember that the ashes of 10,000 prostitutes were buried in this way at a site in Arakawa Ward near the boundary with Taitō Ward. In the same vein, the area near Minami Senju was the principal execution ground during the shogunate of criminals and political opponents. This was done by beheading, crucifixion or burning. Many of the victims had their severed heads put on stakes for display. By 1868 more than 200,000 individuals had been disposed of in this way. At about the time the excecution site was established, another highlight of Arakawa's history, if highlight is the right word, took place: the decision in 1669 by more than 20 temples from closer to the center of the city to put up consolidated cremating facilities at Minami Senju. It was a logical site because it was then outside the limits of urban development and near the shogun's killing fields. Other crematoria soon followed, as did settlements of employees, almost all of whom were members of a feudal-era outcaste group called *hinin*. It was *hinin*, for example, who assisted with executions and took the bodies away for disposal.

The topic of outcaste groups in Japan, especially in contemporary society, is a delicate issue about which there are no official statistics and few people who are willing to talk. Yet it is well-known that so-called 'status discrimination' is still practised against the descendants of *hinin* and other outcaste groups, even though the individuals who were thus labelled were supposedly emancipated shortly after the modernization of Japan began in 1868 (Hane, 1982; Suginohara, 1982; Yoshino and Murakoshi, 1977). Although the problem is identified mostly with the Kansai region (Osaka and Kobe), it is also present in Arakawa, Taitō and other lower-status places of Tokyo. It is whispered that employees of the big crematorium

near Machiya include descendants of *hinin*, and that the residential population of Arakawa and Taitō Wards includes numerous descendants of
hinin and another outcaste group, an untouchable caste once called *eta*
('filth') but now more commonly referred to (but still in hushed tones) as
burakhumin ('the hamlet people'). The presence of this population is said
to explain the concentration of such industries in the Sumida Wards,
especially in the vicinity of Minami Senju and next to the crematorium, as
leather-working and rag- and scrap-picking. These are occupations traditionally assigned to the outcastes (Wagatsuma and DeVos, 1980, p. 215).

Yet another significant characteristic of this 'other side of Tokyo', is a
steady, long-term decline in population. This is in contrast to most other
wards (except the CBD) which gain in numbers and are exceedingly cramped
for space. The population of Arakawa Ward declined from 247,013 in 1970
to 198,126 in 1980, and to 190,061 in 1985. Trends for Taitō Ward and
Sumida Ward are similar (Table 5.1). Related to this is a high rate (by Tokyo
standards) of housing vacancy. For example, a 1983 housing survey shows
that in Arakawa Ward 10.9 per cent of all dwellings were unoccupied and
that in Taitō Ward it was 12.0 per cent (*Tokyo Statistical Yearbook, 1987*,
p. 174). This reflects the fact that many people move out of this part of the city
if they can afford it, and comparatively few young people move in, despite all
the housing pressures elsewhere. So the population is disproportionately
aged, another distinguishing characteristic of the Sumida wards area (see
Table 4.3). Such demographic trends have apparently so alarmed Taitō Ward
officials that they have recently instituted a possibly first-of-its-kind policy to
pay young newly-weds to live there. The offer, so far limited to 200 couples,
is for up to 50,000 yen per month in rent subsidies; it requires that neither
partner be over 40, the combined ages of the couple be under 70 and that the
income level of the household be less than 8 million yen annually (*Japan
Times*, 17 June 1990, p. 20).

Table 5.1 Recent population trends, Sumida River Wards versus West
Side Wards, 1970–1985

	1970	1980	1985
Sumida River Wards			
Arakawa Ward	247,013	198,126	190,061
Taitō Ward	240,769	186,048	176,804
Sumida Ward	281,237	232,796	229,986
Kōtō Ward	355,835	362,270	388,927
West Side Wards			
Shibuya Ward	274,491	247,035	242,442
Setagaya Ward	787,338	797,292	811,304
Suginami Ward	533,016	542,449	539,842
Nerima Ward	527,931	564,156	587,887
23 Wards Total	8,840,942	8,351,893	8,354,615

Source: Tokyo Statistical Yearbook, 1987, p. 24–35.

Epitome districts

Shitamachi nostalgia

I don't want to dwell too long on the negative. This is because still another distinguishing feature of the Sumida wards, one that deserves at least as much attention as each of the previous descriptions, is its rich cultural traditions. Indeed, this is the focus of the vast majority of its literature, be it written in Japanese, English or other languages. There is presently a revival of interest in national history and traditional culture among the public in Japan, as well as renewed interest in seeing and experiencing some of the city's older neighborhoods and historic centers. One indicator of this is the commercial success of the city's several new guidebooks that emphasize the historic sites of *shitamachi*. One such book, by Enbutsu Sumiko, is in English and is especially good (Enbutsu, 1984). Another indicator is the immense recent popularity of a film series shown in movie houses, on television, and on rental video about 'Tora-san,' a middle-aged itinerant peddler from Shibamata, an aging blue-collar neighborhood in Katsushika Ward at the eastern edge of *shitamachi*. There have now been more than 40 episodes, a typical one showing Tora-san wandering the countryside in search of adventure and the quintessential warm spirit of Japan, and then tearfully returning home to family and neighbors and proclaiming that what he was looking for was there all along. So, too, we see new interest in urban nostalgia reflected in the popular series of pen-and-ink postcards called 'Old Tokyo Today' by artist Kiritani Itsuo. The simple, austere drawings of old houses and shops along the back streets of various *shitamachi* neighborhoods are haunting records of a fast-disappearing past and a special kind of urban beauty (Kingston, 1988). Figure 5.11 is an example from one of Yanaka's back streets, a tightly-knit old neighborhood in Taitō Ward.

Some parts of the *shitamachi* area are becoming increasingly popular as places for day trips and urban explorations. This is particularly true for small enclaves of well-preserved old-style houses and traditional local shops that still exist within the larger residential areas such as Kanda, Shiba, Tsukiji, Nezu and Tsukishima (Fujimori, 1987a, p. 417). In Tsukishima, for example, an Edo-era fishing village on a landfill island in Tokyo Bay close to the CBD that is still reasonably intact, aficionados like to stroll the old streets and alleyways for a flavor of bygone days, to visit the strikingly beautiful Shinto shrine, Sumiyoshi Jinja, tucked away next to a tiny harbor of fishing boats, and to sample a popular food (*tsukudani*, small fish or seaweed boiled down over many hours in soy sauce) that originated in this settlement. In mid-July, people from many parts of the city like to come here for *bon'odori*, a joyous religious festival celebrating the annual return of the souls of one's ancestors, observed during the summer months in cities and towns all over Japan. It always involves singing, dancing and colorful traditional costumes. The event in Tsukishima is said to be especially well-staged, and has been designated an 'Intangible

Figure 5.11   A back street in Yanaka, Taitō Ward. (Courtesy of the artist Kiritani Itsuo)

Cultural Asset' by the Tokyo Metropolitan Government (Enbutsu, 1984, pp. 141–5).

For many Tokyoites the best place to go for a dose of traditional culture is Asakusa. This became the principal entertainment center of Edo, thriving during the Meiji era and Taisho as a busy theater district before destruction in the 1923 earthquake. The numbers are enormous: 1.7 million visitors to its main temple at the New Year; two million visitors to a mid-May festival called the *sanja matsuri*; almost one million to see the fireworks along the Sumida River at the end of July. Even non-traditional events in this neighborhood are becoming popular: there is an annual samba festival in Asakusa now which was recently attended by an estimated half a million individuals (Simmons, 1988, p. 39). All this represents a big turn-around in the fortunes of the district, which had declined markedly after the 1923 disaster, and then declined again in the 1950s and 1960s when new subway lines began to compete with Asakusa's Ginza Line and take passengers to other sections of the city. As Tokyo shifted westward to centers such as Shinjuku and Shibuya, Asakusa was left behind. Its revival is attributed to heightened public interest in investigating the old sections of the city, as well as to skilful promotion and dedicated work on the part of merchants, residents and local public officials. There is a civic association comprised of about 45 proprietresses of local shops called *Asakusa Okamisan Kai* ('the Asakusa Women's Association') that has been instrumental in bringing about the beautification of Rokku, a century-old theater sub-district of Asakusa, and the restoration of some of its historic buildings. A recent achievement was the reopening in November 1988 of the Asakusa Toki-waza, a once-prominent Meiji entertainment palace that closed down in 1984 after a long period of hard times.

Asakusa's major landmark is the famous temple called Asakusa Kannon, or Sensōji. It is actually a fairly new building, having been built of ferro-concrete in 1958 to replace the Edo structure destroyed in the air raids of 1945, but its history is much older than the city itself, going back perhaps to the year 628 when two fishermen brothers are said to have caught a small golden statue of the goddess Kannon in their nets in the Sumida. The temple was built to safeguard that image, which may or may not be buried somewhere beneath it. This detail does not matter much in practice, because Kannon, the goddess of mercy, has a large public following, and believers continue to flock to her shrine as they have for centuries. Because of the traditional design of the temple building itself, the layout and design of other structures in the temple precincts, and the evident devotion of the many believing visitors, Sensoji is a 'don't miss it' attraction for tourists.

The entry to Sensōji is through a huge decorative wooden gate called Kaminarimon. Translated as 'The Gate of the God of Thunder', the gate guards the temple complex, and is itself a significant Tokyo landmark. It is distinguished by the terrifying images of the gods of thunder and wind to either side of the opening, and by a giant red lantern hanging overhead. Because it is the subject of an extremely well-known 1857 *ukiyoe* print by

Figure 5.12 Worshippers at Sensōji Temple in Asakusa

Hiroshige, almost every Japanese recognizes the lantern and associates it and the famous gate with Edo's *shitamachi*. So, too, the long commercial street leading from Kaminarimon almost to the steps of Sensoji itself is a part of the 'Edo experience' that visitors to Asakusa expect. Called Nakami-se-dōri, 'the street of the inside shops', it is lined, just as it was two centuries ago, with small shops of every variety. Many of them are old and famous, and offer such fare as traditional foods or snacks, delicate ivory carvings (still being sold in Japan), Edo-period firemen's banners or beautiful *kimono*. Others have today's products (see Chapter 1). The street is gaily decorated, especially during the festival season, conveying the same sense of pleasure that visitors must have experienced during earlier times when Asakusa was the most popular gathering place in the city (Figure 5.12).

Gentrification of *shitamachi?*

One other aspect of the growing interest among the public in the city's old neighborhoods, and perhaps an inevitable one, is a developing trend for a 'return to the city' type of migration. There are no statistics that I know of, and the movement still seems to be pretty small, but it is clear in some of the *shitamachi* neighborhoods that increasing numbers of young professional people are moving in from outside the area and settling in old houses by choice. From my own contacts, a disproportionate number seem

181

to be artists, writers, educators, architects and other professionals. They are attracted, it seems, by the central location, the historic ambience of certain specific neighborhoods, a relatively sizable stock of old housing with interesting architecture and lower prices. I have also heard new arrivals talk excitedly about the 'wonderful social mix' that exists in *shitamachi*: young people and old, rich and poor, professional and blue-collar, lots of traditional craftsmen. This is in welcome contrast, I am told, to the social and architectural homogeneity of new housing developments in other parts of the metropolis, especially the aesthetically sterile and greatly overpriced apartments and *manshon* abounding in the fashionable west side. More than once I have heard it said that because of the squeaky-clean tiles covering the surfaces of so many new buildings, the new Tokyo was coming to look like a public toilet rather than a city. Some of the preferred alternatives are Yanaka in Taitō Ward, Nezu at the border between Taitō and Bunkyō Ward, and the Minowabashi area, where Tokyo's last trolley line ends, in Arakawa Ward.

All this sounds very familiar to me, like the time when the so-called 'urban pioneers' re-invested in the inner-cities of greying American urban centers because it was both what they could afford and preferred. Their arrival was a welcome infusion of new blood and physical improvements to neighborhoods that had previously lacked both, but in most cases it was followed by profit-seeking developers who changed old neighborhoods overnight into hot property, displacing long-term residents and routines. It would be terrible if the same happened in *shitamachi*. What distinguishes this area as 'the other side of Tokyo' is that, unlike most of the rest of the city, it has not been hot property, and is, therefore, in all its good and bad points, different. Unfortunately, in some of the preferred neighborhoods there are plenty of signs that it is going to be a hard fight to preserve the ambience of the past and the social mix. There are more and more squeaky-clean *manshon* popping up among the old houses, as well as more high rises and other intrusive developments. Sometimes these are erected by the biggest of builders. So it is not inconceivable that, as old prejudices about 'good' versus 'bad' sides of the city die, and as the problem of housing supply and cost persists, this 'other side of Tokyo' will be swallowed up by overdevelopment in much the same way as has happened to parts of the west side. The key that will determine which path endangered areas of *shitamachi* will take – traditional residential districts or fast-developing pieces of the new Tokyo – will depend on the outcome of struggles between citizens and developers such as the fight over Shinobazu Pond.

The underside of Tokyo: Sanya

There is one neighborhood within this 'other side of Tokyo' that is so different from the rest that it needs to be considered separately. It is called Sanya, a name written with the Chinese characters for 'mountain' and 'valley', and Tokyo's closest equivalent to a slum. Located in Taitō Ward and overlapping the boundary with Arakawa, it is a place few people from other sections of the city know and that almost no one goes to except those who live and the few who work there. It is the secret 'underside of Tokyo', a place inhabited in large fraction by the cast-offs of society and ignored by almost everyone else. Most maps of the city fail to identify it, and either use formal place names only for the *chōme* in the area or, more often, are designed to have boxed map titles or legends where Sanya would have been.

The approach to Sanya is through Namidabashi, now a street intersection but originally the name of a bridge that crossed a small river. On one side of the river was the city; on the other was Kozukappara, the shogun's bloody excecution grounds. Namidabashi thus separated the doomed from the rest of Edo; it was where families said their final farewells to relatives who were about to die. Hence the name for the bridge: Namidabashi, 'Bridge of Tears'. There is now a narrow pedestrian bridge in the vicinity leading from the closest train station across the tracks in the direction of Sanya. It is no exaggeration to say that in walking the few tens of meters in that direction, down to the main street of Sanya, a street that locals sometimes call the 'Street of Bones', one still leaves the familiar world of the city and enters a sad place where Tokyo seems to end.

I can think of several examples that show unequivocally that, for the Japanese at least, the neighborhood is clearly beyond the limits of safe entry. On a number of occasions I have gone to Sanya with some of my students, all Japanese, to teach them about the place, and have noticed how nervous and apprehensive they get during the approach as they read the cues of an unknown landscape. I'll never forget one particular incident when one of the students, speaking for the small group as a whole, begged in a voice choked with fear that we did not cross the Namidabashi intersection, but that we look in on Sanya instead from across the street. In a similar vein, James Fallows, for several years the Tokyo correspondent for *The Atlantic* and one of the few people to write about this neighborhood, also described a Japanese friend who felt afraid to enter this realm (Fallows, 1988, p. 16). Finally, a friend of mine from Sanya, an American who was one of the subjects of an ABC News piece on the area in 1988, reported to me that the American journalists who interviewed him had to bring a camera crew from abroad, because the Japanese cameraman who usually worked with them (and who had previously covered combat in Southeast Asia) was afraid to enter.

There are about 45,000 people living in Sanya, most of them, in Fallows' words, 'normal working-class Japanese', but about 7,000 of whom are 'flophouse occupants' and people who live on the streets (p. 16). This is skid row, a neighborhood of vagrants and alcoholics, of day laborers and night-time drinkers. Most of the occupants are men, the majority of whom are middle-aged or older, and many of whom will be in Sanya for a long time, perhaps the rest of their lives. Others are drifters. They come from

183

elsewhere in Tokyo or to Tokyo from the hinterlands for a variety of reasons, most of them familiar stories in skid-row areas in general: family problems, broken romances, lost jobs, failed businesses, trouble with the law, mental illness. Those who work do so on a temporary basis, usually lining up positions through one of the local employment agencies that takes a commission for providing the services of unskilled labor, or by standing early in the morning on the main street and waiting to be selected for work at some construction site by employers who drive by in vans whenever they are short of labor. Those who wait at curbside to be selected for work are called *tachinbō*, 'standing pole' (Caldarola, 1968–9, p. 513). All the hiring is said to be controlled by *yakuza*, Japan's gangsters. The work is sometimes dangerous and workers' benefits are nil. It is also seasonal. In recent years there has been increased competition for the better jobs from younger men from Third World countries such as Bangladesh and Pakistan, both legally in Japan and illegal, who also work for low wages and minimal benefits.

Housing in Sanya reflects its poverty. For those who have some money, generally the youngest and healthiest inhabitants of Sanya, there are dozens of cheap hotels and rooming houses. The top end of the scale is a tiny private room with a color television and a shared toilet and bath that rents for about 2,500 yen per day. Prices for these units have been going up lately, because wages have risen due to a labor shortage. At the bottom end of the scale, or about 500 yen, one can go to one of the several shelters that rents mats on the floor of large rooms shared by 20 men or more. These are generally old buildings, crowded and dangerous. Many other Sanya men, especially the worst-case alcoholics, stay outdoors. They live on the sidewalks, in doorways, on the side streets and in a small local park. The 'Street of Bones' is lined with such men, often arranged in small clusters around a fire. Others are found alone on the pavement (Figure 5.13). There is little help from the government and not nearly enough charity from the public at large; every winter some people die from exposure after passing out drunk. An excellent survey of the population and a study of its daily routine is the research carried out in Sanya in the early 1980s by Eguchi, Nishioka and Katō (1985).

That there is also a Sanya in nearly every other great city in the world is beside the point. I include this description not just to represent Tokyo more fully in its various aspects, but also to stress that even here, at the very bottom of the urban scale, the city is being shaped by powerful traditions and unchanging beliefs. The piece of real estate that is Sanya became tainted a long time ago when Ieyasu Tokugawa selected a site nearby for executions. It has never recovered. It was a place no one wanted, and inevitably became the place where, one after the other, successive waves of outcaste groups would settle. Not just the *hinin* and *burakhumin* from feudal times, but in Meiji times there were the descendants of these groups, superannuated prostitutes from Yoshiwara, criminals and many of the city's poor, no matter what their background. The arrival of the last

Figure 5.13 Homeless men trying to keep warm on the street in Sanya

of these categories increased after 1895, when a tough law was put into effect to chase cheap lodging houses from most parts of the city and confine them in designated districts such as Sanya. In this century, the population swelled at different times with Korean laborers and with soldiers returning to Japan after World War II. Many of the latter had lost their homes and families, or they felt shame about Japan's defeat and went into self-exile. It is said that much of the construction force that prepared Tokyo for the 1964 Olympics came from these ranks. A large part of Sanya's reputation for heavy drinking stems from the after-hours activities of returned veterans.

It is interesting that a vastly disproportionate amount of the charity that goes to this district comes from the small proportion of foreign residents in Tokyo. This is the case for the operation of the largest 'soup kitchen' in Sanya, a free medical clinic, and for a large fraction of the donations of clothing, blankets and food. Some of the Western churches in the city and the well-heeled membership of the Tokyo American Club have been particularly generous. A number of the few social services volunteers who work in the neighborhood are foreigners, too, particularly Christian missionaries (Betros, 1985b). There are, however, a small number of remarkable Japanese individuals who are exceptions, and who also work in Sanya and share with its poor their considerable talents in medicine and counselling, often as volunteers without pay. The article by Fallows includes an interview with one such individual. Most other Japanese have chosen to ignore this problem, as indeed do most other societies in their own backyards. However, in Japan, Sanya has the added stigma of being 'poisoned ground' and a concentration of social castes that, despite the advent of modern times, are still discriminated against and generally avoided. Sanya is now, as it always has been, 'a safe distance away.'

Along the Chūō Line: a look at suburbia

It is not possible in this brief review of 'epitome districts' to represent every type of neighborhood in Tokyo. The city is simply too big and too varied. However, there is at least one critically important aspect of Tokyo not yet adequately represented: that of the suburban areas such as the Tama region of *Tokyo-to* and in neighboring prefectures. This in itself is a complicated topic because the area is so big, with a great variety of places to be found there. We saw in Chapter 4 that the suburban ring includes planned new towns, factory cities, *danchi* estates, college towns and at least one famous neatly laid-out garden city, as well as places that mix these and other characteristics. So I plan to focus on what seems to be most typical. To do so, we can return to the Chūō Line, the super-crowded commuter train line, and look at some details about communities along its course through the western suburbs.

A good place to begin is the vicinity of Musashisakai, a moderate-sized train station in Musashino City 23 minutes (eight stations) west of the giant commuter interchange at Shinjuku. This is an area in the Tama district of *Tokyo-to*, a few minutes west of Tokyo's western-most wards. It is a highly mixed suburban district that itself reflects the complexity of Tokyo; it includes a diverse population and a wide range of housing types, commercial centers, workplaces and recreation facilities. There are other similar places along the Chūō and other lines, so it seems representative. My practical reason for choosing it is that it is where I moved after leaving the neighborhood near Shinjuku. What I observed during one year of living at Musashisakai is that (1) there is a different, but complementary, set of daily routines from those in closer-in neighborhoods and business districts; and (2) that except for an awful morning train commute and some minor annoyances, suburban Tokyo can be extremely pleasant and comfortable. I make the latter point especially because it differs from the impression one gets with a first look at the suburbs, when one notices mostly the displeasing aspects of endless urban sprawl and look-alike developments.

The focus of activity in the Musashisakai area is, like the focus of so much else in urban Japan, the train station and its adjacent blocks. In the mornings on workdays we can see the extent to which the neighborhood is a bedroom appendage to inner Tokyo, as thousands of commuters zero in on one or other other of the station's two entrances to board the Chūō Line's *nobori densha*. The march to the station starts before 6:00 am and builds to a peak about two hours later when the downtown-bound platform becomes dangerously overcrowded and every car on every one of the trains that come by three minutes apart is hopelessly jammed. It is not until well after 9:00 that the rush period slows and crowds thin out enough to make room on trains and in-bound loading platforms. The commuters converge on the station on foot, by bicycle, by motorcycle and by bus, as well as by another train, a short line that is part of the Seibu Railway empire's reach into the suburbs (see Chapter 4), that uses one of the tracks at Musashisakai as a terminus. On average, more than 50,000 people board Chūō Line trains at Musashisakai each day (*Tokyo Statistical Yearbook*, 1987, p. 230).[11] As we can imagine from such a total and the various ways that commuters travel to the station, the catchment area of Musashisakai Station is quite large. I do not have an exact measure, but from the routes of feeder buses it is clear that it includes, at a minumum, all the western part of Musashino city as well as big sections of neighboring towns such as Mitaka, Fuchū and Koganei, and that the population is in the range of 300,000 or so.[12]

The morning exodus through the station substantially changes the sex and age structure of the population of the neighborhood. As is typical of bedtown suburbs, the majority of people who leave Musashisakai for the city during the morning rush period, perhaps as many as two-thirds of the total, are men aged between their 20s and 60s on their way to work. Most of them wear conservative suits, ties and white shirts, and fit the stereotype of the Japanese salaryman (*sarariman*). They are white-collar employees who put in long hours of dedicated work in exchange for the security of lifetime employment with a trusted company, and who spend comparatively little time at home. Other commuters are women, especially young women without children who work as 'office ladies' ('OL') and in the retailing sector until they start families of their own, and students of all ages and both sexes. Mothers stay behind, as do most younger children and elderly people. The neighborhood belongs to them (and to shopkeepers) all day, and it is these categories of people almost exclusively whom one sees around the neighborhood until the evening rush home. Because the Musashisakai area is a mature neighborhood, having been built up as a suburb some decades ago (much of it even before World War II), it has a substantial fraction of older people. Many of them are 'empty-nesters' who have already raised their children and now live alone as older couples or widows or widowers. They are especially visible during the day in the neighborhood's shops and supermarkets, and in street-side conversations between neighbors in the residential precincts.

The area closest to the station is a commercial district. This is also the case for just about every other busy rail station in the metropolitan area. At Musashisakai, which has tens of thousands of daily riders (as well as

[11] This is an average based on 18,828,000 riders getting on at Musashisakai each year, and includes both in-bound and out-bound traffic.

[12] Although this number is big enough to constitute a substantial city or town, the station itself, with its 50,000 daily riders, is only moderate in size on the scale of Tokyo.

Figure 5.14 A station-front shopping center in the suburbs. The example is from Musashisakai Station in Musashino City on the Chūō Line

thousands of shoppers who do not board trains), the commercial center is on the scale of a small downtown. It is marked by a cluster of taller buildings – six and seven stories – and a variety of retail stores, restaurants and drinking places, banks and other offices, entertainment facilities and other commercial land uses. It is divided neatly into two halves, one on either side of the rail tracks, reflecting at one train station the two principal styles of shopping center design at suburban commuter centers. The north side has the older fashion: an extended shopping street lined on both sides with a great variety of stores, most of them well-established family-run operations, as well as some shopping on the side streets that intersect with the main shopping street. The other side of the tracks is a newer style shopping center (Figure 5.14). It is actually one big building, five stories plus a basement and a rooftop level, that is a huge department store, a large supermarket (the basement), an assortment of restaurants and some other businesses (mostly the top floor), and a sports club with tennis courts (the roof). The building is one of a chain of similar developments that some giant retailing corporations (in this case, Itō Yokado) have opened recently at preferred sites in the residential rings around Tokyo and other large cities.

In a pattern that is a microcosm of the city as a whole, the blocks nearest the commercial core are themselves becoming commercial and high density. In just the one year that I have kept track, five or six new mid-rise office buildings have opened within a two-minute walking radius of the station. Tenants include branch banks, real-estate companies, professional offices such as doctor's offices, and the ubiquitous private cram schools called *juku*.[13] So, too, there are several new mid-rise (seven stories on the average) apartment and condominium (*manshon*) buildings in this area. This reflects the much higher land values in the vicinity of busy train stations, and the premium that commercial users and residents alike pay for being located within a short walk of station exits. A negative consequence of this is that, just as in the city, there are long-time residents who find their preserves outside the city are no longer quiet, and that urbanization engulfs them. Thus, the sight of an older house completely surrounded by stores and tall buildings is quite common at places like Musashisakai. Likewise, there is a beautiful temple garden where I like to sit that is walled in on three sides by tall buildings. It reminds me of my previous hideaway in the old neighborhood, where the giant City Hall towers have pierced the sight line and loom over the peaceful enclosure.

The rest of suburbia lies beyond this nucleus. It is mostly residential, but not homogeneously so, and also contains a variety of other land uses. Table 5.2 compares land-use distribution in Musashino City as a whole with other jurisdictions. In the area around Musashisakai (western Musashino City, parts of Mitaka City), which is largely a middle-class district with lots of families, the typical street is a short, quiet residential lane with newer single-family houses hidden behind walls and barriers of greenery (Figure 5.15). It is similar to the quiet residential streets in the better neighborhoods of the central city, except that the houses tend to be somewhat more substantial in size and farther apart, and their gardens are bigger. Other aspects of the residential landscape are apartments, including some stands of *danchi* erected by companies to house their employees and their families, and condominiums. As in the city as a whole, the latter are ever more prevalent, and are continually being built in the vacant spaces between existing developments and on redevelopment sites. There are also still some aging wooden farmhouses standing amid small orchards and remaining patches of farmland. In some sections, generally on larger land parcels further away from the station, there are sizable tract developments of similar single houses aligned close together in straight rows. These are some of the newest suburbs, reflecting in their higher densities and quick construction the high cost of land in the Tokyo area and the great demand for housing.

There is also a considerable amount of non-residential land. The most important examples include large tracts given to industry and to institutions such as college and university campuses. This has been the case since the

---

[13] Once I looked through the door of a small school that teaches English and saw the teacher explaining the sentence 'I help pigs' that she had written on the board.

Figure 5.15 A typical suburban single house on a typical residential street on a rare snowy morning. This is Kyōnancho in Musashino City

Table 5.2 Land use in Musashino City and other jurisdictions, 1988 (hectares)

	Musashino		23 Wards		Tokyo-to	
Total land area	700		33,857		108,633	
Total land area for building	604		31,240		52,567	
Commercial land (%)	53	(8.8)	3,346	(10.7)	4,071	(7.7)
Industrial land (%)	22	(3.6)	3,065	(9.8)	5,098	(9.8)
Residential land (%)	529	(87.6)	24,799	(79.4)	41,892	(79.7)
Other building land (%)	0	(0)	30	(0.1)	1,504	(2.9)
Paddy fields	0		220		1,128	
Ordinary fields	52		1,558		13,267	
Forests	1		73		29,960	
Other	44		766		11,711	

Source: Tokyo Statistical Yearbook, 1987, pp. 2–3.

early part of the century, as the initial growth of the Musashisakai area (together with several other Tama district suburbs) is attributed more to the presence of large factories and other sizable employment centers than to service as a bedroom community for the central city. Their inducement was ample land and good freight-rail connections to Tokyo and the port of Yokohama, as well as the added advantage for some firms of plentiful water supplies (Allinson, 1979, p. 55). The most famous company in the area in the past was the Nakajima Aircraft Corporation. It opened two large plants in Musashino on the north side of the Chūō Line tracks in 1937 and 1938, and then became one of the largest manufacturers of military planes and engines during the World War II. The entire complex was destroyed by US planes in 1945 and the site is now housing, a park, some commercial blocks and other community facilities.

One of the biggest firms close to Musashisakai today is the Subaru automotive company, which operates a large engineering and testing facility in Mitaka a few minutes south of the station. Other companies in the general area, although not necessarily closest to Musashisakai Station, are manufacturing plants of Yokogawa Electric, the Citizen Watch Company, Nissan Motors and Fuji Heavy Industries. The campus of the International Christian University is also close to Musashisakai, as is Asia University, Musashino Women's University and Seikei University. The presence of these factories and most of the educational institutions reflects long-standing policies by Tokyo's government to encourage decentralization of large employers. The result is a stronger local tax base for Musashino and other cities in the Tama district, and less reliance on long-distance commuting to work in central Tokyo. Many residents of the Musashisakai area and places like it work locally, travelling there by bus, by bicycle or by car. There is also noticeable reverse commuting, as workers and students take outbound trains (or private automobiles) from central Tokyo to their companies or schools in the Tama area.

The commercial center at Musashisakai Station is a local center only. There are also larger, regional shopping centers distributed further apart. One is the center of Tachikawa City, a larger industrial and bedroom suburb six stations further out on the Chūō Line, while another is Kichijōji, in Musashino, two stations closer to central Tokyo than Musashisakai. Both have several competing department stores within a short walk of their respective stations, as well as dozens of other stores, restaurants, coffee shops and movie theaters. In Kichijōji, much of this is arranged along streets closed to vehicular traffic and made into pleasant pedestrian arcades (Spivak, 1987). There is always a lot of activity when the stores are open, but the busiest time is at weekends. This is when families have time together, and take care of shopping needs or use the opportunity to stroll and browse. The fact that there are large public parks within walking distance of both stations adds to the appeal of these centers for such outings (Figure 5.16). There are also great throngs of teenagers who visit these shopping centers, particularly on weekends and during after-school hours. Kichijōji is especially popular, and is fast developing a reputation as not just a suburban shopping center, but as an outlying version of Shibuya. It has many of the same stores and fashions and is a favorite date-night hangout.

The automobile has a strong and visible role in the suburbs of Tokyo, although not to the extent that characterizes suburban areas in the United

Figure 5.16 Photographing the wildflowers in Shōwa Park, Tachikawa City, in Tokyo's suburbs

States and some other countries. Rates of car ownership now exceed 60 per cent of all households in the suburbs and are rising, and most houses and apartments have off-street parking. The increasing car culture is seen in the weekend traffic jams and long lines to enter parking lots at Tachikawa, Kichijōji, and other shopping centers, in the big parking lots surrounding suburban factories and some college campuses, and in car-oriented commercial 'ribbon developments' along the busy streets and highways crisscrossing suburbia. Unlike the station-front commercial centers, the landscape there is one of big, new supermarkets, brightly lit discount appliance stores, spacious family restaurants (more Denny's), all-night convenience stores and video rental shops all strung out at irregular intervals along busy arterials and offering free off-street parking. Most noticeable are the pachinko parlors, so bedizened with flashing neon and tasteless statuary that they remind one of the Las Vegas strip. There are also plenty of bright, clean multi-pump gas stations, rows of automobile dealerships and used car lots, and learn-to-drive schools with their own enclosed practice courses. Even the love hotels are designed with the car in mind, and offer secluded interior parking to enhance privacy. Young people seem to be especially car-conscious. In a reflection of the affluence Japan now enjoys, many older teenagers, college students, and others of that generation drive fancy sports cars or other new vehicles, and show them off in cruising,

California style, around the shopping malls and past favorite drive-in hang-outs.

The point of all this is to emphasize that just outside the limits of central Tokyo there exists a physical environment and life-style quite different from what was described for the 23 wards. It is hard to generalize, because the suburban ring is so big and varied, but on the whole we see a pleasant, comfortable existence in an environment of lower density, less crowded housing and more use of private automobiles. Where I live is convenient to the center of the city, to a choice of local and regional shopping centers, and to many other facilities. It is also incredibly quiet, clean, safe and well-serviced. Instead of the light from a restaurant that intruded into my old house and the all-night motorcycle races on Yamate-dōri, the Musashisakai night is dark and quiet, the only outside sounds coming from crickets and the rustling of bamboo. There are also some welcome reminders from time to time that one is not alone. On cold winter nights, usually shortly after 10:00pm, the itinerant baked-sweet-potato salesman makes his rounds down our small street, calling out again and again in a deep singsong: *Ishiyakiimo, oishii desyoo* ('baked potatoes, they're delicious'). It is one of the traditional foods to help you stay warm and sleep better, distributed in a time-honored way that was once one of the sounds of the feudal Edo night. However, instead of walking behind a pushcart, today's *ishiyakiimo-san* drives a Toyota pick-up with a charcoal stove on the back; his voice is on cassette tape and comes through a speaker system.

6
Planning directions

City planning in Tokyo: introduction

Perhaps more so than in most other cities of the world, city planning has come to be a topic of lively interest among the citizenry of Tokyo. This is especially true for large redevelopment and other new construction projects relating to the planning of land use. We see this interest in the bookshops where paperbacks about grand schemes for the waterfront or urban design for the 21st century compete on the shelves with popular novels and top magazines; in daily newspapers which devote prominent space to details of government policy for controlling the price of land, the building of new residential estates, commercial centers, industrial districts, or the planning of new highways to ease a chronic traffic problem; and in the popularity of occasional television specials on public as well as commercial networks discussing urban problems and necessary action. Much of the population seem informed, at least in a general way, about how Tokyo is expected to change in the future, and up-to-date about the principal characteristics of many current redevelopment proposals and other large constructions.

Such awareness about planning stems from several factors. Certainly Tokyo's great size and extraordinary expansion in recent years, as well as its rapid economic growth, its high potential for environmental disaster, and other fundamental characteristics of the city in themselves call for attention to planning. So, too, the great tragedies that befell the city in 1923 and 1945 brought on rebuilding programs that increased awareness among citizens about alternatives for the design of urban landscape, requiring considerable cooperation from the public with the directives of planners and managers of construction projects. Moreover, public interest in planning is closely tied to the pride many Tokyoites have in their city, and to the special interest in local affairs one would expect where many citizens identify strongly with both the city as a whole and with their own neighborhoods. Finally, high levels of citizen awareness are also related to their high level of literacy, and to their often-observed voracious appetite for reading (Christopher, 1983, pp. 193–210).

However, all this is not to say that Tokyo has been a model of how city planning should work. In fact, perhaps the opposite is true. As Tange Kenzō has observed in a call for radical redesign of the city: 'Tokyo has formed as a result of totally planless spontaneous growth on the basis of self-assertion of the inhabitants. [There has been an] irritating . . . lack of leadership on the part of governments in enforcing a rational plan for Tokyo (Tange, 1987, p. 8). In this city, as indeed in many places across the world, urban development has been propelled largely by the interests of private capital. Those who stand to profit most are generally closest to decisions about land use; while they often use their influence to promote what they see as the public good, they also exploit the planning process, such as it exists, to increase the value of their own businesses. For the most part, there is fairly little significant citizen input, despite such established mechanisms for participation as needs assessments, attitude surveys about city services, and public hearings (Figure 6.1). Instead, the public in Tokyo is mostly a passive, albeit interested, body, and accepts the new urban development projects that are announced in newspapers and on television as necessary or inevitable, and most probably in its own best interests.

This is a familiar pattern in many countries. In Tokyo, however, lack of planning has posed special problems because of some of the city's distinctive characteristics. The city is so big and the potential for disasters, particularly from earthquakes, so great, that it would be foolish not to try to correct the course of urban development. So, too, some kind of planning is needed to do something about the problems of extraordinarily high land prices. Otherwise, even the uncontrolled land development practices of the profit-making sector would be impossible. Consequently, there is great demand in Tokyo for some sort of rational, comprehensive and long-term plan that will solve the city's many problems and avoid the chaos many observers fear might be just around the corner.

Tho Tokyo Metropolitan Government believes it has developed such a plan. This is the so-called 2nd Long-term Development Plan released in 1986 and presently in force. It is the latest in a series of plans, and attempts at plans, developed at various times over much of this century; it represents the thinking of Governor Suzuki Shunichi's administration about the kind of city Tokyo should be. There is also a larger-scale master plan in force for the entire Capital Region covering the whole of Tokyo, plus seven neighboring prefectures. Moreover, there are quite a number of other plans, such as those for individual wards in Tokyo and for nearby towns and other local jurisdictions. Finally, there are also a number of creative and visionary ideas for the not-too-distant future for Tokyo as a whole, or for specific sites, by concerned architects and urban designers. Some of the best-known of these plans are spectacular proposals for new cities and transportation networks on landfill in Tokyo Bay, and various bridges and tunnels to connect these with the main part of the city.

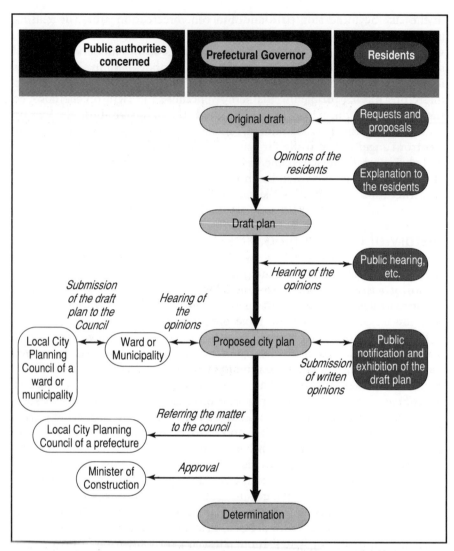

Figure 6.1 Chart of the city planning procedure in Tokyo. (Tokyo Metropolitan Government, 1988, p. 18)

The objective of this chapter is to review some of these plans and discuss their principal features. I am especially interested in redevelopment projects in and near the city center and in the new construction begun nearby in Tokyo Bay. This is greatly transforming the core of Tokyo, and setting a course for a totally different look for the city. I shall also discuss planning outside the central area, including areas that are now the rural-suburban fringe but that will soon become part of the urbanized area. A significant theme is an apparent conflict of goals: on the one hand, much of the attention of planning in Tokyo is given to improving the 'quality of life' in the city by increasing parkland and other recreation areas, decreasing population density, reducing commuting times, cleaning the air and water, reducing noise, caring for the aged and other constituencies with special social service needs; and so on. It is also clear that planning in Tokyo is intended to make Tokyo even bigger than it is already. Even though so many of Tokyo's problems exist simply because the city so enormous, in the plan the urban mass will be permitted to expand in all directions: up to new heights of tall buildings; down to what planners called the 'geofront', and out into the far reaches of the Kantō Plain and the waters of Tokyo Bay. The discussion will begin with an introduction to the history of city planning in Tokyo and a short overview of present-day administrative structure and enabling legislation relating to planning.

History of city planning

Despite the fact that city planning has been generally poorly developed in Tokyo, it has a long and interesting history. Many of the most significant chapters of this story stem from the episodes of destruction that periodically visit the city and then create a need to rebuild. In some cases, notable improvements to Tokyo have resulted from carefully planned reconstruction, but in many others the history of planning is most notable for missed opportunities and the failure to rebuild on a more-or-less clean slate according to some more rational urban design. On the other hand, given that so many heavily planned cities in the world, ranging from Brasilia to Moscow to Singapore, are perhaps too orderly in their designs and somewhat sterile, it might be a good thing that Tokyo missed some chances in the past and rebuilt itself, in large part, in the old way.

We can trace the history of planning in Tokyo at least as far back as 1590, when Ieyasu Tokugawa arrived in Edo, saw a town in great disrepair, and initiated a series of remarkable public works' projects that changed the place forever. This included the reclamation of marshland at Nihombashi and other low-lying shore areas to enlarge the city; the construction of a canal to bring fresh water about 20 kilometers from Lake Inokashira; and major reconstruction of the previous castle, moats and surrounding fortifications. Social space was manipulated to emphasize the hierarchy of classes and to protect the shogun and his closest retainers. Thus, we recall that the overall form of Edo as determined by Ieyasu's plan was an irregular clockwise spiral, reminiscent of the *hiragana* symbol for the syllable *no*, that unwound outward from the castle to the edge of the city through districts of ever-lower social classes.

Other notable examples of early planning are seen in various efforts during Edo to check the spread of the periodic fires that swept the city. After the huge Meireki inferno of 1657 there was a co-ordinated effort to plaster the straw and shingle roofs of the city with mud. After 1720, following still other conflagrations, the preferred roofing material was changed by another civic improvement project to tiles. So, too, efforts were made during Edo to enhance the effectiveness of streets and watercourses as firebreaks and to reduce the density of the built-up area by opening new districts for urban expansion. The results at best, however, were only partly successful. Even the rebuilt districts were mostly congested tinderbox, and the so-called 'flowers of Edo' continued to storm across the city every few years to destroy buildings and lives.

The beginning of modern city planning in Tokyo, like so many other things in Japan to which the adjective 'modern' is applied, is traced to the Meiji Restoration. The great Ginza fire of 1872, only four years after the start of the new era, was occasion for yet another rebuilding of a key part of the city. This time, however, the modernization of Tokyo in the Western image was a prime objective. Thus, the entire Ginza district was refashioned in red brick, not just to better protect against fire, but also to plan Tokyo as a showpiece for foreigners by giving it a more European flavor (Smith, 1978, p. 54). Other examples of planning for a Western-style city during Meiji included the construction of the government buildings' complex at Kasumigaseki, and the famed Mitsubishi Londontown development of the 1890s. The latter was a brick-faced commercial center designed by Josiah Conder for the Mitsubishi trust and patterened after architecture in the British capital.

Another product of Meiji modernization was the first legislation in Tokyo to facilitate city planning. This was the 'Tokyo Urban Improvement Ordinance' of 1888, a 16-point initiative that created a city planning board with responsibilities for policy formulation and execution, and that set in motion various improvements to infrastructure, especially in the downtown area. The greatest attention was given to road building projects. This is seen in the priorities of Tokyo governor Yoshikawa Akimasa as expressed in his written appeal in 1884 to Central Government calling for planning in the city:

The primary need is for roads, bridges and canals. Water, housing and sewers come afterwards. Thus, if plans are determined for roads, bridges and canals, which are the fundamental needs, it will facilitate the attainment of the other objectives (Tokyo Metropolitan Government, 1972, p. 8).

Accordingly, in the first three years after funds were made available, some 80 to 90 per cent of the total outlay went for the paving and straightening of the 'confused maze-like spaces' that comprised the center of the city (Ishizuka and Ishida, 1988, p. 13). However, because of cholera outbreaks, some increased attention was given in subsequent years (the mid–1890s) to supplying water and removing sewerage. The principal objective of focusing so much on infrastructure was to solidify Tokyo's hold on its role as national capital, as well as to surpass Osaka as a center of commerce (Tokyo Metropolitan Government, 1972b, p. 8).

The next city planning law in Tokyo, called the 'Town Planning Act', was adopted in 1919 during the rule of the Taishō emperor. It followed a time of unusually rapid urbanization and industrial expansion, and was one of the first uses in Japanese of the term 'city planning' (*toshi keikaku*). Again, the emphasis was on infrastructure to establish a modern, competitive economic base. This included construction of roads, railways, port facilities, and similar projects, as well as provisions to identify districts within the city for special planning, to delineate fire prevention zones and for modifications to the city's river system. It also provided for land adjustment such as the straightening of roads and property lines in suburban areas that were soon expected to change from farms to houses. Companion legislation in the same year, the Municipal Area Building Law, established the first zoning provisions in Tokyo. In large part this was to separate industry that was a fire hazard or a source of pollution from other sections of the city.

The first true test for these advances came with the Great Kantō Earthquake of 1923. In reducing some 60 per cent of Tokyo to ashes, this disaster provided planners with an enormous opportunity to restructure the city according to the most modern standards. Gotō Shimpei, a national figure who had proposed grand plans for the city while he was mayor just before the emergency, was put in charge of reconstruction and once again drew up impressive plans. This included laying out new street lines and wider streets, reorganization of the rail network, improvements to water and sewer systems, creation of open spaces and other upgrading. However, because the cost was to have been considerable, and because of angry opposition by powerful landowners who felt threatened by the new design, only a few elements of the total scheme were actually completed.

Something of the same can be said about what happened to entirely new sets of rebuilding plans put forward after destruction of the city by American bombing in 1945. For example, Ishikawa Eiyo, the Tokyo government's chief planner, prepared a 'War Damage Rehabilitation Plan' that included a symmetrical radial and ring road network for Tokyo, strategically spaced greenbelts and separation of land uses through zoning. Once again the costs proved to be prohibitive, especially in the light of the nation's ruined economy after the hostilities. Moreover, there was such a rush of population to Tokyo after the war – citizens who had previously evacuated the city, military personnel from fighting zones and Japanese from lost colonies abroad – and the press for housing and other space so great, that schemes on paper for urban reorganization were simply impractical. Thus, more effective planning for the city would be deferred until later when new problems in a worsening urban environment would make ameliorative measures absolutely unavoidable, and rising incomes would make planning goals more attainable.

Planning directions

The Post-War Period

Post-war recovery in Japan was a time of extraordinary growth in Tokyo. As the population of the 23-ward area exploded from a wartime low of 2.8 million in 1945 to 5.4 million in 1950, and then to 8.9 million by 1965, it became clearer than ever that exceptional methods to control expansion and regulate patterns of development were required. Thus, from the mid–1950s, the first in a long and sometimes confusing series of steps toward improved planning were put into effect. This involved various levels of government spread over a large area of rapid urbanization. The national government took a leading role in this planning by creating a cabinet-level Capital Region Development Commission in 1956. This facilitated co-operation between numerous political jurisdictions, including Tokyo Metropolitan Government, the governments of neighboring prefectures, and government in such localities as urban wards and smaller towns and villages. The Commission also provided a framework, albeit a weak and inexperienced one, for dealing with the many competing development initiatives that were being put forward by private sector interests such as land development companies and private railway corporations.

One of the Commission's first achievements was publication in 1958 of the National Capital Region Development Plan. This was a comprehensive, general plan addressing all major categories of land use and various types of social needs, that encompassed a huge territory with a radius of some 100 kilometers centered on the 23-ward nucleus. In many respects it was based on Sir Patrick Abercrombie's 1944 concept for London (Hall, 1984, pp. 33–4 and 39–44). The main feature was a greenbelt zone about 16 to 27 kilometers from the center of Tokyo.[1] Development of all types would be greatly restricted within this belt, while housing and other building projects would be directed to a more distant zone located between 27 and 72 kilometers from central Tokyo. This outer zone would include a number of new satellite towns to house much of the region's population growth and to provide centers for economic expansion. The plan also called for the construction of an integrated network of expressways and arterial highways connecting the newly urbanized areas of the Kantō Plain, as well as to link them to the center.

There was also considerable attention in the 1958 plan on the need to direct growth within Tokyo itself. Thus, provisions were made for various redevelopment projects in the central city to reduce crowding and encourage more efficient use of land, as well as to alleviate the extremely vexing problem of overdevelopment and excessive land costs at the city's principal business district. A specific step in these directions was to encourage growth in the station-front districts of Shinjuku, Ikebukuro, Shibuya, Ōtsuka, Gotanda and Kinshichō, as strategically sited alternatives to the CBD. Further-

---

[1] The provision for greenbelts was actually a revival of a 1939 plan for Tokyo called the Tokyo Green Space Plan. Like the 1958 idea, it too was based on an English model, but it was interrupted by the war and never put into effect.

more, there was a law passed in 1959 prohibiting construction of factories and universities within the 23-ward area. Both uses were understood to be among the major attractions for migrants to Tokyo, and therefore were steered by this regulation to designated areas in the outlying zone. However, because other places in the Tokyo area besides the 23 wards were also suffering from too much growth, the establishment and enlargement of industries and universities was also restricted in the 1958 plan from Musashino, Mitaka and parts of Yokohama, Kawasaki and Kawaguchi. These were previously existing central cities in the Tokyo orbit, and were referred to by protective planners as 'mother towns' (*haha toshi*) (Ishizuka and Ishida, 1988, p. 28).

The 1958 plan was substantially revised in the 1960s. Development pressure from an overcrowded Tokyo was simply too great to maintain a greenbelt so close to the city. Moreover, the plan itself had almost no powers to enforce any compliance with ideals. A good example of this was the Japan Housing Corporation, a public agency established in 1955 to ameliorate housing shortages in urban areas, which was using the greenbelt zone for many of its housing development sites. Consequently, in recognition of what real-estate developers were doing anyway on their own, a revised document issued in 1965 erased the greenbelt altogether and marked its zone for suburban growth. A year later the outer boundaries of the Capital Region planning district were substantially extended beyond the 72-kilometer limit. This too was in recognition of on-going development patterns. The new boundaries encompassed some 36,500 square kilometers within an area with a radius of approximately 150 kilometers from Tokyo's center. The large, open spaces that had been the objective of the greenbelt were reduced to vestigial units often well beyond the built-up area and along the floodplains of rivers. Another change from the 1958 plan was the abolition in 1963 of building-height restrictions in the 23 wards. This too reflected the intense pressure on space that existed in Tokyo and launched the city into an era of skyscraper construction. The first of these was the Kasumigaseki Building, completed in 1968.

The 1964 Summer Olympics provided a special stimulus for detailed planning in Tokyo. The Japanese viewed the Games as their world debut after the war, and made certain of presenting their city in the best possible light. Consequently, there was considerable public support for ideas contained in another planning document, this one called 'Tokyo Plan 1960' and released in 1961, that simultaneously proposed to ready the city for the Olympics and solve its numerous long-standing urban needs. Its main author was the city's budding urban design superstar, Tange Kenzō. Thus, following an energetic redevelopment campaign, Tokyo received a much-expanded road system within the 23-ward area, new parks and recreation facilities, an augmented system for water supply, a major national rail line (the 'bullet train' Tōkaidō Line), the famous monorail to Haneda Airport, major expansions in its subway system, several new Western-style hotels, and, of course, the Olympics facilities themselves. The most striking landmark, often presented as a symbol of modern Tokyo, was Tange's own magnificent National Gymnasium complex in Yoyogi Park, illustrated in Figure 3.13.

As impressive as many of the results of the Olympics construction were, most of Tokyo remained rather backward. The needs of residential neighborhoods had been given short shrift during every point in planning since the 1888 and 1919 landmark laws that favored infrastructure projects and the downtown. So, too, the neighborhoods were lower priority during reconstruction following the 1923 earthquake and the wartime bombing. For the most part, such basic needs as improved housing, sanitary sewers, and spaces for recreation were deferred, while emphasis was given to the larger goal of putting the city's economy back into shape. In the words of then Prime Minister Ikeda Hayato, explaining about the persistence of residential crowding, poor public services and chronic air pollution: 'We must first make the pie bigger' (Tokyo Metropolitan Government, 1972, p. 10). So little was being done at that time to build a better living environment that the severe water shortage during the Olympics summer should have been no surprise (Tokyo Metropolitan Government, 1972, p. 10).

It was in this context that planning in Tokyo began to move in new directions after the mid-1960s. The immediate reason was that citizens had become fed up with their poor conditions and the slow pace of improvements to their neighborhoods, voting out of office the conservative municipal government that had long held sway. The principal victim of their wrath was the Governor of Tokyo, Azuma Ryūtarō, 'the Olympics governor' who had the good sense not even to try for re-election. He was in trouble anyway because of scandals involving voter fraud and financial misdealings, but then received an even greater setback in the 1965 summer when a noisome plague of black flies descended on the blue-collar wards east of the Sumida River from late June and into July. They had come from the city's garbage dump in Kōtō Ward, a landfill site with the ironic name of Yumenoshima, 'Dream Island', and came to symbolize his administration's failure to take care of basic public needs (Seidensticker, 1990, pp. 259–60).

Thus, the next gubernatorial election of 1967 was carried by Minobe Ryōkichi, a university professor, longtime critic of the government and leader of a successful Socialist-Communist coalition. He was a skilled lecturer and an experienced TV personality, blessed with an infectious smile, the 'Minobe *sumairu*' as it was called, that couldn't help but get him votes. His campaign, captivated the public with nostalgic stories about what the city was like during his boyhood, and promises of an alternative image for Tokyo. He talked about clean rivers and blue skies, charming urban districts not yet covered over with concrete, and, as an alternative to garbage flies, butterflies, dragonflies and fireflies (Lockheimer, 1967, p. 13). He promised to work toward a healthier Tokyo, and became an extremely popular two-term governor (until 1979) who reoriented much about planning in the city and priorities in government spending. Unfortunately, he is also remembered as the person who so favored expensive urban programs that he almost brought the city to bankruptcy.

The goals of the Minobe-era planning are spelled out in the aptly-titled 'Tokyo for the People', a booklet produced in English to inform a wider public about the city's new order. It promised to 'guarantee all citizens . . . the minimum standards necessary to live a decent life' (Tokyo Metropolitan Government, 1972, p. 7), setting out an ambitious program to improve housing, promote social programs and clean the environment. The plan sought to construct some 200,000 new high-rise apartment units within the city, to develop attractive, new multi-function residential community centers at other sites, and to eliminate the tens of thousands of unsound, fire-prone wooden houses still standing in Tokyo. In doing so, the plan promised to increase floor space in the new units, extend sewer systems to all districts, and to provide for such community needs as schools and kindergartens, libraries, sports facilities, parks and playgrounds. Other parts of the housing plan addressed location problems, stressing the need to reduce the time that Tokyoites spent commuting on crowded trains. There were also programs to separate residential environments from industrial pollution and other noxious sites. Still other parts of the plan considered improvements to roads and other transportation, open space, waste disposal and the return to Japan of US military bases within Tokyo. For all these aspects, there were noteworthy provisions that instituted mechanisms for citizen participation. This was a new component to planning in Tokyo, directly reflecting the social activism that brought Minobe to power and characterized the times.

'My Town Tokyo'

The plan that is now in force for the Tokyo Metropolis is called the 2nd Long-Term Development Plan. Released in November 1986, it is the brain child of the administration of Governor Suzuki Shunichi, a member of the Liberal Democratic Party that replaced Minobe in 1979. It is called the '2nd' plan rather than the first because it is a revised, updated version of an earlier document put out in 1982. Even though it replaces 'Tokyo for the People', its contents reflect much of the same concern for assuring citizen participation in planning and addressing their specific needs that distinguished the previous administration. There is also a return of attention to glamour projects in and near the downtown that serve big business and show off Tokyo as an international metropolis. This is something that the Minobe administration had played down. Thus, the 2nd Long-Term Development Plan tries to strike more of a balance between the immediate needs of citizens in the residential areas of the city and plans for bolstering Tokyo's economic influence on a wider scale.

The slogan distinguishing the 2nd Long-Term Development Plan is 'My Town Tokyo'. This motto of the Suzuki administration is often repeated (in English) in the text of the plan itself, as well as in various brochures, posters and other promotional material by the Tokyo government. The words are supposed to convey a sense that the city is both humane and intimate. As the editors' preface to the plan explains, this is to counter the 'tenuous relationship' existing between the city and its residents because of 'top-down' urban development that alienated citizens in the past. Thus, 'My Town Tokyo' promises to 'retrieve' the city for its residents and to plan for the future with their needs in mind first (Tokyo Metropolitan Government 1987b, p. 3). As it does so, the plan will emphasize what it calls 'respect for humanity' and 'ideas born of regional communities' (p. 13). These are high-sounding terms in the peculiar jargon of public servants; they mean that planning is intended to be both people-oriented and sensitive to the specific needs of different communities.

I am especially interested in analysing urban plans as cultural records (Cybriwsky, 1986; Cybriwsky, Ley and Western, 1986) and the *2nd Long-Term Development Plan* for Tokyo is no exception. Instead of dismissing prefatory material in such 'slick and glossy' planning office publications as so much empty public relations nonsense, which it often is, we can focus instead on a content analysis to tell us more precisely about the kind of city the plan envisions. This is an approach I learned from the anthropologist Constance Perin and her book about the social context of planning in the United States called *Everything in Its Place: Social Order and Land Use in America* (Perin, 1977). One of its principal lessons is that careful attention to the language of planning documents, as well as to the details of illustrations contained therein, may reveal the hidden biases of planners (and 'urban decision-makers' more generally), casting new light on their assumptions and deeply held conceptions of the city.

To start with the *2nd Long-Term Development Plan*, we need to look no further than the cover of the published document (Figure 6.2).[2] It is an artist's conception of an ideal for Tokyo that we can examine much as we studied the Meiji era *ukiyoe* about urban change in Ginza in 1874 (see Figure 3.5). In particular, this illustration offers insights in to an idealized overall form or spatial layout that planners have in mind for Tokyo, as well as insights of enduring stereotypes about what is the 'correct' place in both society and geographic space for different social-demographic categories. We see immediately from the illustration that an ideal Tokyo consists of two aspects: one a giant city with super high-rises packed close together and fast communications (such as by futuristic plane) with the rest of the world; another that is, at its base, a fine place for families and older people to live. There are blue skies (on the color cover), ample greenery, clean water and nice homes spaced far apart. While this might all seem too optimistic for this or any huge city because it is an impossible mix, the picture shows in two ways (the rectangular frame and the horizontal line) a clear separation between big-city aspects and the bucolic 'My Town'.

[2] This is the English language edition. The Japanese edition has the same illustration.

Figure 6.2 The cover of the *2nd Long-Term Plan* for Tokyo

This implies that, in reality, the two are located some distance apart from each other. Thus, the form of Tokyo is depicted as essentially two zones: an area for work, shopping and certain types of entertainment, which happens to be the center on the real map of the city, and an area for living, which happens to be the periphery. This is precisely the description of Tokyo I emphasized in Chapter 4.

We also see from the illustration that 'everything is neatly in its place' in terms of social roles that are important in Japanese society. For one thing, no middle-aged men are illustrated among the citizenry of 'My Town'. One can only surmise that they are the providers of the comforts that wives, children and older people who *are* illustrated enjoy, and that they are at their jobs in the big buildings in the background or off in the plane to take care of business elsewhere. The bucolic scene shown is for active children, their mothers (stay-at-home wives) and old people with time to watch the world go by. Students of both sexes, as well as workers who are not middle-aged men, are also missing: presumably they too are off in the distant city. However, how they get there – how Tokyo solves its chronic commuting problem – is not shown either. The problem is avoided perhaps because it reveals an unpleasant aspect of Tokyo, and perhaps because no permanent solution is seen.

Examination of the contents of the *2nd Long-Term Development Plan* reflects attention to both these aspects of Tokyo: the city as a workplace and as a place to live. We see prominent headings about improving residential districts and building new housing; redevelopment in the center of the city; expansion and improvement of other commercial districts; modernization of industrial zones; major improvements to transportation such as roads, subways and train lines; enlarging harbor and airport facilities; redeveloping waterfront areas for residence and recreation; cleaning up environmental pollution; improving disaster-prevention measures; providing new parks and recreation facilities; and many other aspects of the urban scene. There is also considerable attention to social services of all kinds, especially those for an aging population.[3] Some of this variety is summarized in Figure 6.3, a map showing the different types of physical improvements slated for each of the major sections of the Tokyo Metropolis.

It is not my intention to undertake the kind of assessment that measures social needs against what is being done in Tokyo, or that compares in detail what is promised in planning with what is actually realized. These are technical assignments beyond my scope. Instead, I shall summarize the major directions of planning in Tokyo, and describe some of the largest and most important specific planning projects slated for the city and its surroundings. The emphasis is on the changing physical form of the city. I have organized the discussion around three principal sub-topics: (1) development of new commercial sub-centers at strategic transportation nodes to complement the CBD and transform Tokyo into what is being called a 'multi-nodal metropolis'; (2) significant expansion of the urban area into Tokyo Bay and redevelopment of the existing bayfront; and (3) construction of new towns and other sizable urban developments at the edge of the built-up area in the Tama area of Tokyo and in neighboring prefectures. These are the subjects for the next three sub-sections.

Multi-nodal metropolis

As the term suggests, this is an idea to reorient the spatial organization of Tokyo so that the city focuses less on the CBD and more on alternative commercial nodes elsewhere. This is because of overcrowding in the center, excessive land costs and the chronic problem of long-distance commuting. It is an expansion of an idea that was developed first during the Minobe administration to make Tokyo into a 'bi-polar metropolis' focused on the CBD and a cluster of expanded urban centers in the Tama district. It is

---

[3] For the record, I want to mention that the plan says almost nothing about correcting the sexism and stereotypes about age that its cover illustration reflects.

Figure 6.3 Map of plans for physical improvements in *Tokyo-to*

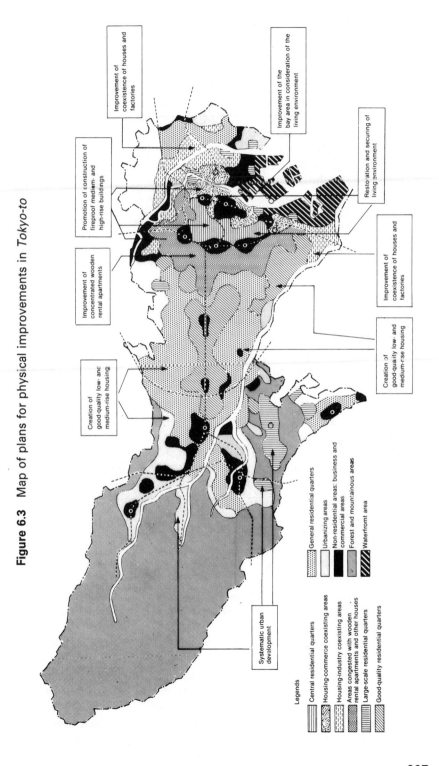

Legends

Central residential quarters
Housing-commerce coexisting areas
Housing-industry coexisting areas
Areas congested with wooden rental apartments and other houses
Large-scale residential quarters
Good-quality residential quarters

General residential quarters
Urbanizing areas
Non-residential areas: business and commercial areas
Forest and mountainous areas
Waterfront area

Improvement of coexistence of houses and factories

Improvement of the bay area in consideration of the living environment

Promotion of construction of fireproof medium- and high-rise buildings

Restoration and securing of living environment

Improvement of concentrated wooden rental apartments

Improvement of coexistence of houses and factories

Creation of good-quality low- and medium-rise housing

Creation of good-quality low- and medium-rise housing

Systematic urban development

Planning directions

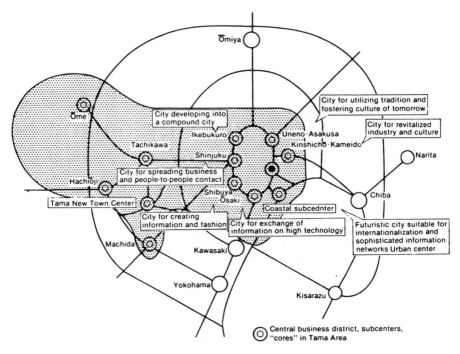

Figure 6.4 The multi-nodal structure of the Tokyo metropolitan area. (*Tokyo Municipal News*, 37, 3, 1987, p. 2)

hard to specify exactly how many new 'sub-centers' (the preferred term) are being planned now, because many things about the multi-nodal concept are still ill-defined and because of certain problems of definition. But recent maps of the scheme issued by Tokyo Metropolitan Government identify as many as 22 such places, 12 of which are within the limits of *Tokyo-to* itself and 10 in the neighboring prefectures (Figure 6.4) Most of these sub-centers are established commercial nodes that have been in existence for some time, such as the CBD of Yokohama, the centers of Tachikawa, Chiba and Ōmiya, and the station-front districts of Shinjuku, Shibuya and other close-in Tokyo districts, and have been singled out as places that should grow to become even more important in the future. Some others, however, notably Tama New Town in *Tokyo-to* and Tsukuba Science City in Ibaraki Prefecture, are more recent developments designed from the start to be growth centers.

The greatest attention in the multi-nodal plan is given to a group of sub-centers that is closest to the CBD and arranged in a ring around the inner wards as stations on the Yamanote Rail Line. This is the all-important loop line that encircles the core of the city and intersects with all of the train and subway lines that run in and out of its heart (see Chapter 2). Each of the biggest stations – Shinjuku, Shibuya and Ikebukuro on the west side of the loop and the Ueno-Asakusa complex to the north and east

— are designated as new nodes for Tokyo, as is a place called Ōsaki, a newly developed commercial center on the southwest side of the loop. A new node for Tokyo is also promised at Kinshichō-Kameido, a mixed industrial-residential area in Sumida Ward and at the waterfront with Tokyo Bay. All seven of these are close enough to the CDB (always well within 10 kilometers) to make it possible to envision their eventual coalescence into one super-giant business core. We have seen in the earlier discussion about the expansion of the CBD (chapter 4) that the CBD and both Shinjuku and Shibuya are all growing together, and that the CBD is also rapidly expanding in the directions of the waterfront and Ueno.

According to publicity about the plan, each of Tokyo's new sub-centers is to be distinctive, based on its history and characteristic economic functions. For example, Shinjuku, which we have already discussed as becoming the principal 'new center' of Tokyo because of the new City Hall, is to emphasize its role as an office and hotel concentration, and as a pre-eminent center for the all-important eating, drinking and entertainment functions that characterize Tokyo's after-work and after-school life. The latter assignment was determined presumably because of the presence in Shinjuku of the Kabukichō district. Shibuya, on the other hand, which we discussed as being especially popular among high school and college students out for a good time, is given the general charge of being 'a town that generates information and fashions'. Some of the other designations seem less specific: Ueno-Asakusa is to be promoted as 'a traditional town that creates tomorrow's culture'; Kinshichō-Kameido is to be 'an activated industrial and cultural town'; and Ikebukuro, which seems to be a little bit of everything, is 'a town expected to grow into a composite city' (Tokyo Metropolitan Government, 1987b, pp. 206–7). Unfortunately, none of these distinctions is particularly well-defined, even though they are repeated everywhere and often in publicity by the Tokyo government (Figure 6.5). Perhaps only time will tell what the results will be in practice.

It is especially interesting here to look more closely at the sub-center being developed at Ōsaki (Figure 6.6). This is an entirely new project, and is being built from the ground up by a partnership between the Japan Railways Corporation (JR), other local landowners, Shingawa Ward and several outside investors at Ōsaki Station on the JR Yamanote Line. This used to be the least-used of all 29 Yamanote stations, and was selected to be a new node for Tokyo in part so that the number of passengers who get on and off there could be increased. Construction of so-called Phase I, on a three hectare site that was previously freight railroad and industrial land, began in 1986 and is almost complete. Phase II, which will cover an additional six hectares, is slated for completion in the mid–1990s. The name given to the development as a whole is 'Ōsaki New City' (also written *Ohsaki* New City). It is touted in the publication by the Tokyo government, cited above, as 'a town for high-tech information exchanges'. A currently popular television drama *Sora ni hoshi ga aru yōni* ('As if There Were Stars

個性を生かした副都心の育成
Buildingng Up of Subcenters with Individual Character

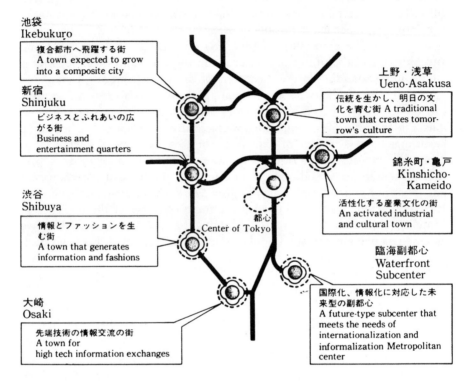

池袋
Ikebukuro

複合都市へ飛躍する街
A town expected to grow
into a composite city

新宿
Shinjuku

ビジネスとふれあいの広
がる街
Business and
entertainment quarters

渋谷
Shibuya

情報とファッションを生
む街
A town that generates
information and fashions

大崎
Osaki

先端技術の情報交流の街
A town for
high tech information exchanges

都心
Center of Tokyo

上野・浅草
Ueno-Asakusa

伝統を生かし、明日の文
化を育む街 A traditional
town that creates tomor-
row's culture

錦糸町・亀戸
Kinshicho-
Kameido

活性化する産業文化の街
An activated industrial
and cultural town

臨海副都心
Waterfront
Subcenter

国際化、情報化に対応した未
来型の副都心
A future-type subcenter that
meets the needs of
internationalization and
informalization Metropolitan
center

Figure 6.5 The close-in sub-centers of Tokyo and their 'individual character' as described by Tokyo Metropolitan Government. (Tokyo Metropolitan Government, 1990a)

in the Sky'), is set there, I am sure, in part to publicize the existence of the place and promote its development.

If we go to Ōsaki New City we see very little yet that is actually 'high-tech information exchange' or anything else that would seem to make this sub-center distinctive from the others. Instead, the place looks much like any of a number of other developments in Tokyo and, indeed, other Japanese cities. There is a certain style of building design and project layout that seems to be spreading so widely in the country that it is now a cliché for its modern urban environment. Thus, at Ōsaki New City we see four high-rises (the tallest is 21 stories) that not only look like each other, but also much like the new commercial buildings at the Sunshine 60 complex in the Ikebukuro sub-center at Ark Hills (see Chapter 4), at Tama New Town (Chapter 4), and all over the CBD. As seen from a distance, they

Figure 6.6 Ōsaki New City and Osaki Station on the Yamanote Line. The background shows industrial facilities and warehouses near Tokyo Bay. (Courtesy of Ōsaki New City, Information Office)

are big, light-colored blocks that stand on end. Three of the Ōsaki buildings are office buildings and one is an hotel, one of a major chain. A fifth, one low in profile, is a rather standard indoor shopping mall. Although some tenants have been in Ōsaki for many years, the mall is mostly given over to chain stores. There is a Humpty Dumpty Crêpe House at one of the entrances, and a squeaky-clean McDonald's in the center of the mall. Between the buildings is a plaza, paved with square tiles in a white and grey checkerboard pattern, with some stands of potted trees and other landscaping, two bubbling fountains, a modern-art sculpture of a shapely young woman (along with seagulls, the most common theme for public art in Japan's newest redevelopment projects) and a plaque that tells distances and directions to various capital cities in the world. The only 'high-tech' in evidence is a futuristic-looking pedestrian bridge from the train station and the chrome-plated mechanical sculptures found along its length. It is all nice, clean and comfortable – and very predictable.

Waterfront planning

The largest of the sub-centers in the multi-nodal scheme is to be developed at the Tokyo Bay waterfront. This is the direction the city has always gone

Figure 6.7 A barge carrying fill material for Tokyo Bay heading downriver on the Sumida. The twin towers represent an expanding edge of the CBD

in the past when it needed room to expand, and where much fanfare for the future is directed (Figure 6.7). This is because the coastal sub-center is supposed to be not just another giant business center like the others, but also an entirely new city with a mix of workplaces, residences and recreation sites. When this happens, it will be a significant change for Tokyo, because since at least Edo times, the city has never fully exploited its waterfront for amentities. Tokyo ranks far behind almost all other large cities in industrialized societies in waterfront planning, and stands alone for having almost no public access to the water, very little waterfront parkland and almost no amenities such as marinas for recreational boating or a beach for swimming. There are not even any restaurants, waterfront hotels or Rouse-type malls at the waterfront. This is especially strange, given that now is a time of revitalization by commercial interests of waterfront districts in cities worldwide in general, and that Tokyo itself is the world's greatest concentration of restaurants, hotels and shopping centers. For the time being, what we find instead at the Tokyo waterfront is a landscape of industry and warehouses, docks, rail sidings and cement walls that protect against floods and tidal surges.

The proper name for the coastal sub-center is Tokyo Teleport Town. This is meant to suggest that the place will be a highly futuristic city with advanced telecommunications technology. According to the publicity, this is where Tokyo will concentrate its greatest efforts to become *the* international business center for the 21st century. The details are yet to be

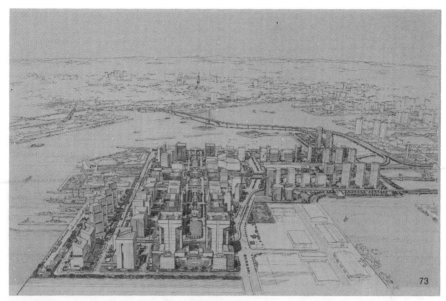

Figure 6.8 Artist's rendering of the Teleport concept for Tokyo Bay. (Courtesy of the Office of Information, Tokyo Metropolitan Government)

worked out, but plans call for being in instant touch with other global cities through fiber optics' technology and satellites, and for having state-of-the-art technology for information processing and office automation. Teleport is also to be highly advanced in the design of its buildings, in technology for providing utilities and removing wastes, traffic control and many other aspects of urban development. In fact, official publicity speaks grandly about this being an 'ideal' urban environment and the 'frontier for developing the cities of the 21st century' (*Tokyo Municipal News*, 40, 1, 1990, pp. 1–2). A widely circulated artist's conception of what Teleport might look like in a few years is given in Figure 6.8.

The specific location of Teleport is an island in Tokyo Bay about six kilometers from the center of the CBD that, for now, is unceremoniously called No. 13 Reclaimed Land. The site is 440 hectares, almost all of which are owned by the Tokyo Metropolitan Government, and is made from municipal waste and landfill brought in from construction sites all over the metropolitan area. There is not much to see there yet except for a rather lonesome park, an isolated maritime museum, tennis courts, a popular disco with plenty of parking spaces and various industrial and warehousing facilities. There are also lots of well-fed sea gulls and, in summer, the same plagues of flies from garbage dumps that once infested the Sumida River wards from the 'Island of Dreams'. However, in the future, perhaps by 2010, planners expect that some 115,000 people will work at Teleport and 44,000 people will live there (*Tokyo Municipal News*, 37, 3, 1987, p. 1). This is a mix that accurately reflects what the center of Tokyo and all its sub-centers is to be about: despite occasional words to the contrary, it is planned as more a magnet for commuters than a place of residence.

One of the reasons for the slow development at Teleport has been poor transportation links with Tokyo proper. So the first phase of the plan's construction, scheduled for completion in 1993, will be to extend the Yūrakuchō subway line from the heart of Tokyo and to complete a 4.3 kilometer expressway over water (called the 'No. 12 Metropolitan Express-way') from the waterfront area of Shibaura. There are also plans to build rapid connections with both Haneda Airport, which itself is to be relocated to newly reclaimed land in the Bay, and the airport at Narita. The fact that the Teleport site is on a line with both airports gives it an advantage as a gathering place for international contacts. Planners hope that after such connections are in place, companies will scramble to build in Teleport, and that income from rents and land sales can offset the investment costs. To promote development, the Tokyo Metropolitan Government has recently announced plans to host a major international event at Teleport in 1994. To be called 'Tokyo Frontier', it will focus on solutions to urban problems. If all goes well, city officials hope to show off Tokyo to the world as the leading 21st century city. This is much like 1964 when the Olympics were used to unveil Tokyo's recovery from the war and to announce its entry into the emerging global economy.

As big and important as the Teleport project is expected to be, it is but one of several major developments taking shape at the waterfront (Figure 6.9). Some of the other landfill islands have also been targeted for the construction of offices, hotels and high-rise residences, as have large stretches of the shoreline (itself made of landfill) and several areas immediately behind the shoreline. The biggest projects have been proposed for three large rectangular islands that lie between the Teleport site and the core of the city: Tsukushima, Harumi and Toyosu. Most of the land uses there now are related to the port, but the future would reorient this area to be an extension of the CBD. At Toyosu, for example, which is now 105 hectares of petroleum storage tanks and other industrial facilities, the plan would create a giant cluster of sleek office and commercial buildings and high-rise residences not unlike the cluster planned for the No. 13 site. Examples of projects in this vein on the shoreline include redevelopment of the Hinode and Takeshiba Pier areas into high-rise cities, the construction of an offices and hotels complex at Tennosu to be called Bay City Towers, and the redevelopment of the neighboring Shibaura factory and warehouse district to include a mix of offices, shopping centers, public institutions and some housing. The electronics industries concentrated in this area are to have the lead in this by relocating factories outside the city and erecting company offices in their places. We have already seen in the discussion of CBD expansion that the giant Tōshiba Corporation has done this by building a tall headquarters tower near the waterfront close to Hinode Pier.

A general description of what is to be at these various sites is the

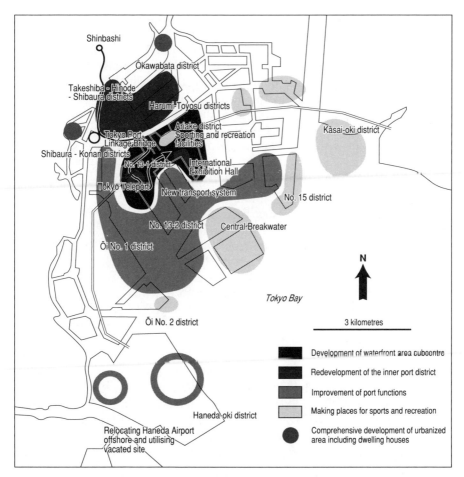

Figure 6.9 Waterfront area development plan for Tokyo

paragraph below. It is taken from a publication (in English) by the Tange architects' group, and was written specifically to describe what Toyosu, the landfill island mentioned above, might look like in the future. What strikes me most about it, is that in a few words this one paragraph incorporates all the buzzwords characterizing contemporary planning in the center city of Tokyo, and thus encapsulates the image that planners have for the area as a whole in years to come. That is, we can substitute the word 'Toyosu' with 'Number 13 Reclaimed Land', 'Harumi', 'Tsukushima', 'Hinode' or any of several other waterfront place names, and still be fairly accurate about the plans:

In terms of the great demand for office space in Tokyo, Toyosu [or whatever place] can be a central, dense, internationalized and information-oriented business district. In addition, it will include good-quality urban-style housing, international business and convention facilities, a commercial zone making good use of the waterfront, and recreational functions. With all of these amenities the Toyosu district will occupy an important position in the waterfront region and the entire city of Tokyo in the twenty-first century, (Tange, 1987, p. 26).

There are, in fact, more than 40 different projects under way now in Tokyo Bay designed to extend the city and improve its environment. As Table 6.1 shows, not all of them are physically within *Tokyo-to*: the waterfront extends in one direction and the other into Kanagawa and Chiba Prefectures, and not all are oriented to enlarging the CBD. Other projects enlarge business districts elsewhere or create new business centers; still others address land-use needs that are altogether different. Examples of important projects within the jurisdictional limits of Tokyo include improvements to piers and other port facilities such as warehousing and distribution centers at Ōi and Shinagawa Wharfs, on Tsukushima (the innermost landfill island) and other places in the inner waterfront; the construction of River City 21, a large residential complex at one of the edges of Tsukushima; expansion of sports fields and other recreation facilties on a reclaimed island named Ariake; the relocation of Haneda Airport to a much larger site in the bay and redevelopment of the present site; and the improvement to housing and recreation facilities at Kasai in Edogawa Ward and along the waterfront in Ōta Ward. Projects in neighboring prefectures include improvements to harbor facilities in Yokohama, Kawasaki and the industrial areas of Chiba; construction of large blocks of apartments in Urayasu City near the Tokyo Disneyland complex (Chiba Prefecture); a new 70-hectare 'Sea Park' in Yokohama; a large new international conference center ('Shōnan International Village') in the Yokosuka area in Kanagawa Prefecture; and the construction of a new city center with a high-tech, international focus in Makuhari City, Chiba Prefecture. A selection of these projects is described below.[4]

Perhaps the most highly publicized project of all, one that exemplifies the scope and spirit of most of the planning at the Tokyo Bay waterfront, is a project called Minato Mirai 21. This is a giant new urban center being built on a 186-hectare site on the waterfront near the Yokohama CBD. Its name means 'port of the future for the 21st century'. What is being done there could well have been described in the all-purpose paragraph above. The project combines redevelopment of the existing shoreline (60 per cent of the site) with considerable freshly reclaimed land; it promises to be a rather impressive-looking district of neatly arranged commercial, residential and waterfront recreation land uses. Because it is adjacent to Yokohama's extremely busy port, and because of the city's history as an international trade center, Minato Mirai 21 is expected to be especially important as a business center related to shipping and as an international

[4] For a discussion of the environmental impact of development in Tokyo Bay, see Short, 1988.

Table 6.1 Important waterfront development projects along Tokyo Bay (arranged geographically from the west side of the bay in Kanagawa Prefecture near the bay mouth, north through the Tokyo waterfront, to the east side of the bay in Chiba Prefecture)

1 **Shōnan International Village**
Hayama town Yokosuka, Kanagawa Prefecture. 185.0 hectares.
Comprehensive facilities for international academic, cultural and technological exchanges.

2 **Marine community-polis**
Off Sarushima, Yokosuka, Kanagawa Prefecture.
A new man-made island that is to be a 'park-like' city.

3 **Sea Park**
Kanagawa Ward, Yokohoma, Kanagawa Prefecture. 70.0 hectares.
A new public park.

4 **International Trade Island**
Off Kanazawa, Yokohama, Kanagawa Prefecture.
Land reclamation for distribution, recreation and industrial facilities.

5 **South Honmoku Wharf**
Naka Ward, Yokohama, Kanagawa Prefecture. 98.2 hectares.
New cargo wharf.

6 **Honmoku D Land Lot**
Naka Ward, Yokohama, Kanagawa Prefecture. 70.8 hectares.
Wharfs and distribution facilities for container cargo.

7 **Kitanaka-dori**
Naka Ward, Yokohama, Kanagawa Prefecture. 11.0 hectares.
Redevelopment to improve trunk roads.

8 **Minato Mirai 21 (MM21)**
Naka and Nishi Wards, Yokohama, Kanagawa Prefecture. 186.0 hectares.
A huge new town on the waterfront to add to the city's cultural and commercial centers.

9 **Portside Area**
Kanagawa Ward, Yokohama, Kanagawa Prefecture. 25.0 hectares.
Redevelopment for commercial, business and housing facilities.

10 **Daikoku Wharf, second phase**
Tsurumi Ward, Yokohama, Kanagawa Prefecture. 100.0 hectares.
New wharfs and distribution facilities.

11 **Civil Port Island**
Kawasaki Ward, Kawasaki, Kanagawa Prefecture. 442.0 hectares.
Improvement of harbor facilities and construction of energy and industrial facilities.

12 **Ukishima Land Lot**
Kawasaki Ward, Kawasaki, Kanagawa Prefecture. 92.5 hectares.
Land reclamation for waste materials dumping; improvement of thoroughfares; construction of parks.

13 **Marinepolis Project**
Kawasaki Ward and off Hajima, Kawasaki, Kanagawa Prefecture. 480 hectares.

Table 6.1 *Continued*

Construction of an offshore island through waste materials dumping and development of a new city.

14 Kawasaki Riverside
Kawasaki Ward, Kawasaki, Kanagawa Prefecture. 130.0 hectares.
City-center redevelopment; remodeling of industrial sites; new research and development area.

15 Kawasaki Technopia Project
Kawasaki and Saiwai Wards, Kawasaki, Kanagawa Prefecture. 47.0 hectares.
Improvements to the center of Kawasaki and redevelopment of the commercial area around Kawasaki Station.

16 Relocation of Haneda Airport
Ōta Ward, Tokyo. 1,100 hectares.
Relocation of the overcrowded airport to new reclaimed site in Tokyo Bay.

17 Haneda Airport Site Reuse
Ōta Ward, Tokyo. 200.0 hectares.
New uses for the present airport facility.

18 Ōi Market
Ōta Ward, Tokyo. 60.0 hectares.
Vegetable and fish warehouses and distribution facilities.

19 Ōi Community Zone
Yashio, Shinagawa Ward and Tokai, Ōta Ward, Tokyo. 56.0 hectares.
Sports, recreation and cultural facilities.

20 Tennosu Bay City Towers
Higashi Shinagawa, Shinagawa Ward, Tokyo. 20.0 hectares.
Office towers and hotels complex.

21 Shibaura-Konan
Shibaura and Konan, Minato Ward, . 500.0 hectares.
Comprehensive redevelopment of the area, with emphasis on transportation, warehouses and industry.

22 Takeshiba, Hinode and Shibaura Wharfs
Kaigan, Minato Ward, Tokyo. 36.8 hectares.
Improvement of harbor facilities at three wharfs.

23 Tokyo Harbor Number 18 Land
Minato, Chūō and Kōtō Wards, Tokyo. 150.0 hectares.
Construction of Tokyo Teleport and other facilities of a high-technology offshore new town.

24 Chūō Breakwater
502.2 hectares in Tokyo Bay.
Land reclamation project for future uses.

25 Riverside Redevelopment
Tsukuda, Chūō Ward, Tokyo. 27.9 hectares.
Construction of housing, commercial and cultural facilities on previously industrial land.

Table 6.1 *Continued*

26 **Tsukishima Area**
Tsukishima, Chūō Ward, Tokyo. 20.1 hectares.
Redevelopment of a crowded, old residential and commercial district.

27 **Harumi Area**
Harumi, Chūō Ward, Tokyo. 77.0 hectares.
Redevelopment of industrial facilities for residential and cultural uses.

28 **Toyosu Area**
Toyosu, Kōtō Ward, Tokyo. 88.0 hectares.
Comprehensive redevelopment of an industrial district.

29 **Ariake Comprehensive Sports Recreation Area**
Ariake, Kōtō Ward, Tokyo. 30.0 hectares.
Improvement of sports and recreation facilities.

30 **Tatsumi District (No. 7 Land)**
Tatsumi, Kōtō Ward, Tokyo. 40.0 hectares.
Improvement of the area's environment.

31 **Wakasu District (No. 15 Area)**
Wakasu, Kōtō Ward, Tokyo. 75.0 hectares.
Marine park.

32 **Reclaimed Land off Kasai**
Kasai, Edogawa Ward, Tokyo. 348.0 hectares.
Improvement of housing, distribution and recreation facilities on
reclaimed land.

33 **Urayasu Area**
Urayasu, Chiba Prefecture. 563.4 hectares.
Housing and industrial sites.

34 **Ichikawa Area, Second Phase (Marine Garden Ichikawa)**
Ichikawa, Chiba Prefecture. 540.0 hectares.
Cultural facilities and waterfront recreation.

35 **Western Funabashi**
Funabashi, Chiba Prefecture. 64.0 hectares.
Improvement of wharfs and other port facilities.

36 **Keiyō Area, Second Phase**
Funabashi, Chiba Prefecture. 370.0 hectares.
Improvement of wharfs and other port facilities.

37 **New Makuhari City Center**
Makuhari, Chiba Prefecture. 437.7 hectares.
Construction of new city center with international focus.

38 **Makuhari Messe-Techno Garden**
Makuhari, Chiba Prefecture. 25.0 hectares.
Construction of a permanent international trade fairground, and of
research and development facilities.

39 **Chiba Station Area**
Chiba, Chiba Prefecture.
Redevelopment of the commercial district around Chiba Station.

40 **Chiba Port Area**
Chiba, Chiba Prefecture. 160.0 hectares.
Improvements to the area in and near the port of Chiba.

Table 6.1 *Continued*

---

41   Jōsō New Research and Development City
Kisarazu, Chiba Prefecture.
Construction of centers for academic research and high-technology facilities.

42   Futtsu Area
Futtsu, Chiba Prefecture. 643.8 hectares.
An industrial area centered on distribution and processing.

Source: Business Tokyo, May 1987, p. 25.

conference complex. The proposed daytime population is 190,000 and the number of residents 10,000. One large piece of Minato Mirai 21, a section called Block 25 to be developed by the Mitsubishi Estate Company, the giant conglomerate from Tokyo's Marunouchi district, is to have a super landmark office and hotel tower that, at 70 stories, would become the tallest building in Japan.

The River City 21 complex, in Tokyo near the mouth of the Sumida River, is also especially important and deserves extra mention (Figure 6.10). What makes it special is that unlike all the other new projects nearby, it is primarily a housing development, and one on a prime site at that. This is a departure from the trend of expanding the CBD in every direction,

Figure 6.10   River City 21 under construction at the tip of Tsukushima, one of the close-in reclaimed islands in Tokyo Bay. Unlike most other new high-rises in Tokyo, the tall buildings here are residences. The background is the Sumida River and its celebrated bridges, and Kātō and Sumida Wards. (Courtesy of Ōkawabata River City 21 Kaihatsu Kyōgikai and Mami Miyamato.)

including to the waterfront, and is therefore one of the few places in the center of Tokyo where a serious effort is being made to increase, rather than decrease, the residential population. Moreover, because it is mostly housing (2,500 units; 7,000 residents), it is not supposed to be a magnet for commuters like Teleport or Minato Mirai 21. Instead, the project is intended to cut down on the number of commuters to Tokyo, because its residents will be able to walk to work, or take a short bus or subway ride to the CBD or to one of the new waterfront commercial projects. Because it is such a radical idea for Tokyo, River City 21 (the '21' means it is a 21st-century idea), is a pet project for its planners at the Tokyo Metropolitan Government and the Housing and Urban Development Public Corporation.

The site of River City 21 is a former industrial tract on the tip of Tsukushima, precisely where the Sumida River enters Tokyo Bay and splits into two equal distributaries. Because this is an extremely visible place from riverbanks and various bridges, the project is coming to be quite well-known in Tokyo. This is precisely what its creators wanted. The design, as seen from a distance, is a cluster of distinctive high-rises that look to be a cut above the big blocks standing on end that dominate so much of the rest of the city. This, too, calls attention to the project. The view from the high-rises is superb and is also a selling point: the whole center of Tokyo is visible, as are the Sumida River with its well-known series of historic bridges, the islands and bridges of Tokyo Bay, and the comings and goings of ships in the inner harbor and planes at Haneda Airport. The realtors who sell the River City 21 units like to point out that in the evening you can even see the Electric Parade at Tokyo Disneyland through the windows.

The site plan is even more impressive. Although less than half the project is finished, there is already a lot of open space and greenery between the buildings, several pleasant winding paths, playgrounds and small parks, and the beginnings of what promises to be a super waterfront promenade. There is also local shopping, a new elementary and middle school and other community facilities. These are shared with an historic neighborhood that is immediately adjacent: an area of older houses, many of them wooden, squeezed in between factories and what is left of a fishing fleet harbor. All these features, and the quiet one gains from city noise by virtue of being at the tip of a peninsula, convey a sense of relaxed living (Figure 6.11). So it is not surprising that there is a long waiting list for units in this project, and that prices even by Tokyo standards are very high. In fact, there has been so much recent demand for units at River City 21 that extraordinary measures have been needed to keep out the kind of speculators who would buy there just to make a profit from fast resale (Yada, 1989a, p. 28).[5]

If we go in either direction along the shoreline from the innermost part

[5] Unfortunately, it seems that the high standards of design that marked River City 21 during the first stages of its development have been relaxed. The buildings that are going up now are much closer together and ugly, and the public spaces and recreation facilities between them are small and undistinguished.

Figure 6.11   Children at play at River City 21

of the waterfront, we see recent planning projects dealing with the industrial aspects of Tokyo and its working harbor. They are not as showy as the sleek, commercial high-rises or a fancy new residential town, but they are equally spectacular in their own way. For example, Ōta Ward, south of the center of the city, is one of the areas where the Tokyo government is investing most heavily in improvements to piers and other facilities for the Port of Tokyo, and where an expansive new district of warehouses, distribution facilities, container cargo terminals, and other facilities relating to shipping and trucking have been developed on reclaimed land. Quite a few of the major manufacturing companies of Japan, especially electronics firms with a large export trade, have facilities here. There is also a huge new wholesale market for produce and marine foods, operated by the Tokyo Metropolitan Government. Like the other facilities in the area, it benefits from an efficient network of new access roads and bridges, as well as from attractive landscaping (Figure 6.12). In fact, the immediate neighbor of the Ōta Wholesale Market is a new public park of more than 30 hectares. It is the Tokyo Port Wild Life Park, a beautiful, restful place that is a sanctuary for many species of birds, and a marvelous addition to this district of warehouses and industry.

In the other direction from the center of the city, where Edogawa Ward borders Chiba Prefecture, is another new section of waterfront and still a different use of the land. This is the Kasai area, where the Tokyo government has developed a large new public park with an aquarium and a wide,

Figure 6.12 Warehouses and industrial plants at the Tokyo Bay harborfront south of Ōi in Shinagawa Ward.

Figure 6.13 The new beach at Kasairinkankōen in Edogawa Ward

new sandy beach (Figure 6.13). Called Kasairinkankōen, the park measures 185 hectares, and is close to some huge tracts of subsidized apartments (*danchi*) put up by the Japan Housing Corporation for workers at the industrial waterfront and their families, as well as for other residents. It is most quickly reached from the city by a new train line, the Keiyō Line which extends to the cities and industrial areas of coastal Chiba Prefecture, and is only 15 minutes away from the terminal at Tokyo Station. This is close enough for workers from the CBD to sneak off to the beach during an extended lunch break or after hours on a long summer day. I was there recently on a hot July afternoon and saw small groups of salarymen strolling along the water's edge, shoes and suit jackets in hand. The park is also convenient by new expressway. Tokyo Disneyland (actually in Chiba Prefecture) and its new complex of waterfront hotels is one station away from Kasairinkankōen, and is clearly visible from the beach. This makes for a wider recreation-tourism district, and adds to the appeal for visitors. Because so much of the other construction along the waterfront (and elsewhere in Tokyo) is of high-rise/high-density urban material, this park is an especially welcome addition to the city, and a significant step toward remedying its overall lack of outdoor recreation spaces.

The Tama area

The other direction of Tokyo's growth, in addition to enlargement of the CBD and designated close-in commercial sub-centers, and expansion into the bay, is outward to the suburbs and beyond. There are literally hundreds of planning projects of all kinds scattered over Tokyo's Tama area and its neighboring prefectures of Chiba, Kanagawa and Saitama, including several that are quite spectacular because of their size and ambitions. Some of the most notable of these are large-scale 'new town' developments combining thousands of new residences and workplaces at sites that were previously non-urban, as well as new or expanded commercial centers of various types that, collectively, represent an 'outer-ring' complement to the inner-ring commercial sub-centers described earlier. The effect of all this is to expand the Tokyo metropolis to newly gigantic proportions, well beyond the limits of the already huge extent of the built-up area; and to fill in any gaps in urbanized land that are still found between the core of Tokyo and the urbanized areas of nearby satellite towns.

Perhaps the best-known and most established of these projects is the Tama New Town development that I introduced earlier in discussing sub-urbanization trends (Chapter 4). This project was started in 1965 on 2,200 previously undeveloped hectares in the Tama Hills area west of Tokyo proper by Tokyo Metropolitan Government and two public development corporations (the Tokyo Metropolitan Housing Supply Public Corporation and the Urban Development Public Corporation) to provide housing and community services for overflow population from the central city (Figures

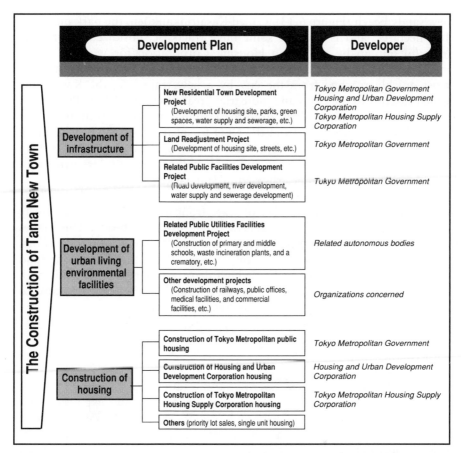

Figure 6.14 The construction of Tama New Town. (Tokyo Metropolitan Government)

6.14 and 6.15). It is one of several notable 'satellite town' projects designated for the 'Central Tama' section of *Tokyo-to* after enactment of the 1958 Law for Town Development in the National Capital Region, and was originally intended to be a major focus of business and commercial functions as well as a residential concentration. The other projects, which, together with the center of Tama New Town, were to comprise part of a 'second pole' to Tokyo, included smaller new towns at nearby Hachiōji and Akirudai (also called 'Akiru Plateau' in some English language publications), and major reconstruction in Tachikawa, particularly at a repatriated US air base that now has several areas of planned housing developments and a large, attractive, multi-use public park (Hall, 1984, pp. 192–4).

Some 101,000 residents currently live in Tama New Town, but as new

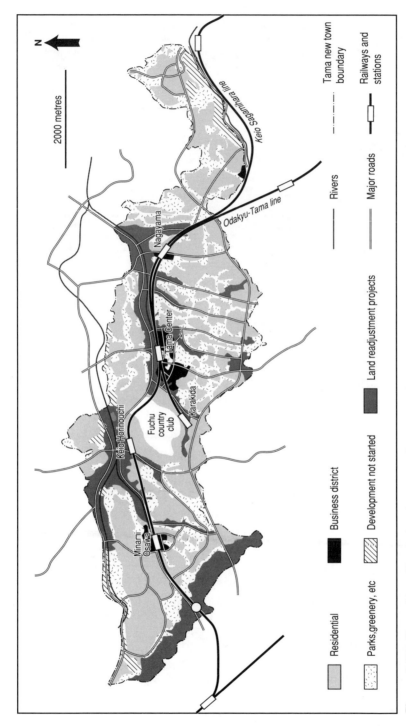

Figure 6.15 Tama New Town development plan

Figure 6.16 Tama New Town

housing is added, the total is eventually expected to exceed 300,000.[6] Housing consists of distinctive clusters of townhouses, mid-rise multi-family buildings, and attractive suburban-style single-family structures not unlike those on display at the model home park in Shinjuku; it is arranged in neat neighborhood groupings separated by greenery and recreation spaces. There is also a new planned town center with department stores, large supermarkets and many other shops and facilities built around two adjacent train stations (the competing Keiō and Odakyū Lines) connecting the development directly with Shinjuku; there are lots of parks, playgrounds, bike paths, streams and ponds, and public fountains and sculptures for residents to enjoy. While one could fault the design for being too conspicuously clean and orderly (and therefore not especially stimulating for true cityphiles), the place succeeds as an escape from urban crowding for growing families and a chance for comfortable, reasonably affordable housing (Figure 6.16). A survey of residents' opinions about the place shows rather high scores on most 'quality of life' indicators (Table 6.2) (Hovinen, 1988). However, the town has not developed much of a local employment base, as the early publicity had promised, and is instead mostly a commuters' town within the orbit of central Tokyo.

[6] The size of the Tama New Town area will be expanded from 2,200 hectares to over 3,000 hectares.

Table 6.2 Evaluation of the quality of life in Tama New Town by residents, 1987

Quality of life indicator	Score
Abundant green space	1.32
Clean air	1.39
Sunny and breezy	1.40
Drainage and sewer system	1.50
Parks	1.52
Garbage disposal	1.53
Assembly facilities	1.71
Appearance of buildings	1.76
Friendliness	1.86
Safety of transportation	1.89
Community activities	1.97
Crime prevention, public morals	2.04
Housing	2.08
Noise, vibration	2.08
Convenience of shopping areas	2.22
Convenience of transportation	2.35
Medical facilities	2.37
Retail prices	2.81

The questionnaire was designed so that 1.00 was 'good'; 2.00 was 'rather good'; 3.00 was 'rather bad'; and 4.00 was 'bad'.

Source: Hovinen, 1988, p. 55, after the report in Japanese of a survey conducted by local government in Tama New Town.

Hachiōji, on the other hand, has had more success at becoming an important employment nucleus. This is partly because of the long history of this outlying town as a factory center specializing in textiles, but the more important reason is the establishment there of numerous colleges and universities after 1959. This is the year when a Tokyo growth-control ordinance was enacted to prohibit new campuses from opening within the boundaries of the 23 wards, and when tight controls were put on the expansion of existing campuses. Hachiōji became a preferred location for higher education because of its pleasant surroundings, and because it was thought to be far enough away from the center of Tokyo to help reduce the crowding problems caused by the overconcentration of education functions, but near enough so that students and educators could enjoy the capital's benefits and attractions. There are now more than a score of *daigaku* in and near this city, employing several thousand individuals and having thousands and thousands of students, both residents and commuters. In addition, because of the higher education base, Hachiōji has recently emerged as a significant center for high technology research and development.

Hachiōji New Town is the newest phase of this development. Located on 390 hectares in the southern ward of Hachiōji City, it is a plan by Tokyo government for a carefully designed, self-contained community that will have some 28,000 residents, a full range of attractive community facilities, and numerous new workplaces in various high technology fields. The goal is to strengthen the role of Hachiōji, and indeed the Central Tama region in general, as a major concentration of growth industries, and in so doing to lessen the need for residents in the western outlying zones of Tokyo to commute long distances to work. The plan was announced in 1980; construction was just beginning in 1991, so there is not much to report yet in the way of results. In fact, several key parcels that can 'make or break' the project are still untaken by developers. However, the ground plan for the New Town as a whole described in publicity brochures promises a pleasanter environment than most urban land around Tokyo, and features a balanced mix of residential neighborhoods next to landscaped office and industrial parks and school campuses. The fact that Hachiōji has achieved a reputation as a fashionable Tokyo suburb, and the shortage of housing in the Tokyo metropolis as a whole, will doubtlessly help to make this development a commercial success.

Neighboring prefectures

Each of the prefectures that border *Tokyo-to* have variations on the planned urban development taking place in Central Tama. For some of the best examples, we can go to the opposite side of Tokyo to Chiba Prefecture where what is called the Chiba New Industry Triangle Concept is taking shape amid suburban satellite towns, paddy fields and wooded hills (Figure 6.17). This is another emerging high-tech zone to be built around a grouping of designated, close-together towns. As the proper name suggests, three towns in particular are most important: Makuhari, a rather ambitious new town on Tokyo Bay between Tokyo and Chiba City (Otani, 1990); Narita, the historic temple-town-in-the-farmlands, turned in the 1970s amid considerable turmoil into the site of Tokyo's giant new international airport (located a famously inconvenient 60 kilometers from the center of the city); and Kazusa, a 1,000-hectare site in the broken terrain of Chiba Peninsula that is supposed to become a model research and development town with numerous private laboratories, especially in medicine. The similarity of this concept to the Research Triangle area in North Carolina in the US is intended. In fact, the official guide book to these developments gives a photograph of a university scene in North Carolina in the absence of completed buildings in Kazusa (Chiba Nipposha, 1989, p. 177). So, too, the Silicon Valley of California has been a model for this development. We see this in a new nickname for the prefecture: 'Chiba-fornia' (Otani, 1990, p. 458).

The plan for Makuhari is especially well-publicized. The town is to be a 'ground-up' new town on 522 hectares of reclaimed land in industrial Chiba City, expected to house 26,000 residents and to have some 15,000 full-time employees (Table 6.3). The focus is a huge international-scale

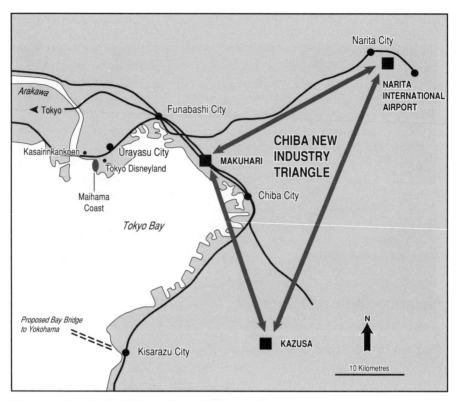

Figure 6.17 Chiba New Industry Triangle

convention facility, formally named the Nippon Convention Center but more commonly called Makuhari Messe,[7] near the waterfront (Figure 6.18). Its main features are three gigantic structures for meetings and exhibitions that, in profile, are supposed to suggest a traditional Japanese village set in front of a backdrop of misty mountains. In keeping with more general goals for improving public use and access to Tokyo Bay, other parts of the waterfront are given to open space recreation, such as a beach, and a 30,000 seat stadium for baseball and other sports. Makuhari also has a sizable 'Business Research Zone', in which several prestigious companies, both Japanese and foreign, have already begun to construct showy office towers and other facilities. Prominent examples include NTT, IBM-Japan, Tokyo Gas Company and BMW Japan. The residential area, much of which is also to be near the waterfront, is to have 8,100 housing units in buildings ranging in height from 5 to 40 stories. The fact that the project

[7] The nickname Makuhari Messe is eagerly promoted by Chiba government and other developers of the project because, according to them, the words 'messe' and 'convention' 'are used in much the same way in the international community', and both 'mean a place for comprehensive communication, integrating people, objects and information' (Chiba Nippōsha, 1989, p. 103).

Figure 6.18 Makuhari New Town. (Courtesy of Makuhari New Metropolis Planning Division)

is only a few minutes from central Tokyo by new train line and by expressway, as well as close to such attractions as Tokyo Disneyland, the Maihama resort hotel strip on the water at Urayasu City, and the popular shopping center in Funabashi City called Lala Port (because 'Lala literally means "lively or active mind", according to the English language brochure), adds to the appeal of Makuhari and contributes to its fast growth.

Tsukuba Science City

There is one other new town project I want to introduce, even if it is further from central Tokyo than all the other projects described. It is separated from the nearest edges of the Tokyo built-up area by long stretches of farmland and other non-urban terrain. Tsukuba is one of the most famous and largest of Japan's new towns, and a leading center for basic research in fields ranging from high-energy physics, to biology, medicine, computer technology, building materials, earthquake prediction and social policy. Sometimes referred to in Japan as 'the City of Brains', Tsukuba now has a daytime population of over 150,000, of whom some 30,000 are researchers, students, administrative staff and their families (Tatsuno, 1986, p 100). It is located in a foothills area of Ibaraki Prefecture close to Mt Tsukuba, a little more than 60 kilometers from central Tokyo,

Table 6.3 Land use and population objectives, the Makuhari New Town Plan

Number of employees	10–15,000
Number of residents	26,000
Total area	522.0 hectares
Project development area	437.7 hectares
Town center	24.4 hectares
Business research zone	50.3 hectares
School zone	85.4 hectares
Residential land	44.8 hectares
Park and green zone	85.8 hectares
Public facilities	21.9 hectares
Roads, etc.	125.1 hectares
Housing units	
Housing for families	4,900 units/ 19,600 persons
Housing for one person households	1,600 units/ 1,600 persons
Housing for couples	800 units/ 1,600 persons
Housing for extended families	400 units/ 2,000 persons
Housing for foreigners	400 units/ 1,200 persons
TOTAL	8,100 units/ 26,000 persons

Source: Chiba Nippōsha, 1989, pp. 119, 145, and 174.

and was conceived in the early 1960s to be a vital national research center that would feed the high-growth economy of Japan with competitive advantages and new ideas. The reason for building it so far from the city was to avoid the high cost of urban land and the increasing congestion and pollution of 'business-first' Tokyo. The goal was also to provide researchers with a pleasant environment in which to work and live. Lessons for this are said to have come from site visits in March 1966 by Japanese government officials to renowned science cities and research parks around the world such as Stanford Industrial Park, Research Triangle in North Carolina, Sophia Antipolis and South Ile in France, and Louvain Science City in Belgium (Tatsuno, 1989, p. 97).

I want to make two particular points about Tsukuba. First, it seems clear that despite the fast growth of this city and the huge sums spent on construction (central government alone has spent over $1 billion on the project), it is not generally regarded as a popular place to be. There is greenery, streams, vistas of hills, and other natural beauty, but many residents and visitors think the project is contrived and sterile, a poor alternative to Tokyo's excitement and cultural stimulation. In fact, there were some rather well-publicized protests by university faculty and other skilled professionals in the 1970s against plans by their employers to relocate them there from the capital. While this situation has improved considerably in recent years, especially because Tsukuba has matured as a city and because of increased services and public facilities, there are still many workers who choose not to live there, but prefer the long commute (about two hours each way) from Tokyo. My point is that Tsukuba, large and famous as it is, and expensively planned as it has been, is still at many levels below that of overgrown, congested, unplanned Tokyo in desirability. There seems to be a lesson here for those who build new towns in each and every direction around the center of Tokyo, and demolish older sections of the city to make room for new towns in town.

Second Tsukuba illustrates something about the tremendous reach of the Tokyo metropolis. Even though many miles of farmland still separate Tsukuba from the outer edges of what are clearly bedroom suburbs of Tokyo, the new town is less and less the isolated think tank in the mountains that designers want it to be, and more an outer outpost of Tokyo. Not only is rail and highway access to the central city quicker, but the built-up area around Tokyo, and particularly around its outlying growth nodes such as Narita, is beginning to spread beyond the inner ring of suburban prefectures (Chiba, Kanagawa and Saitama) to an outer ring that includes, as in this case, Ibaraki Prefecture.

Geofront

We have already seen the expansion of Tokyo in various directions: up to new heights in ever-taller skyscrapers; out to new islands in Tokyo Bay; far into the distance to the outer reaches of the Kantō Plain. We now turn to the newest direction of growth, down below ground to what is being called the 'geofront'.

There are already many expressions of sub-surface development in Tokyo, particularly within the 23 wards. First, there is the city's celebrated subway system. With more than 10 different lines and over 200 kilometers of track, this is the world's most extensive underground transportation network. So, too, the sub-surface has elaborate networks of water lines, sewer lines, electrical cables, gas pipes and many other elements of urban infrastructure. Other below-the-surface examples include underground shopping promenades beneath busy commercial centers (most notably at Shinjuku and the Yaesu exit of Tokyo Station) and the growing numbers of high-rise buildings with extensive basement-level commercial space. Especially in high-rent shopping and entertainment areas such as Shibuya, Harajuku and Shinjuku, there are many new buildings with two or three (and sometimes more) distinct basement levels (called 'B1', 'B2', 'B3', etc.), full of the kinds of shops and eating and drinking places that abound at street level and on the upper floors of the multi-story commercial arcades.

What 'geofront' means is that Tokyo will continue to grow down to new depths below the surface, and will include there various new facilities and other new uses. To make this possible, the national Diet has recently passed legislation that limits ownership of land to a depth of 50 meters. The effect of this is to enable the construction of subway lines, subterranean highways and other underground projects without having to compensate the landowners above. This avoids one of the most expensive components of any construction project in Tokyo, opening the way for numerous capital improvements at reduced cost. Already, a new subway line, the No. 12 Shinjuku-Nerima Metropolitan Subway Line, and a new highway, a 10 kilometer stretch of the Chūō Kanjō Highway in the vicinity of Shinjuku, are under construction with benefits derived from this legislation (*Japan Times*, 20 March 1988, p. 16). Other ideas for the deep sub-surface include 'underground rivers' to bring in fresh water, other rivers to take away wastes, high-speed inter-city rail systems, and earthquake-safe storage facilities for valuable documents, records and computing equipment under conditions of constant humidity and temperature. There are also more distant possibilities for underground residential complexes, shopping centers, offices, factories and other urban activites. There are some rather impressive drawings of what this might look like by city planners in Tokyo, and by artists in the employ of the same giant construction companies that have previously expanded Tokyo upward and outward (Ojima, 1989).

7
Epilogue

It is amply clear that Tokyo has improved substantially in recent years as a place to live, and that many of the horrendous urban problems that had characterized the city during its economic reconstruction in the post-war period have also been improving. People are more comfortably housed now, they have more time and more facilities for recreation, the air and water are cleaner, and there are more protections from environmental disasters. The 'pie' that reconstruction era Prime Minister Ikeda had said must first become bigger before 'quality of life' issues could be addressed is now quite large indeed (see the beginning of Chapter 6), and the citizenry as a whole shares in its rather generous slices. Not only are there the many 'glamour projects' such as those that I emphasized in the previous chapter, there are also hundreds of other capital improvements in *Tokyo-to* and surrounding prefectures that are less noticeable or that have a more local nature. Depending on which part of the metropolis you visit, there are new community centers, new neighborhood parks, improved roadways, extensions to subway lines and new stations; pedestrian bridges over rail tracks and busy roads; enlarged facilities for sewage treatment and garbage disposal; flood control improvements; landscaping for streets, sidewalks and station-front plazas; new neighborhood shopping arcades; public swimming pools, designated bicycle paths and other welcome changes. In being someone who comes from a crumbling American city with a woeful lack of funds to solve its many great problems, I can't help but be more than a little impressed (and envious) with what I see going on in Tokyo.

On the other hand, I am genuinely astounded by what seems to be a fundamental weakness in the planning strategy for Tokyo, a weakness that should not be there. It seems that planning is helping the city, already greatly overgrown, to be become even bigger. The growth is in all directions: out into the Kantō Plain and into Tokyo Bay, up to taller buildings and down below ground. There is hardly a suggestion in the 'My Town Tokyo' document that, with over 11.8 million people on just over 2,000 square kilometers of land, Tokyo as a whole might have a problem of overpopulation, and no hint whatsoever about limiting the size of the metropolis or directing some of its growth to other regions. There is not even a word about such time-honored approaches to controlling the pace or direction of metropolitan growth as zoning or the selective withholding of water and sewer lines or road construction. In fact, the plan anticipates even more population in *Tokyo-to*, as much as a half million more people by the year 2000, but mentions this only very matter-of-factly, as if it were inevitable and nothing could or should be done to try to change it. Thus, the tone of the *2nd Long-Term Development Plan* is 'build, build, build,' and attention is given only to providing the infrastructure and community facilities needed to support an enormous population. If we add to the Tokyo total the fact that neighboring prefectures (Saitama, Chiba and Kanagawa) are expected to grow by some 2 million additional people by the year 2000, and that this, too, is being accepted as inevitable, then we see the urgency for some of the gigantic construction projects and mega-plans that now characterize Tokyo and its vicinity.

I hate to conclude this book on a cynical note but I feel that I have to. The bottom line is that Tokyo has become, now more than it ever was in its past, the domain of privileged business interests. Despite all the rhetoric about 'My Town Tokyo' and how the city is to be primarily a place for community life, and despite all the good intentions (and impressive results) of enhanced planning in the metropolis, the emphasis in Tokyo continues to be corporate profits. What actually gets built, be it via freewheeling private enterprise or under the auspices of government plans and regulations, is done first and foremost to serve the needs of powerful commercial interests. While this is also true for many other cities, including my troubled American hometown, the situation in Tokyo is exceptional. The number of construction projects by huge private-sector developers slated for the city, and in some cases their inordinately immense proportions, promise to make Tokyo, already probably the most profitable piece of real estate in the history of the world, even more profitable for them. They will continue to high-rise the city, and to squeeze on to its limited and shake-prone land ever more places of business and ever more residences for a growing workforce.

The public justification for this has two interrelated components: (1) the pressing need to solve Tokyo's continuing problems of crowding and high land costs; and (2) the important goal of making Tokyo an ever more competitive locale for the conduct of international business. We see this in quotations from powerful movers and shakers in Japanese society. In speaking about the need to have large waterfront redevelopment projects in Tokyo, Ishikawa Rokurō, Chairman of the Kajima Corporation (a giant construction firm) and a key member of the Japan Product Industry Council, recently said in a candid magazine interview:

Unless something is done to redevelop Tokyo and make it more attractive to foreign businessmen as Asia's center of commerce, nothing will prevent them from going off to Hong Kong or Singapore (*Business Tokyo*, May 1987, p. 20).

In what sounds like pretty much the same voice, Tange Kenzō, the noted architect and urban designer to whom I have referred often in this book, has written:

Tokyo is burdened with the fatal flaws of congested automotive traffic and lack of personal communication caused by excessively great commuting distance. Moreover, from the viewpoint of foreign enterprises contemplating the idea of opening outlets and offices there, the unprecedented and unparalleled high cost of land in Tokyo puts Japan in what looks like a state of hopeless isolation. If nothing is done to remedy this situation in the next four or five years, Tokyo will no longer be qualified to bear the responsibility of one of the world's urban poles. Indeed, some Western information-oriented and finance related business are already seriously contemplating Hong Kong, Singapore, or Shanghai as possible alternative locations (Tange, 1987, p. 11).

These are the kinds of arguments that carry a great deal of weight in Japan, because they speak to national economic interests. If Tokyo is not remade according to what these other experts advise business interests require, then the nation as a whole will lose steps in its race against foreign competitors. I see continuity here with debates that took place more than a century ago, when ambitious projects to remodel Edo-Tokyo were undertaken to meet the challenges of the foreign presence after the arrival of Perry's black ships.

However, none of this is to say that there is unanimity in Japan about a need to expand Tokyo. There are plenty of voices to the contrary – the direction of deconcentrating the city (Itō, 1988; Tamura, 1987). Some of the most convincing emphasize the folly of having so much of Japan's commercial and political power centered in one city, when it is known to be at great risk from earthquakes. Even more, these critics note that the concentration greatly favors one part of the city, the CBD and its environs, which because of geological conditions is itself a higher-risk zone than most of the rest of the Tokyo metropolis. What would happen to national interests, the critics say, if a powerful earthquake suddenly destroyed the center of Tokyo, taking with it the lives of many of the country's political leaders, its top business executives and a great many of its valued workers? The fact that Japan is in the forefront of research about earthquake-proof architecture and other measures to save lives and property in the event of disaster is small comfort given the enormity of what is at stake.

Other critics of Tokyo's increasing size point to the need to distribute national investment more fairly among the various regions of the country, and especially to assist the economic development of prefectures with slow economic growth and problems of population decline. Indeed, this has been a politically popular approach that, as we saw in Chapter 2, has been articulated at the highest levels of government. For example, deconcentration of Tokyo was a stated objective in former Prime Minister Tanaka's widely-quoted plan for the nation called *Building a New Japan: Remodeling the Japanese Archipelago* (Tanaka, 1972); and it continues to be a central feature of the most recent (1987) Comprehensive National Development Plan (the 'Fourth' such plan, the '*Yonzensō*'). However, as is often the case, there is a distinction to be made between what the government says, or even honestly intends, and what is actually accomplished. Thus, despite significant investments made in other regions, especially in industry, the Capital Region as a whole continues to be favored with growth, and Tokyo's considerable primacy in the nation remains unabated.

This is why there has been much recent discussion about moving Japan's capital away from Tokyo (Yawata; 1988; Maekawa and Takezawa, 1988). This could be done either in whole or in part, if some, but not all, government ministries or branches were to relocate. Either way, this would not only reduce the economic base and, therefore, the rate of population growth in Tokyo, it could also result in a more secure site for national government and considerable economic advantages for other regions. Moreover, if the government moves, this would be an example (and perhaps an incentive) for certain private sector enterprises also to relocate. Supporters of this idea like to point out that Japan has moved its capital a number of times before (most recently in 1868), and that a move now would fit with historical tradition to relocate government when the need to do so becomes great.

Where to move the capital is another question. Not surprisingly, this is a topic of great popular interest: one that has spawned many proposals for sites and the specific configuration that the government should have, if national administrative functions were to be shared among several cities. Some of the specific ideas, summarized in the essay by Yawata (1988), include relocating the capital to a smaller metropolis such as Nagoya or Sendai (both of which happen to be lobbying for this); sharing capital functions among various sites along a newly developed 'maglev megalopolis' that would extend along a high-speed rail corridor from Tokyo to Osaka; returning the capital to Kyoto; building a new, planned capital city somewhere close to the population center of Japan, such as in Shizuoka Prefecture, or in a region that especially needs an economic boost, such as the northeast of Honshū; or having several 'sub-capitals' in various parts of the country. Another proposal, by the celebrated architect Kurokawa Kishō (see below), would relocate government offices to a huge new island to be built in the middle of Tokyo Bay. There is a high-level government commission now sorting through such ideas, expected to make recommendations soon.

However, even in a climate of 'relocation fever',[1] Tokyo continues its expansion. This, I emphasize, is the dominant trend for Tokyo, and the direction in which it seems likely to continue despite the good arguments to the contrary. A prominent example of what is more likely to come than

---

[1] The term is from an editorial in *Japan Echo*, XV, 2, 1988, p. 5.

any significant shifting of capital functions away from Tokyo is a recent proposal, announced in January 1988 by the powerful Mitsubishi Estate Company, to completely redevelop the Marunouchi district. You might recall that this is the strategically located sub-district of the CBD sitting between the main gates to the Imperial Palace and the principal entrance of Tokyo Station, that has come to be one of the most important office districts in the city (see Chapters 3 and 4). It was first established almost exactly 100 years ago by the forerunners of the famous Mitsubishi *zaibatsu*, and is still largely controlled by Mitsubishi companies. The buildings are not so old – most of them were built after the 1945 disaster – but they are not particularly tall and do not command the kind of rents per land parcel that owners believe are possible. Consequently, the suggested plan is of true Tokyo scale: it would more than double the floor space to land ratio to about 20:1, and consist of 60 (yes, 60!) high-rise office buildings, all between 40 and 50 stories, and all neatly aligned in rows and columns over a 113-hectare site (Matsuda, 1988). Not surprisingly, this proposal has sometimes been called the 'Manhattan Plan'. Because the Tokyo Station building would be dwarfed by it all, one version of the plan, a short-lived idea pretending to support the preservation of that historic landmark, actually proposed that the whole structure be lifted to the roof line of the high-rise towers that would be built on its site!

It is not certain exactly what will come of the Mitsubishi-Manhattan plan. Even without the bizarre touch of putting a landmark in the sky, there has been considerable public displeasure about the scheme as a whole. For example, the English-language newspaper, *Japan Times*, carried an editorial, 'A Tokyo Without Heart', in which the plan was blasted as being 'Appalling, absolutely'. According to the writer, the plan's 'bank of skyscrapers, several rows deep . . . appeared like a scene of a graveyard . . . precisely the correct symbolism' (*Japan Times*, 24 January 1988, p. 16). On the other hand, every analysis of market demand for office space in and near the CBD supports gargantuan projects (Mammen, 1990). Because of this, and because of the great influence that the Mitsubishi family of companies has in Japan, there will probably be some substantial redevelopment. After all, most of Marunouchi *is* Mitsubishi land and Mitsubishi interests are intent on its redevelopment. While the final site plan might be a significant improvement over the unpopular 'first draft', and the new buildings might ultimately be attractive, what is not addressed is whether Tokyo should have any of this at all. The CBD is already greatly overcrowded and all the commuter routes feeding into it are jammed well beyond capacity. Yet Mitsubishi-Manhattan would make the CBD even bigger and cause still more workers to funnel into the center.

In a similar vein, there are proposals for the Tokyo Bay waterfront that are huge beyond all logic. We have already considered the plan to build Tokyo Teleport Town on reclaimed land as one of the city's several important commercial sub-centers (see Chapter 6). With 400 hectares and projected populations of 44,000 residents and 115,000 workers by 2010, all

Epilogue

located within a few minutes of the existing CBD, the scheme seems enormous enough already. Yet there are already various ideas for expansion of Teleport, even as construction of the original project is in the early stages. One of these ideas, put forward by Tange, calls for adding to both the Teleport plan and to the several redevelopment projects slated for bayfront piers and islands, and making a new city, called the Coastal City of Tokyo, right next to the existing city. This, too, would be a high-rise city covering some 2,000 hectares of landfill. The projected population would be 640,000 workers and 1.4 million residents. As if that were not enough, the Tange architects have an even bigger proposal as the next stage: the 'Tokyo Bay City' plan. This would require a complicated series of new islands to be fashioned in the bay from inner Tokyo all the way to Kisarazu in Chiba Prefecture, covering some 7,000 to 8,750 hectares.[2] The working population would be between 1.5 and 2.3 million and the resident population between 2.7 and 3.9 million. There would also be a new 1,600-hectare 24-hour international airport in the bay (Tange, 1987, pp. 8–15). Still another idea, this one advanced by a research group sponsored by the national Ministry of International Trade and Industry (MITI), calls for four large new islands totalling 10,000 hectares to be made in the bay, and for a giant city of indeterminate population to be built there called Tokyo Bay Cosmopolis (Takami, 1988, p. 16). There seems to be no end to such schemes: the so-called 'New Tokyo Plan, 2025' by Kurokawa, the famous architect mentioned above, proposes to fill in almost all the upper bay, and to develop it and much of the adjacent land area in Chiba Prefecture into a gigantic addition to Tokyo (including new space for capital functions) with room for several millions of new residents (Kurokawa, 1987).

Thus, it seems that, in Tokyo, progress has been defined as growth, and that growth is in all directions: up, down, and out to ever more distant reaches of land and bay. Even as experts talk about 'the Tokyo problem' and propose solutions such as moving the capital, it seems clear that the future of the city, at least for the time being, is one of an even more gigantic urban center, and of growing numbers of high-rises in more and more neighborhoods. This was the image of Tokyo that dominated our orientation from Tokyo Tower (Chapter 2), and the one that most remains with us after having examined the city more closely. The Tokyo imperative is to never sit still as a city, but continually to build and rebuild a constantly changing profile. This is a long-standing trait that has roots of 400 years, when Tokugawa Ieyasu arrived on the scene and rebuilt Edo. Its most current expression, which has dominated the life of the city during the six-plus years since 1984 that I have been studying this giant metropolis, is what I referred to in Chapter 4 as 'the third rebuilding of Tokyo' during the 20th century.

It is accepted that the center of the city, – the CBD and its environs –

[2] By way of comparison, the ward area of Tokyo itself, including existing islands, is 33,857 hectares. *Tokyo-to* as a whole is 108,633 hectares.

Figure 7.1 A view of Tokyo's new vernacular. This is Minato Ward as seen from Tokyo Tower

is at the forefront of this rebuilding. This is similar to what is also true in many other cities in other advanced countries where downtown redevelopment has been a major recent trend. But in Tokyo it seems that no place is untouched by this, and that the rebuilding is everywhere and thorough. While there are still some traditional neighborhoods left, and apparently growing numbers of citizen activists who fight for their preservation, old buildings in almost all sections of the city are constantly being razed and replaced forever by a new vernacular. If it is not high-rise office and other commercial buildings, then almost everywhere else it is mid-rise *manshon*, crammed one next to another seemingly without pattern, and taller apartment buildings and *manshon* that pop up higher and higher from among them. The photograph from Tokyo Tower across a largely residential section of Minato Ward seems to tell this story particularly well (Figure 7.1). In an area of tens of thousands of residents, it is hard to see whether there are any single houses left, even though there were many just a decade ago.

I learned that no place is untouched by Tokyo's rebuilding at Shioiri, a relatively inaccessible small neighborhood in Arakawa Ward, located beyond some industrial and freight rail tracts and tucked into a bend of the Sumida River. Two friends, experts on Tokyo, took me there when I was beginning this book, with the advice that I should get to know it and follow its development. It was like a tiny village within the city, a place where, as much as is possible in Tokyo, time had stood still. Here was a compact maze of narrow, winding streets; old wooden houses with a traditional look; small private gardens behind and beside the houses, and potted plants in front; folksy 'ma-and-pa' shops near the bus stop and along the central street; a quaint old *sentō* (public bath house); a small but beautiful old temple; and other various charms. Neighbors, many of them elderly, were in conversation seemingly everywhere; all of them always noticed the foreigner-stranger who kept returning periodically to walk the streets and take pictures. It was a nice little community I came to think of as one of my 'secret places' in Tokyo, where I proudly took some of my students and some foreign visitors to show them a hidden face of the great city.

Tange Kenzō has also found Shioiri. The man who has done so much to build up Tokyo over these past decades of great growth has determined that it too shall be high-rises. His plan, which I first saw detailed in an issue of *Japan Architect*, calls for the whole neighborhood to be made over into what so much of the rest of Tokyo is becoming (Tange, 1987, pp. 36–7; see also Yada, 1989a, pp. 200–2). Called 'Kawanote New City Center' ('*kawanote*' is a play on the name of the historic district '*yamanote*', meaning 'in the direction of the river'), the proposal is for a sizable (175 hectares) mixed-use development of commercial and residential high-rises set among planned green spaces, institutions and recreation facilities. Construction is already well underway on land that was vacant at the edge of the old village, and the days of Shioiri itself seem numbered. One of my students, Shimizu Aoi, wrote a thoughtful paper for my class that effectively conveyed the sadness of residents that it will soon be their turn, as it was the turn of people in other neighborhoods before them, to make way for the progress of Tokyo. Their lament is reflected in Figure 7.2.

It is natural to be critical of all the high-rise building that is going on, and to lament the loss of historical urban fabric. This is an understandable and a correct reaction. However, as I hope I have successfully explained in the preceding pages, the very essence of Tokyo is change: not staying still. Certainly more than any large urban center that I know, this city is process and not artifact, and deserves to be evaluated as such. There are ways, sometimes distinctively 'Tokyo ways,' in which the past is retained in the city and held deeply inside, even as the surface changes completely in profile. I think the good student of Tokyo recognizes this, and admires Tokyo both for its unsurpassed dynamism and for its ever-present traditions (Figure 7.3).

Figure 7.2 A broadside posted on a wooden fence in Shioiri. It reads: 'The approval of residents should come before decisions about development planning'

Figure 7.3 Two schoolgirls painting pictures of a pagoda in the Asakusa temple district as part of a class project about the history of Tokyo and traditional architecture

References

There is no extended bibliography of English-language materials about Tokyo. I hope that the following is a step toward correcting that short-coming. It lists the material that I used and cited in the text (including some items that are in French), plus additional readings that I consulted and recommend as useful for readers who want to learn about the city. A separate section of the references lists sources in Japanese. It is a shorter list and consists only of those books and periodical articles that contributed directly to the text.

Alden, J. 1984: 'Metropolitan Planning in Japan', *Town Planning Review*, 55, 1, pp. 55–74.

Alden, J. 1986: 'Some Strengths and Weaknesses of Japanese Urban Planning', *Town Planning Review*, 57, 2, 1986, pp. 127–34.

Allinson, G. D. 1975: *Japanese Urbanism: Industry and Politics in Kariya, 1982–1972.* Berkeley: University of California Press.

Allinson, G. D. 1978: 'Japanese Cities in the Industrial Era', *Journal of Urban History*, 4,4, pp. 443–76.

Allinson, G. D. 1979: *Suburban Tokyo: A Comparative Study in Politics and Social Change.* Berkeley and Los Angeles: University of California Press.

Allinson, G. D. 1984: 'Japanese Urban Society and Its Cultural Context', in *The City in Cultural Context*, J. A. Agnew, J. Mercer and D. E. Sopher (eds), pp. 163–85. Boston: Allen & Unwin.

Arisue, T. and Aoki, E.: 'The Development of Railway Network in the Tokyo Region from the Viewpoint of the Metropolitan Growth', in *Japanese Cities: A Geographical Approach*, S. Kiuchi et al. (eds), pp. 191–200. Tokyo: The Association of Japanese Geographers.

Ashihara, Y. 1987: 'Chaos and Order in the Japanese City', *Japan Echo*, XIV, Special Issue, pp. 64–8.

Ashihara, Y. 1989: *The Hidden Order: Tokyo through the Twentieth Century.* Tokyo and New York: Kodansha.

Awata, F. 1988: 'Disneyland's Dreamlike Success', *Japan Quarterly*, 35, 1, pp. 58–62.

Awata, F. 1989: 'Making Magic Pay', *Look Japan*, 35, 401, August, pp. 4–7.

Barr, P. 1968: *The Deer Cry Pavilion: A Story of Westerners in Japan, 1868–1905*. New York: Harcourt, Brace & World, Inc.

Barthes, R. 1982: *Empire of Signs*. London: Jonathan Cape.

Bennett, J. W. and Levine, S. B. 1977: 'Industrialization and Urbanization in Japan: The Emergence of Public Discontent', *Habitat*, 2, No. 1/2, pp. 205–18.

Bestor, T. C. 1989a: *Neighborhood Tokyo*. Stanford, California: Stanford University Press.

Bestor, T. C. 1989b: '*Tokyo no Daidokoro*: Research on the Tsukiji Wholesale Fish Market', *Japan Foundation Newsletter*, XVII, No. 4, pp. 17–21.

Bestor, T. C. 1990: 'Tokyo Mom-and-Pop', *Wilson Quarterly*, XIV, 4, Autumn, pp. 27–33.

Betros, C. 1985a: 'Down and Out in Tokyo', *Japanalysis*, 1–2, February, pp. 20–1.

Betros, C. 1985b: 'The Shepherds of Sanya', *Asahi Evening News*, 25 January 1985, p. 3.

Betros, C. 1988: 'Tsukiji: Afishionados', *Look Japan*, 34, 391, pp. 54–5.

Booth, A. 1985: *The Roads to Sata: a 2000-Mile walk through Japan*. New York: Weatherhill.

Bureau of Reconstruction and the Tokyo Institute for Municipal Research, 1929: *The Outline of the Reconstruction Work in Tokyo and Yokohama*. Tokyo: Sugitaya Press.

Burks, A. W. 1984: *Japan: A Postindustrial Power*. Boulder and London: Westview Press.

Busch, N. F. 1962: *Two Minutes to Noon*. New York: Simon and Schuster.

Caldarola, C. 1968–9: 'The *Doya-Gai*: A Japanese Version of Skid Row', *Pacific Affairs*, XLI, 4, pp. 511–25.

Center for Urban Studies (ed.) 1988: *Tokyo: Urban Growth and Planning, 1868–1988*. Tokyo: Tokyo Metropolitan University Center for Urban Studies.

Chapman, C. 1987: 'Denenchōfu: An Oasis of Spacious Living', *Look Japan*, 33, 377, pp. 38–9.

Christopher, R. C. 1983: *The Japanese Mind*. New York: Fawcett.

City Planning Association of Japan (ed.) 1969: *City Planning in Japan*. Tokyo: Sugitaya Printing Co.

Clay, G. 1973: *Close-Up: How to Read the American City*. Chicago: The University of Chicago Press.

Coaldrake, W. H. 1986: 'Order and Anarchy: Tokyo from 1868 to the Present', in *Tokyo: Form and Spirit*, M. Friedman (ed.), pp. 63–75. Minneapolis: Walker Art Center/ New York: Harry N. Abrams Inc.

Collcutt, M., Jansen, M. and Kumakura, I, 1988: *Cultural Atlas of Japan*. New York: Facts on File.

Connor, J. and Yoshida, M. 1984: *Tokyo City Guide*. Tokyo: Ryuko Tsushin.

Cybriwsky, R. 1986: 'The Fashioning of Gentrification in Philadelphia', *Urban Resources*, 3, 3, pp 27–32 and 53.

Cybriwsky, R. 1988a: 'Shibuya Center, Tokyo', *Geographical Review*, 78, 1, January, pp. 48–61.

Cybriwsky, R. 1988b: 'Takadanobaba: The Shogun and the Show Girl', *Look Japan*, 34, 392, pp. 38–9.

Cybriwsky, R., Ley D. and Western, J., 1986: 'The Political and Social Construction of Revitalized Neighborhoods: Society Hill, Philadelphia and False Creek, Vancouver', in *Gentrification of the City*, N. Smith and P. Williams (eds), pp. 92–120. London, Boston and Sydney: George Allen & Unwin.

Daniels, G. 1975: 'The Great Tokyo Air Raid, 9–10 March 1945', in *Modern Japan: Aspects of History, Literature and Society*, W.G. Beasley (ed.), pp. 113–31 and 278–9. Berkeley and Los Angeles: University of California Press.

Davies, B. et al. 1990: 'Up on a Property Seesaw', *South*, No. 112, February, pp. 13–16.

References

Dempster, P. 1967: *Japan Advances: A Geographical Study*. London: Methuen.

Dogan, M. and Kasarda J. D. 1988: 'Introduction: How Giant Cities Will Multiply and Grow', in *The Metropolis Era, Vol. 1: A World of Giant Cities.*, M. Dogan and J.D. Kasarda, (eds) pp. 12–29. Newbury Park, CA: Sage.

Doi, T. 1968: 'Japan Megalopolis: Another Approach', *Ekistics*, 26, 152, July, pp. 96–9.

Dore, R.P. 1958: *City Life in Japan: A Study of a Tokyo Ward*. Berkeley and Los Angeles: University of California Press.

Enbutsu, S. 1984: *Discover Shitamachi: A Walking Guide to the Other Tokyo*. Tokyo: The Shitamachi Times Inc.

Fallows, J. 1986: 'The Japanese are Different from You and Me', *The Atlantic*, 258, 3 September, pp. 35–41.

Fallows, J. 1988: 'The Other Japan', *The Atlantic*, 261, 4 April, pp. 16–18 and 20.

Fallows, J. 1989: 'Tokyo: The Hard Life', *The Atlantic*, 263, 3 March, pp. 16–26.

Fawcett, C. 1986: 'Tokyo's Silent Space', in *Tokyo: Form and Spirit*, Mildred Friedman (ed.), pp. 179–91. Minneapolis: Walker Art Center/ New York: Harry N. Abrams Inc.

Forbis, W. H. 1976: *Japan Today: People, Places, Power*. Tokyo: Charles E. Tuttle.

Friedman, M. (ed.) 1986: *Tokyo: Form and Spirit*. Minneapolis: Walker Art Center/ New York: Harry N. Abrams Inc.

Fujii, N. 1987: 'Directions for Growth', *Japan Echo*, XIV, Special Issue, pp. 12–19.

Fujimori, S. 1984: 'Kanto's Main Problem is Growing Urbanization', *Asahi Evening News*, September 29, 1984.

Fujimori, T. 1987a: '*Shitamachi*, In Tokyo's Left Hand', *Japan Quarterly*, 34, 4, October/December, pp. 410–17.

Fujimori, T. 1987b: 'Urban Planning in the Meiji Era', *Japan Echo*, XIV, Special Issue, pp. 45–9.

Fujimoto, K. 1987: 'Trying to Save Tokyo Station', *The Japan Times*, 15 November, 1987, p. 8.

Fujioka, W. 1989: 'Learning to Live the Good Life', *Japan Echo*, XVI, 2, Summer, pp. 30–4.

'Future City on the Sea', *Tokyo Municipal News*, 37, 3, 1987, pp. 1–3.

Gill, T. 1990: 'Sanbanchō's Last Stand', *Tokyo Journal*, 9, No. 11, February, pp. 82–6.

Gluck, P. 1977: 'Shinjuku', *Architectural Record*, 162, September, pp. 101–4.

Greenbie, B. B. 1988: *Space and Spirit in Modern Japan*. New Haven and London: Yale University Press.

Guillain, R. 1981: *I Saw Tokyo Burning: An Eyewitness Narrative from Pearl Harbor to Hiroshima*, W. Byron (trans.) Garden City, N.Y: Doubleday & Company Inc.

Haberman, C. 1987: 'Tokyo Aims to Reshape Itself as a "World Class City" ', *The New York Times*, 8 February 1987, p. 14.

Hall, P. 1984: *The World Cities*. London: Weidenfeld & Nicolson.

Hane, M. 1982: *Peasants, Rebels and Outcastes: The Underside of Modern Japan*. New York: Pantheon Books.

Hattori, K., Sugimura, N. and Higuchi, S. 1980: 'Urbanization and Commercial Zones', in *Geography of Japan*. Association of Japanese Geographers (ed.), pp. 320–46. Tokyo: Teikoku-Shōin.

Hayase, Y. 1974: *The Career of Gōtō Shinpei: Japan's Statesman of Research, 1857–1929*. Ph.D. Dissertation, Florida State University.

Hebbert, M. 1986: 'Urban Sprawl and Urban Planning in Japan', *Town Planning Review*, 57,2, pp. 141–58.

Holloway, N. 1988: 'Tokyo: Time to Tame the Monster of the Capital', *Far Eastern Economic Review*, 16, June, pp. 53–5.

Honjō, M. 1975: 'Tokyo: Giant Metropolis of the Orient', in *World Capitals: Toward Guided Urbanization*. H. W. Eldredge (ed.) pp. 340–87. Garden City, New York: Anchor Press/Doubleday.

Hovinen, G.R. 1988: 'The Search for Quality of Life in Japanese Planned Communities', *Proceedings of the Middle States Division of the Association of American Geographers*, 21, pp. 47–56.

Imaoka, K. 1988: 'Regional Tribute-Bearers in the Capital', *Japan Echo*, XV, 3, pp. 55–8.

Inouchi, N. 1987: *Tokyo*. Tokyo: International Society for Educational Information.

Ishida, Y. 1988a: 'Chronology on Urban Planning in Tokyo, 1868–1988', in *Tokyo: Urban Growth and Planning, 1868–1988*. Center for Urban Studies (ed.) pp. 37–68. Tokyo: Tokyo Metropolitan University Center for Urban Studies.

Ishida, Y. 1988b: 'Ougai Mori and Tokyo's Building Ordinance', in *Tokyo: Urban Growth and Planning, 1868–1988*. Center for Urban Studies (ed.) pp. 83–6. Tokyo: Tokyo Metropolitan University Center for Urban Studies.

Ishimizu, T. and Ishihara, H. 1980: 'The Distribution and Movement of Population in Japan's Three Major Metropolitan Areas', in *Geography of Japan*. Association of Japanese Geographers (ed.) pp. 347–78. Tokyo: Teikoku-Shōin.

Ishizuka, H. and Ishida, Y. 1988: 'Tokyo, the Metropolis of Japan and its Urban Development', in *Tokyo: Urban Growth and Planning, 1868–1988*. Center for Urban Studies (ed.) pp. 3–35. Tokyo: Tokyo Metropolitan University Center for Urban Studies.

Isoda, K. 1987: 'Tokyo and the Mythology of Modernity', *Japan Echo*, XIV, Special Issue, pp. 59–63.

Isomura, E. 1960: 'Tokyo: An International City', *New Japan*, 12, pp. 26–8.

Itakura, K. and Takeuchi, A. 1980: 'Keihin Region', in *An Industrial Geography of Japan*. K. Murata and I. Ota (eds) pp. 47–65. New York: St Martin's Press.

Itō, M. 1988: 'Coming to Terms with the Tokyo Problem', *Japan Echo*, XV, 3, pp. 50–4.

'Japanese Property: A Glittering Sprawl', *The Economist*, 3 October 1987, pp. 25–8.

Jefferson, M. 1939: 'The Law of the Primate Cities', *Geographical Review*, 29, pp. 226–32.

Jinnai, H. 1987: 'Tokyo Then and Now: Keys to Japanese Urban Design', *Japan Echo*, XIV, Special Issue, pp. 20–9.

Jinnai, H. 1988: *Ethnic Tokyo*. Number 72 of *Process: Architecture*, Tokyo.

Jones, H.J. 1980: *Live Machines: Hired Foreigners and Meiji Japan*. Tenterden: Paul Norbury.

Katayama, O. 1989: 'The Spice of Life', *Look Japan*, 34, 394, January, pp. 4–7.

Katō, H. 1979: 'Comparative Study of Street Life: Tokyo, Manila, New York', *Occasional Paper No. 5*. Tokyo: Gakushuin University for Oriental Cultures.

Katō, H. 1987: 'Tokyo Comes of Age', *Japan Echo*, XIV, Special Issue, pp. 8–11.

Kauffman, R. 1988: 'Tokyo's Housing Dilemma: Who's Paying the Price?' *Tokyo Journal*, 8, 1, pp. 78–83 and 104.

Kawai, K. 1960: *Japan's American Interlude*. Chicago: University of Chicago Press.

Kawamoto, S. 1987: 'Ōkubo: Ethnic Melting Pot', *Japan Echo*, XIV, Special Issue, pp. 73–6.

Kawazoe, N. 1987: The Flower Culture of Edo. *Japan Echo*, XIV, Special Issue, pp. 53–8.

Kennedy, R. 1988: *Home, Sweet Tokyo: Life in a Weird and Wonderful City*. Tokyo and New York: Kodansha International.

Kennerdell, J. 1988: 'Golden-Gai', *Tokyo Journal*, 8,4 (supplement), p. 13.

Kingston, J. 1988: 'Artist Captures the Charm of Old Tokyo', *The Japan Times*, 18 December 1988, p. 5.

References

Kirwan, R.M. 1987: 'Fiscal Policy and the Price of Land and Housing in Japan', *Urban Studies*, 24, pp. 345–60.

Kishi, N. 1987: 'On the Waterfront', *Business Tokyo*, May, pp. 18–21 and 25.

Knox, P. 1982: *Urban Social Geography: An Introduction*. London and New York: Longman.

Kojiro, Y. 1986: 'Edo: The City on the Plain', in *Tokyo: Form and Spirit*, Mildred Friedman, (ed.) pp. 37–53. Minneapolis: Walker Art Center/ New York: Harry N. Abrams Inc.

Kosai, Y. 1986: *The Era of High-Speed Growth: Notes on the Postwar Japanese Economy*. Tokyo: University of Tokyo Press.

Kornhauser, D. 1982: *Japan: Geographical Background to Urban-Industrial Development*. London and New York: Longman.

Kurokawa, K. 1987: 'New Tokyo Plan, 2025', *The Japan Architect*, 367/378, pp. 46–63.

Kurokawa, N. 1990: 'Getting Serious About Land Prices', *Japan Quarterly*, 37, 4, pp. 392–401.

Lane, R. 1978: *Images from the Floating World: The Japanese Print*. Secaucus, New Jersey: Chartwell Books.

Lee, C. and DeVos, G. 1981: *Koreans in Japan: Ethnic Conflict and Accommodation*. Berkeley and Los Angeles: University of California Press.

Levin, Mike 1986: 'Staunching the Flow of Pornography: "Band-aid on a Bullet Wound" ', *Tokyo Journal*, 6, 8, pp. 46-8.

Levy, D., Sneider, L. and Gibney, F. B. 1983: *Kanban: Shop Signs of Japan*. New York and Tokyo: Weatherhill.

Lewis, M. 1989: 'How a Tokyo Earthquake Could Devastate Wall Street and the World Economy', *Manhattan, Inc.*, June, pp. 69–79.

Lewis, P. F. 1976: *New Orleans: The Making of an Urban Landscape*. Cambridge: Ballinger Publishing.

Lockheimer, F.R. 1967: 'The People's Choice: Ryōkichi Minobe', *East Asia Series* (American University Field Staff), XIV, 4 (Japan), pp. 1–18.

Longstreet, S. and Longstreet, E. 1988: *Yoshiwara: The Pleasure Quarters of Old Tokyo*. Rutland, Vermont and Tokyo: Yenbooks.

Ma, K. 1989: 'Parking Lot or Pond', *The Daily Yomiuri*, 11 September 1989.

Maekawa, M. and Takezawa, K. 1988: 'Two Cities Bid for the Capital', *Japan Echo*, XV, 2, pp. 22–7.

Mammen, D. 1990: 'Toward an Urban Policy for Central Tokyo', *Japan Quarterly*, 37, 4, pp. 402–14.

Marlin, J.T., Ness, I. and Collins, S. T. 1986: *Book of World City Rankings*, (New York: The Free Press).

Masai, Y. 1986: *Atlas Tokyo: Edo/Tokyo through Maps*. Tokyo: Heibonsha.

Masai, Y. 1990: 'Tokyo: From a Feudal Million City to a Global Supercity', *Geographical Review of Japan*, 63 (Ser. B), No. 1, pp. 1–16.

Masler, D. 1987: 'Tsukudajima: An Island in Time', *Look Japan*, 33, 237, July, pp. 38–9.

Matsuda, K. 1988: 'A Bold Plan to Remodel Tokyo's Business Center', *Japan Echo*, XV, 2, pp. 28–30.

Matsushita, M. and Lo, J. 1988: 'Selling Culture: Department Stores – Cross-Cultural Comparisons', *Look Japan*, 34, 393, December, pp. 7–9.

Meech-Pekarik, J. 1986: *The World of the Meiji Print: Impressions of a New Civilization*. New York and Tokyo: Weatherhill.

Morris-Suzuki, T. 1985: *Shōwa: An Inside History of Hirohito's Japan*. New York: Schocken Books.

Munsterberg, H. 1982: *The Japanese Print: An Historical Guide*. Tokyo: Weatherhill.

Murata, K. and Ōta, I. (eds). 1980: *An Industrial Geography of Japan*. New York: St Martin's Press.

Nagaharu, H. 1988: 'The Tsutsumi Brothers, Feuding Magnates', *Japan Quarterly*, 35, 2, pp. 192–5.

Nagai, K. 1972: *A Strange Tale from East of the River and Other Stories*. E. Seidensticker (trans.). Rutland, Vermont and Tokyo: Charles E. Tuttle.

Nagashima, C. 1967: 'Megalopolis in Japan', *Ekistics*, 24, 140, pp. 6–14.

Nagashima, C. 1968: 'Japan Megalopolis: Part 2, Analysis', *Ekistics*, 26, 152, p. 95.

Naitō, A. 1987: 'Planning and Development of Early Edo', *Japan Echo*, XIV, Special Issue, pp. 30–8.

Nakamura, H. and White, J. 'Tokyo', in *The Metropolis Era: Mega-Cities, Volume 2*. M. Dogan and J. D. Kasarda (eds) pp, 123–56. Newbury Park, California: Sage.

Nishida, K. 1963: *Storied Cities of Japan*. Tokyo: Weatherhill.

Nishibe, S. 1989: 'Defending the Dignity of the Symbolic Emperor', *Japan Echo*, XVI, 2, pp. 22–7.

Noguchi, K. 1988: 'Construction of Ginza Brick Street and Conditions of Land-owners and House Owners', in Center for Urban Studies (ed.) pp. 76–86. *Tokyo: Urban Growth and Planning, 1868–1988*. Tokyo: Tokyo Metropolitan University Center for Urban Studies.

Nouët, N. 1990: *The Shogun's City: A History of Tokyo* (translated from the French edition by J. and M. Mills). Sandgate, Folkestone, England: Paul Norbury.

Nussbaum, S. P. 1985: *The Residential Community in Modern Japan: An Analysis of a Tokyo Suburban Development*. Unpublished Ph.D. Dissertation, Cornell University.

Ōtani, K. 1990: 'Makuhari New Town', *Japan Quarterly*, 37, 4, pp. 451–8.

Perin, C. 1977: *Everything in Its Place: Social Order and Land Use in America*. Princeton: Princeton University Press.

Phalon, R. 1988: 'Land Poor', *Forbes*, November 14, pp. 56–62.

Pons, P. 1984: 'Shinjuku, Le Kaleidoscope Babylonien', *Autrement*, No. 8, pp. 32–9.

Pons, P. 1988: *D'Edo à Tokyo: Memoires et Modernités*. Paris: Gallimard.

Popham, P. 1985: *Tokyo: The City at the End of the World*. Tokyo: Kodansha International.

Reischauer, E. O. 1977: *The Japanese*. Cambridge and London: The Belknap Press of Harvard University.

Relph, E. 1987: *The Modern Urban Landscape*. Baltimore: The Johns Hopkins University Press.

Robertson, J. 1987: Affective City Planning in Kodaira City (Tokyo). Unpublished paper prepared for the annual meeting of the Association of American Geographers, Portland, Oregon, 22–26 April, 1987.

Rozman, G. 1973: *Urban Networks in Ch'ing China and Tokugawa Japan*. Princeton: Princeton University Press.

Sabouret, J-F. 1984: 'Tokyo, Boulot, Ghetto', *Autrement*, 8, pp. 310–11 and 314–17.

Satō, M. 1988: 'Shinkawa: A City Center is Born', *Japan Echo*, XV, 2, pp. 31–3.

Seidensticker, E. 1983: *Low City, High City: Tokyo from Edo to the Earthquake*. Rutland, Vermont and Tokyo: Charles E. Tuttle.

Seidensticker, E. 1990: *Tokyo Rising: The City Since the Great Earthquake*. New York: Alfred A. Knopf.

Shibusawa, K. 1958: *Japanese Life and Culture in the Meiji Era*. C. S. Terry (trans.). Tokyo: Ōbunsha.

Short, K. 1988: 'Tokyo Bay: An Ecosystem in the Clutches of Development', *The Japan Times*, 24 February, 1988, p. 16.

References

Simmons, D. 1988: 'Asakusa: Into the Twilight Zone', *Look Japan*, 33, 386, pp. 38–9.

Smith, C. 1988a: 'Paying for Past Neglect', *Far Eastern Economic Review*, 16, June, pp. 49–51.

Smith, C. 1988b: Tokyo: 'Retain the City, but Shift the Functions', *Far Eastern Economic Review*, 16, June, pp. 55–6.

Smith, C. 1988c: 'Japan's Regions: Solving the Development Imbalance', *Far Eastern Economic Review*, 16, June. p. 56.

Smith, H. D. II. 1973: 'The Tyranny of Tokyo in Modern Japanese Culture', *Studies on Japanese Culture*, 2, pp. 367–71.

Smith, H. D. II. 1978: 'Tokyo as an Idea: An Exploration of Japanese Urban Thought Until 1945', *The Journal of Japanese Studies*, 4,1, pp. 45–80.

Smith, H. D. II. 1979: 'Tokyo and London: Comparative Conceptions of the City', in *Japan: A Comparative View*. A. M. Craig (ed.) pp. 49–99. Princeton: Princeton University Press.

Smith, H. D. II. 1986: 'Sky and Water: The Deep Structures of Tokyo', in *Tokyo: Form and Spirit*. M. Friedman (ed.), pp. 21–35. Minneapolis: Walker Art Center/ New York: Harry N. Abrams Inc.

Smith, T.C. 1973: 'Pre-Modern Economic Growth: Japan and the West', *Past and Present*, 60, pp. 127–60.

Spivak, M. 1987: 'Kichijōji: What More Could You Want?' *Look Japan*, 33, 378, pp. 38–9.

Stanley, T. A. 1983: 'Tokyo Earthquake of 1923', in *Kodansha Encyclopedia of Japan, Vol. 8*, p. 66. Tokyo: Kodansha.

Steiner, K. 1965: *Local Government in Japan*. Stanford: Stanford University Press.

Sternberg, R. 1985: 'Shibuya Town Playguide', *Tokyo Journal*, 5, May, pp. 56–8.

Storry, R. 1960: *A History of Modern Japan*. New York: Penguin Books.

Suginohara, J. 1982: *The Status Discrimination in Japan: Introduction to Buraku Problem*. Kobe: The Hyogo Institute of Buraku Problem.

Sugiura, N. 1987: 'The Urbanization of Nostalgia: The Changing Nature of Nostalgic Landscape in Postwar Japan'. Unpublished paper prepared for the annual meeting of the Association of American Geographers, Portland, Oregon, 22–26 April 1987.

Suzuki, E. 1988: 'Makichō Avenue Project and Excess Condemnation', in *Tokyo: Urban Growth and Planning, 1868–1988*. Center for Urban Studies (ed.), pp. 87–91. Tokyo: Tokyo Metropolitan University Center for Urban Studies.

Swinbanks, D. 1988a: 'Conflicting Views on Extent of Earthquake Threat to Tokyo', *Nature*, 336, 15 December, p. 609.

Swinbanks, D. 1988b: 'Builders Look to "Anti-Quake" Device', *Nature*, 336, 15 December, p. 609.

Symposium Executive Committee (ed.) 1990: *Symposium on Proposed Construction of Shinobazu Pond Underground Parking Lot*, 3 March 1990 (proceedings). Tokyo: Symposium Excecutive Committee.

Taira, K. 1969: 'Urban Poverty, Ragpickers, and the "Ants' Villa" in Tokyo', *Economic Development and Cultural Change*, 17, No. 2, pp. 155–77.

Takami, M. 1988: 'A Myriad of Projects in the Offing', *Japan Times*, 4 February 1988, p. 16.

Takashima, S. 1987: 'Tokyo: Creative Chaos', *Japan Echo*, XIV, Special Issue, pp. 2–6.

Takatani, T. 1987: 'Tokyo Street Patterns: An Historical Analysis', *Japan Echo*, XIV, Special Issue, pp. 39–44.

Takeuchi, H. 1987: 'The Two Faces of Shinjuku', *Japan Echo*, XIV, Special Issue, pp. 69–72.

Takeuchi, M. 1987: 'Edo Style and the Aesthetic of Iki', *Japan Echo*, XIV, Special Issue, pp. 50–2.

Tamura, A. 1987: 'Deconcentrating Tokyo, Reconfiguring Japan', *Japan Quarterly*, 34, 4, pp. 378–83.

Tanaka, K. 1972: *Building a New Japan: Remodeling the Japanese Archipelago*. Tokyo: Simul Press.

Tange, K. 1987: 'A Plan for Tokyo, 1986–', *The Japan Architect*, 367/368, pp. 8–45.

Tasker, P. 1987: *Inside Japan: Wealth, Work and Power in the New Japanese Empire*. London: Penguin Books.

Tatsuno, S. 1989: *The Technopolis Strategy; Japan, High Technology, and the Control of the Twenty-first Century*. New York: Prentice Hall.

'Tokyo Frontier', *Tokyo Municipal News*, 40, 1, 1990, pp. 1–3.

'Tokyo in Torment: The Disoriented City', *The Economist*, 9 April 1988, pp. 21–4.

Tokyo Metropolitan Government, 1969: *Sizing Up Tokyo*. Tokyo: TMG Municipal Library, No. 3.

Tokyo Metropolitan Government, 1970: *An Administrative Perspective of Tokyo, 1970*. Tokyo: Tokyo Metropolitan Government.

Tokyo Metropolitan Government, 1972a: *Tokyo's Housing Problem*. Tokyo: TMG Library, No. 5.

Tokyo Metropolitan Government, 1972b: *Tokyo for the People: Concepts for Urban Renewal*. Tokyo: TMG Municipal Library, No. 6.

Tokyo Metropolitan Government, 1984: *Plain Talk About Tokyo*. Tokyo: Tokyo Metropolitan Government.

Tokyo Metropolitan Government, 1985: *Planning of Tokyo, 1985*. Tokyo: Tokyo Metropolitan Government.

Tokyo Metropolitan Government, 1986: *The Fiscal Outlook for the Metropolis of Tokyo*. Tokyo: Tokyo Metropolitan Government.

Tokyo Metropolitan Government, 1987a: *Plain Talk About Tokyo*. Tokyo: Tokyo Metropolitan Government.

Tokyo Metropolitan Government, 1987b: *2nd Long-Term Plan for the Tokyo Metropolis*. Tokyo: Tokyo Metropolitan Government.

Tokyo Metropolitan Government, 1988: *Planning of Tokyo, 1988*. Tokyo: Tokyo Metropolitan Government.

Tokyo Metropolitan Government, 1989a: *The Fiscal Outlook for the Metropolis of Tokyo*. Tokyo: Tokyo Metropolitan Government.

Tokyo Metropolitan Government, 1989b: *Tokyo: Yesterday, Today and Tomorrow*. Tokyo: Tokyo Metropolitan Government.

Tokyo Metropolitan Government, 1990a: *Planning of Tokyo, 1990*. Tokyo: Tokyo Metropolitan Government.

Tokyo Metropolitan Government, 1990b: *Tokyo Industry, 1990: A Graphic Overview*. Tokyo: Tokyo Metropolitan Government.

Tokyo Statistical Yearbook, 1987: Tokyo: Tokyo Statistical Association, 1987.

Tracey, D. 1985: 'Zushi's Green Revolt', *Japanalysis*, 2–1, February, pp. 16–19.

Trewartha, G. T. 1965: *Japan: A Geography*. Madison: University of Wisconsin Press.

Uchino, T. 1978: *Japan's Postwar Economy: An Insider's View of Its History and Its Future*. Tokyo, New York and San Francisco: Kodansha International.

Udagawa, H. 1988: 'Tokyo Reaches the Outer Limits', *Tokyo Business Today*, April, pp. 34–7.

Ueda, T. 1990: 'Be Prepared!' *Look Japan*, 35, 407, pp. 26–7.

Van Hook, H. 1989: 'Prime Time in Kabuki-Cho', *Tokyo Journal*, 9, 3, pp. 4–9 and 12–17.

Vogel, E. F. 1971: *Japan's New Middle Class: The Salary Man and His Family in a Tokyo Suburb* (second edn). Berkeley, Los Angeles, London: University of California Press.

Wade, D. 1988: 'Shibuya: Old Dog, New Sticks', *Look Japan*, 34, 393, pp. 38–9.

References

Wagatsuma, H. and DeVos, G.A. 1980: 'Arakawa Ward: Urban Growth and Modernization', *Rice University Studies*, 66, 1, pp. 201–24.

Wagatsuma, H. and DeVos, G.A. 1984: *Heritage of Endurance: Family Patterns and Delinquency Formation in Urban Japan*. Berkeley and Los Angeles: University of California Press.

Waley, P. 1984: *Tokyo Now and Then: An Explorer's Guide*. New York and Tokyo: Weatherhill.

Waley, P. 1987: 'Fukagawa: Memories of Edo', *Look Japan*, 33, 373, pp. 38–9.

Waley, P. 1988a: 'The Shinjuku Story', *Tokyo Journal*, 8, 4 (supplement), pp. 14–15.

Waley, P. 1988b: 'The Ginza Story', *Tokyo Journal*, 8, 9 (supplement), pp. 5–7.

Waley, P. 1989a: 'Twelve Storys – Asakusa's Towering Cultural Achievement', *Japan Times*, 24 January 1989.

Waley, P. 1989b: 'Remaining *Nagaya* Serve as Reminders of a Poorer Life', *Japan Times*, 3 September 1989, p. 12.

Wildes, H.E. 1954: *Typhoon in Tokyo: The Occupation and Its Aftermath*. New York: Macmillan.

Witherick, M.E. 1981: 'Tokyo', in *Urban Problems and Planning in the Developed World*. M. Pacione, (ed.) pp. 120–56. New York: St Martin's Press.

'When the Great Quake Comes to Tokyo', *Business Tokyo*, 3, 7, 1989, pp. 5–10.

Whitin Kiritani, E. 1987: 'Nezu: A Quiet Haven', *Look Japan*, 33, 380, pp. 38–9.

Yamaga, S. 1970: 'Urbanization in the Northern Suburbs of Tokyo', in *Japanese Cities: A Geographical Approach*. S. Kiuchi et al. (eds), pp. 73–8. Tokyo: Association of Japanese Geographers.

Yawata, K. 1988: 'Why and Where to Relocate the Capital', *Japan Quarterly*. 35, pp. 127–32.

Yazaki, T. 1963: *The Japanese City: A Sociological Analysis*. San Francisco and Tokyo: Japan Publications Trading Company.

Yazaki, T. 1966: *The Socioeconomic Structure of the Tokyo Metropolitan Complex*. M. Matsuda (trans.). Honolulu: Social Science Research Institute, University of Hawaii.

Yazaki, T. 1968: *Social Change and the City in Japan: From Earliest Times Through the Industrial Revolution*. Tokyo: Japan Publications.

Yoshino, I.R. and Murakoshi, S. 1977: *The Invisible Visible Minority: Japan's Burakumin*. Osaka: Buraku Kaihō Kenkyūsho.

Zetter, J. 1986: Challenges for Japanese Urban Policy. *Town Planning Review*, 57, 2, pp. 135–40.

Sources in Japanese

Chiba, M. 1990: *Nishi Shinjuku o tsukuru kage no shuyaku tachi* (The Behind-the-Scenes Leaders of Nishi Shinjuku). *Tokyo Jin*, 31, April, pp. 76–9.
Chiba Nippōsha, 1989: *Makuhari 2001: Official Guide Book*. Chiba: Chiba Nippōsha (in Japanese with some English text).
Chika Kōji Tokushū (Public Announcement of Land Prices Special Edition), *Asahi Shinbun*, 23 March 1990, supplement, pp. 1–20.
Eguchi, E., Nishioka, Y. and Katō, Y. 1985: *Sanya: Shitsugyō no gendaiteki imi* (Sanya: Today's Meaning of Unemployment). Tokyo: Miraisha.
Fukuda, J. 1990: *Shinjuku maketo no shōrai o uranau* (Predicting the Future of the Shinjuku Market), *Tokyo Jin*, 31, April, pp. 68–73.
Gekkan Akurosu (ed.) 1987: *Tokyo no shinryaku* (The Encroachment of Tokyo). Tokyo: Parco.
Hakuhōdō Institute of Life and Living, 1985: *Town Watching*. Tokyo: PHP Institute.
Ishizuka, H. and Narita, R. 1986: *Tokyo-to no hyakunen* (One Hundred Years of Tokyo). Tokyo: Yamakawa.
Jinnai, H. 1985: *Tokyo no kukan jinruigaku* (The Anthropology of Tokyo Space). Tokyo: Tsukumashobō.
Katō, A. 1986: *Harajuku monogatari* (The Harajuku Story). Tokyo: Sōshisha.
Mitsuoka, K. 1989: *Za-Shibuya kenkyū* (Research about Shibuya). Tokyo: Tōkyū Agency.
Nakawa, M. 1989: *Shinjuku: Tokyo no atarashii kao* (Shinjuku: Tokyo's New Face). *Weeks*, October 1989, pp. 8–21, 23–39 and 41–2.
Ogawa, I. 1989: *Tokyo daitoshi ken no chiiki henyō* (Tokyo Metropolitan Area Changes). Tokyo: Daimeidō.
Ojima, T. 1989: *Tokyo saiseikeikaku to shiteno geofuronto kaihatsu* (Revitilizing Tokyo by Geofront Development). *Newton*, 14 February, pp. 116–24.
Sode, E. 1987: *Tokyo machi bisunesu* (Tokyo Business Towns). Tokyo: Nippon Keizai Shinbunsha.
Tokyo-to (Tokyo Metropolitan Government) 1989: *Tokyo no toshi keikaku hyakunen* (One Hundred Years of Planning in Tokyo Metropolis). Tokyo: Tokyo Metropolitan Government.
Tsutsui, M. 1988: *Tokyo daitenkan* (Major Change of Tokyo). Tokyo: Jyutaku Shinposha.
Tsutsui, M. 1989: *Tokyo Bay Network*. Tokyo: Jyutaku Shinpōsha.

Sources in Japanese

Yada, A. 1987: *Tokyo wa kō kawaru* (How Tokyo is Changing). Tokyo: Asahi Sonorama.

Yada, A. 1989a: *90 nendai no shin Tokyo ken* (New Tokyo Region in the '90s). Tokyo: Nippon Keizai Shinbunsha.

Yada, A. 1989b: *Shin Tokyo ken* (New Tokyo Region). Tokyo: Tokumashoten.

Index

Index

260

Index